48 Hours to Chaos

48 Hours to Chaos

An Engineer Looks at Life and How the World Really Works

JOHN D. WATERMAN

Published by Dennett Ink
129 Bleachery Blvd., Suite 135
Asheville, NC 28805

www.johndwaterman.com

ISBN: 978-0-9831636-0-2

Library of Congress Control Number: 2010942917

Cover Art compliments of Linda Waterman.
"Chaos in a Solar Prominence" acrylic on paper.

Printed in the United States of America

Contents

This book is dedicated to

Linda

without whom
none of this would be possible

PREFACE

LET me say at the outset that I am all in favor of truth, beauty, justice and the American way, and I am opposed to evil and destruction. I would suspect that most of my readers will share this view, regardless of their political persuasion. I have an engineering background, and take a scientific attitude when observing behavior or solving problems. When I look around, I see a world filled with conflict and evil, yet I also see an environment of great wealth where people conduct their lives with respect for others and work hard for their own advancement. How do such opposing concepts coexist in the same society? Why do some people choose a life of crime while others seek to act in virtuous ways and promote peace? Why does a politician who has sworn to uphold his constitution descend into corruption? Questions like these seem to trouble a lot of people, and such concerns motivated me to start seeking answers. Here are a few of the situations that stimulated my curiosity, and eventually led to the writing of this book.

When I was a college student, I heard a professor say that civilization is always a mere forty-eight hours away from chaos. All an enemy would need to do to is find a way to cut off the food supply, and society would be destroyed. After two days without food, all your friends and neighbors would revert to animalism, and the delicate fabric of society would be ripped to shreds along with all those people who are not the strongest and most vicious fighters. The image of that fate stuck to my impressionable young mind, and grew older with it.

Another of my instructors, a grad student, was pleased to announce that he and his new wife would soon accept job offers in industry. This would allow them to finally earn enough money to truly enjoy life. But the graduates were worried about the inevitability of Mother Nature stepping into their lives. The happy couple would soon have babies to care for. Such additional responsibilities would spoil their freedom and put a crimp in the enjoyment of their newfound wealth.

He set me to wondering whether we, as rational human beings, are actually just slaves to our animal instincts. Certainly children would be preventable, with a little forethought and self-discipline.

Have you ever noticed that you spend a significant part of your day eight feet away from certain death? When you drive to work in the morning, and again when you go home at night, you pass numerous vehicles on the road, hurtling along in the opposite direction at a closing velocity of 100 miles per hour. A simple counterclockwise motion of your steering-wheel would spell disaster. How do most of us consistently avoid this ever-present danger?

Sometime during the seventies I was watching an episode of the original Star Trek, where Captain Kirk swaps places with his counterpart in an alternate universe.[1] Due to a transporter malfunction, Kirk arrives in a civilization with a more brutal, animalistic outlook. The starship officers in this other universe advance in rank by undermining or assassinating their superiors. In his quarters Kirk discovers a spying device that can secretly monitor anyone aboard the ship and can also be used to eliminate them. His girlfriend in this episode encourages him to use it to destroy the competition, but he resists the impulse because of his more civilized nature.

How, I wondered at the time, could the people of this alternate universe survive for long in their advanced technological society, if they always practiced such anarchistic behavior? After a little thought I realized that such an attitude has been common in our own world history and is still practiced by those who hold power in dictatorships today. Stalinism is a term we use to describe this school of management practice.

During my career as an engineer in the aerospace industry, I ran across many people who had a different approach to life than I did. I became mildly curious about why they choose their behaviors, when I would have approached a similar situation from a different angle. I decided that these people must have a different understanding of life than I did, or at least used a different method for solving their problems. Some managers were tyrants who chose bullying as a way to make their subordinates toe the line. Some bosses led by example and inspired loyalty in their workers. Some people advanced to positions of power, yet were sorely lacking in competence. Some folks attained their positions by playing office politics, and succeeded despite their shortcomings. Is it not amazing that some organizations continue to function and deliver their products while burdened with such widespread inefficiencies? It is no wonder that every year a whole new set of books about management technique appear in the bookstores.

Perhaps an engineer learns a particular way of approaching and solving problems that is not the same as folks in other career fields. Or maybe people are raised differently by their mothers and start out with an alternate view of life, and how to behave. Some people believe that socialism holds the answers to all the world's problems; others think some form of capitalism would be a preferable way to manage the affairs of mankind.[2]

Thoughts like these percolated in the back of my mind for many years, but during my engineering career I never took the time to think through the entire subject. Once I retired, I undertook the opportunity to make a thorough investigation. Among other things, I discovered that when you go looking for ethical or moral guidance you inevitably end up in religion. God imposes the shalls and shall-nots from His authority on high. Shouldn't there be a way, I thought, to arrive at the same conclusions about the benefits of virtue and love by using the precepts of science and logic? Certainly rational thought should lead us through the temptations of evil to the higher planes of peace and beauty, without reliance on the doctrines of a particular religion or supernatural inspiration.

Throughout history many wars have been fought for the glory of one god over another. This despite the fact that religions teach us that killing is evil. Nevertheless, each army went into conflict convinced that God was on their side. Certainly, in these contests one side or the other was wrong, or both were. Can we conclude that the winner of every battle was the one favored by God? Personally, I cannot agree with that conclusion.

So let us consider the world from an engineering perspective. Take the materials we have available, provided by nature, and use them to build a lasting structure based on the foundations of logic, without resort to miraculous intervention. Let us take a look at how life arose on Earth. Let us analyze how mankind fits into the big picture. Let us consider how the various peoples and cultures on this planet interact and attempt to maintain their civilizations.

The purpose of this book is not to convert you from your current political persuasion to something else. It does not intend to change your religion from whatever you have chosen (or have been forced into) to a different one. The goal of this book is to provide you with a few mental tools, a new perspective, a way of thinking, to use in construction of a better understanding of the world you see around you today.

This is a book about life, and it is based upon the precepts of science. We will avoid conclusions based on religious belief or the command of God. We will not consider the question of life after death. We will consider life on Earth in the here and now, and necessarily the life of our children who follow us into the future. Death is considered the end of life. One's reward or punishment from God or the devil in the afterlife is not addressed herein.

Please note that this is not a book on philosophy. Philosophy books contain terms like: a priori, epistemology, essentialism, existentialism, eschatology, ipso facto, metaphysics, monad, ontological, qua, teleology, vis-à-vis. We will not even bother to define these words because we will not use any of them. Other than this paragraph, you will find no further occurrences of them in this book. Ergo, this is not a philosophy book. Q.E.D.[3]

However, we will take one question that is commonly found in philosophy books and answer it up front, from an engineering perspective. The reader should already have the perception to grasp the actual meaning. "If a tree falls in the forest, and there is no one around to hear it, does it make any noise?" The correct answer, for those of you with any doubts, is: Yes, it makes a lot of noise. And the bigger is the tree that falls, the more noise it makes.

As human beings, the only creatures on Earth possessing the rational thought processes to understand the meaning of such questions, we intend to use our intellect to acquire the answers to even more significant questions. Let's get started.

Notes:

[1] *Mirror, Mirror*, Star Trek episode #39, October 1967.

[2] Disclaimer for purposes of political correctness:
    The terms "man" and "mankind," as used in this book, are certainly
    intended to include woman and child. We don't wish to exclude over half
    our potential audience. We do not wish to offend anyone by our choice
    of using the traditional language reference to "man," rather than the

clumsier sounding terms "humanity" or "persons." The individual reader is free to substitute gender-specific terminology suitable for his or her own taste.

[3] Q.E.D., quod erat demonstrandum, from the Latin meaning, "which was to be shown or demonstrated," commonly used at the conclusion of a mathematical proof.

CHAPTER ZERO

INTRODUCTION

CIVILIZATION has suffered numerous mortal blows throughout the slow march of history, yet always seems able to regenerate from the ashes of its demise, much like the Phoenix of ancient mythology. The population has always bounced back from whatever tragedy it experienced, and subsequently advanced further than it had the time before. Why that should happen at all is one of the themes that motivated this book.

Our purpose here is to give you an enhanced view of civilization, and the world in general. We want to show how to use a set of mental tools, so to speak, for analyzing the events that occur around you, a set of ideas and techniques to employ in observing the attitudes that different people assume in arranging their own lives. This is done from the point of view of an engineer, a highly-trained professional who addresses problems with a technical and analytical frame of mind. An engineer believes in cause and effect, that things happen for a reason, and if he can figure out the reason, he can do something to affect the outcome. His goal is to build better things from the resources at hand, and he is always looking for a different way to do things. He asks why something works this way and not that way. If we change this feature on that machine, will it run faster or more economically?

How, you might ask, is an engineer different from any other student of science? Why should you listen to anything he says? Perhaps an old gag will help illuminate his mindset.

Three men, a physicist, a mathematician and an engineer, were sitting around a lunch table in the college cafeteria arguing about some deep, scientific abstraction.

The physicist looked up from his notes to see a beautiful female professor strolling past with her lunch tray. The eyes of all three men locked on target, watching her sashay to the next table. She sat down and began nibbling her salad.

The physicist leaned closer to his companions and whispered, "I know this lovely woman, and I can arrange to introduce one of you guys to her, but you will have to follow my instructions to the letter."

"Yes, yes?" they urged him on.

"You must approach her in small steps to avoid being rejected, because she doesn't like her men being pushy."

"Of course," they agreed, "tell us more."

"In each step, you may only move closer to her by half the remaining distance, but you can take as many steps as you need."

"Oh, no," said the mathematician, giving up, "even with an infinite number of steps, I could never reach my goal."

"No problem," said the engineer, "I can get close enough!"

Ambiguity

On a more serious note, we need to look at how anyone acquires understanding of a new subject. When we learn something new, we must compare how the new information fits in with things we already know, so we can decide whether to believe it or not. When a subject is entirely new, we need to have a tolerance for ambiguity. We will accept new information temporarily, on the authority of the speaker, until we have enough experience to judge whether it all makes sense. One person can never appreciate all aspects of a subject, because unanswered questions are always nagging at the mind.

When you were a child, your mother told you how to behave in many different situations without giving you any reasons for her directions. You trusted her, and she counted on her authority in giving you instructions. Don't cross your eyes or they'll get stuck like that. Don't stick out your tongue at me. Help me wash the dishes. Don't hit your sister. Don't run out in the street. Brush your teeth every day. Don't run with scissors. Don't talk to strangers.

After a few years you figured out on your own the reasoning behind the instructions. She was trying to teach you to be polite, to show you how to do things, to warn you about the hazards of traffic, or tell you that nasty strangers could be trying to harm you.

By the time you are ready to pursue your engineering degree, you have become socialized and have learned hundreds of rules about how to behave in public. But the fact that you are going to college implies you need to learn many other things before you are ready to practice engineering in the real world.[1] In your math and physics classes, you may safely assume that everything the professor teaches you (about math and physics) is true, and you can safely incorporate this new information into your belief system. However, the things you learn from your history professor must be taken with a grain of salt. After all, a good portion of history has been written by the victors about the losers of previous conflicts, so the bias will favor the existing regime. Political history is most likely to be biased by the opinions of the person telling it to you, and is thus subject to your own interpretation.[2]

This suspicion about the truth of things one learns in school suggests a reason why many students choose to go into scientific fields rather than the humanities. Perhaps many of them would prefer to spend their lives dealing with facts they know to be true, rather than basing their decisions upon opinions of other people, or political expediency.

Therefore, adults in the real world need a healthy tolerance for ambiguity. We need to incorporate new knowledge through our mental filters, provisionally subject to modification as new facts come to light. We use our life experience to judge which things to believe.

This book is intended to guide you on the path to a better understanding of the world around you, while you cultivate your tolerance for ambiguity.

To that end, we may view human life as a long series of conflicts. We see good versus evil, cooperation vs. conflict, friendship vs. hostility, love vs. hate, allies vs. enemies. Each of these opposing forces, and hundreds of other pairs of conflicting attributes, may be visualized by placing them on a diagram, perhaps at the opposite ends of a line, or on opposite sides of a circle. A larger view, in three-dimensions, would place them on different sides of a sphere or bubble.

Consider, for example, love versus hate in a relationship between two people. There are many degrees of emotion between these extremes that we could arrange on our chart. On the side of love we might find friendship, respect, and trust. On the opposite end near hate we could see revulsion, enmity, malice. Somewhere between we might encounter indifference, toleration, or apathy. For each pair of conflicting words we could draw cycles or spheres of revolving ambiguity, like a great conglomeration of bubbles forming a froth of complexity.

Think of your kitchen sink with a stack of dirty dishes after dinner. Turn on the spigot to fill the sink, and squirt in some liquid dish soap. Watch the froth of bubbles gurgle up to cover the dishes and the water's surface, ever higher and thicker. The complexity of this froth may be thought of as an analog for life. It grows as turbulence arises from beneath. It changes form as small bubbles coalesce into larger bubbles, or shrinks when the larger bubbles burst to disappear into nothingness.

Although this idea about a froth of complexity is merely a poetic analogy that has no scientific basis, it may help us to visualize the vast disorder that constitutes the many conflicting forces we observe around us.

As a metaphor, each bubble may be thought to symbolize one individual life, or one life form, or even a collection of life forces, all competing for survival with their neighbors. Some succeed and grow; others burst and disappear. Every bubble will exist for some limited lifetime before it finally pops and is eliminated from the picture.

Let us dive into the bubble bath of life to see if we might splash some enlightenment out of this bathtub of chaos.

Notes:

[1] This is not to suggest, of course, that a college education is necessary for a successful career. Some 55 percent of the U.S. population haven't gone to college, yet these folks prosper in our economy. Any adult, regardless of his formal education, cannot avoid learning new things throughout his lifetime. Everyone is exposed to new products and opportunities in society, and in our diversity of everyday activities.

[2] We are not trying to irritate history professors here. Really. History professors form a valuable segment of our society in performing research and educating students. But we must always consider the source of any information, no matter where it comes from, including history professors, and engineers.

CHAPTER ONE

BEFORE MAN

LET us have a look at what life was like on our planet before the advent of man. We want to observe the interplay between plants and animals before they were affected by the activities of humans. This discussion should illuminate some interesting features of life, and suggest some techniques for understanding the world we find around us today.

Life

First we need to define what we mean by life. The features of life can be observed in an agent, an object or a being of some sort, if it displays directed behavior, as opposed to strictly random behavior. A stone has no life. A stone just sits there doing nothing. An oxygen molecule has no life. It just blows around in the atmosphere randomly bumping into other molecules, like so many tiny stones. Oxygen can combine chemically with other molecules to form different compounds or materials, but that is not directed behavior, thus not life.

The simplest form of life, as far as we will be concerned in this book, is the single celled creature, such as an amoeba.[1] Under a microscope, amoebae can be observed using their pseudopodia to push themselves around in an effort to find food and to seek out more auspicious environments. Perhaps they are looking for better temperatures or pH levels, so they may continue to exist in a suitable host environment. The amoebae reproduce by cell division to make copies of themselves. Thus they grow their communities and propagate their species. It is possible for the amoeba to mutate via random chemical errors in its constituent DNA.[2] A mutation may improve the cell's chances for survival as its environment changes, so it can be considered adaptable. The successful adaptations are propagated in following generations, while unsuccessful adaptations die out quickly. This is natural selection in operation, a concept first proposed by Charles Darwin in his book, *Origin of the Species*, published in 1859.[3]

The amoeba displays directed behavior, growth through metabolism, reproduction and the ability to adapt to the environment. These other features expand our definition of life to an extent which seems reasonable to most people. Examples of higher levels of life are multi-celled creatures, worms, plants, insects, fish, amphibians, reptiles, and mammals, to name a few. Humans represent a highly advanced life form, but we are presently considering the world before the advent of humans, so we will ignore them for the time being.

History

Since life seems to have originated on Mother Earth, and appears to have advanced to an amazing degree, let's see if we can watch it develop over the ages. We can look at the geological history of our planet from the beginnings up to the present time.

Science tells us that the world condensed out of a swirling cloud of matter about 4.6 billion years ago.[4] The chaos of collisions among the smaller lumps of this planet stuff, which eventually stuck together, set the world to spinning on its axis. This rotation defines the length of the day. The force of gravity, acting on all the material, compressed the planet into its spherical shape. The swirling motion in the cloud of matter also left the earth in a stable orbit around the sun, which defines the length of the year.

First Chart

Now that we have a new planet orbiting in the sunshine, let's draw a time-line for its 4.6 billion years of history. Using the top end of the time-line as the beginning, stretch the line down for 100 yards, the length of a football field, where we place the present date. See Figure 1. What events in scientific history can we identify along this time-line, and where do we place their yard markers?

During formation of the early earth, all of those collisions between rocks, ice, dust and gas generated a lot of heat. This, along with the heat generated by radioactive decay, caused the early planet to assume a molten state. During this time, around 4.5 billion years ago, a Mars sized object collided with the planet, causing a large amount of material to go into orbit, and creating the Earth-Moon pair.[5] This earliest event on our figure is indicated at the 2 yard-line near the top.

Nearly a billion years of planetary cooling took place as the earth radiated heat into space. The firm crust solidified approximately 3.6 billion years ago, near the age of the oldest rocks ever found. The marker for this event goes on our figure at the upper 22 yard-line.

The first identifiable feature of life that has survived in the fossil record is the prokaryote, the simple cell without a nucleus. This primitive life form appears 3.2 billion years ago, at our 31 yard-line.

What caused this life form to arise from the primordial ooze is controversial, but we may assume it was a happy coincidence of the right chemicals and amino acids mixing together in some puddle of warm fluid, combined with an energy input from a lightning strike. This is, of course, merely speculation, unsupported by any direct evidence. Many scientists are working to discover the spontaneous development of life from inorganic materials, but a viable theory has not yet been published.[6]

The next major step in the advancement of life is the appearance of the eukaryote, the cell with a nucleus, and the basis of multi-cellular creatures. This event occurs at 2.1 billion years ago, which corresponds with the 46 yard-line on the lower half of our football field, past the halfway point in the history of planet Earth.

After a lengthy period of time, more than 1.5 billion years, the evolution of life produced trilobites. This occurred approximately 530 million years ago, in the Cambrian Period, yard-line 11.5. The trilobite is that famous arthropod with a segmented shell that everyone remembers from high school science class. Fossilized trilobites are commonly found in sedimentary rocks all over the world.

The Cambrian Period, 542 to 488 million years ago, yard-lines 11.8 to 10.6, is noteworthy because of the explosion of new animal life forms in the seas. During this time, plant life was limited to marine algae, while the land surfaces were still barren.

In the remaining ten yards to the goal line of our football field, we find development of the amazing diversity of life forms that created the living environment of our present day planet. This fascinating time of history has been thoroughly described in several fine books, so we will touch here on but a few of the major events.[7]

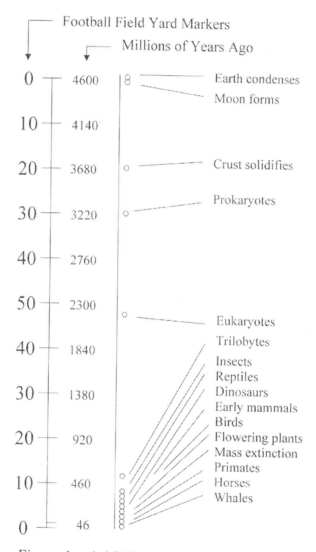

Figure 1.   4.6 Billion to 46 Million Years Ago

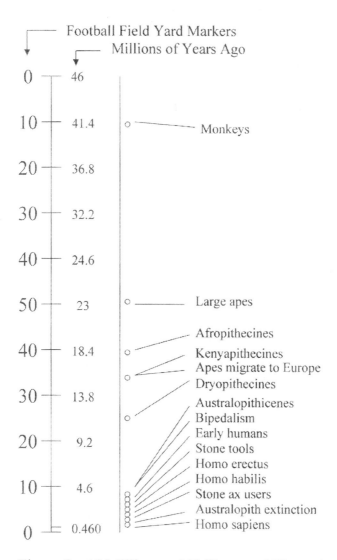

Figure 2   46 Million to 460 Thousand Years Ago

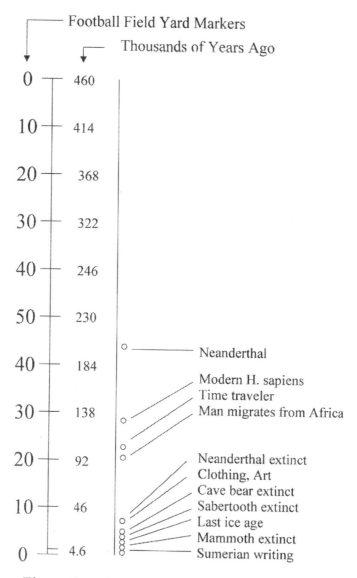

Figure 3. 460 Thousand to 4600 Years Ago

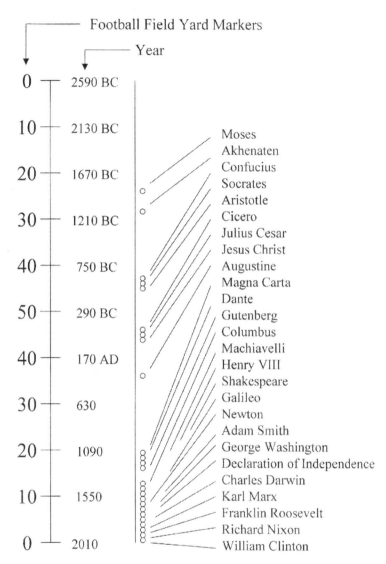

Figure 4. The Sweep of Human History

Event	Million Years Ago	Yard-line
Insects first appear about	400	8.7
Reptiles	350	7.6
Dinosaurs	210	4.5
Early mammals	200	4.3
Birds	150	3.2
Flowering plants	110	2.4

The Mesozoic Era, from 251 to 65 million years ago, is known as the Age of Dinosaurs. The Mesozoic is subdivided into three periods, Triassic, Jurassic and Cretaceous, which have been popularized by displays of dinosaur fossils in many museums.

We should pause at this point in our rush through history to take note of the mass extinction that occurred 65 million years ago. It was a sudden catastrophe that appears in the fossil record indicating the destruction of most life forms. Also known as the K-T boundary, for the dividing line between the Cretaceous and Tertiary periods, this event is now understood to have been caused by the impact of a large meteorite with the planet. The collision caused giant tsunamis in the ocean and threw tremendous amounts of material into the atmosphere, which blocked sunlight from reaching the surface for months. This disruption of climate killed off the dinosaurs and made way for the evolution of mammals. The Cenozoic Era, from 65 million years ago to the present, immediately follows the Mesozoic, and is known as the Age of Mammals.

Event	Million Years Ago	Yard-line
The mass extinction occurs	65	1.4
Primates first appear about	54	1.2

Primates are the apelike creatures that will eventually evolve into man.

Horses first appear about	52	1.1
Whales first appear about	50	1.09

As we near the one yard-line of our historic football field, which corresponds to the time of 46 million years ago, we find we still have an immense quantity of interesting history crammed into this remaining yard of space. Let us expand this remaining one percent of historic time onto a new chart. Hold down the lower goal-line, grab the one-yard-line and stretch it up for 99 yards, like a big rubber-band, thus magnifying this historic interval by 100 times. See Figure 2.

Second Chart[8]

Now the upper 99% of our second time-line stretches from 46 million to 460 thousand years ago. What interesting historical events can we identify in this zone?[9]

Years ago/Yard-line	Event
41M/11	Monkeys first appear.
23M/50	Large ape species.
18M/39	Afropithecines.[10]
15M/33	Kenyapithecines.
	About this time apes have migrated from Africa to Asia and Europe.
12M/26	Dryopithecines.
4.4M/9.6	Australopitecines.
	Bipedalism, the ability to walk on two legs, develops in the apelike creatures that are evolving towards human form.
4M/8.7	The period from 4M to 2M marks the transition from ape to human in evolution.
2.5M/5.4	Oldest fossils in the genus Homo, and the oldest known stone tools. Early Homo extends through 1.6 million years ago.
2M/4.3	Middle Homo begins with Homo erectus, who was the first to discover and control the use of fire. From 2M to 1.6M early humans migrated out of Africa.
1.9M/4.1	Homo habilis.
1.6M/3.5	Stone ax user.
1.2M/2.6	Youngest australopith fossils imply extinction of this creature.
500K/1.1	Paleoanthropologists generally define the earliest Homo sapiens fossils from about 500K where the braincase is larger than that of H. erectus.

460K/1   Our one yard-line defines the transition to the
                          next chart.

Third Chart

Now the upper 99% of our third time-line stretches from 460 thousand
years ago to 4600 years ago. See Figure 3. What notable historical events can
we identify in this zone?

Years ago/Yard-line	Event
200K/43	Earliest Homo neanderthalensis fossils. Neanderthals were man-like creatures that lived during the same time as early H. sapiens in Western Europe and central Asia, and no doubt competed with him for territory and resources.
130K/28	Modern H. sapiens evolved in Africa.
100K/22	Time traveler visit to the Earth of a time before modern man, see Chapter 2.
90K/20	H. sapiens migrates out of Africa to begin settling in other regions.
36K/7.8	Youngest of the Neanderthal fossils implies extinction around this time.
35K/7.6	"People" are wearing clothes, using language, creating art.
27.8K/6	Extinction of the Cave bear.
11.5K/2.5	Extinction of Sabertooth tiger.
11K/2.4	Boundary between the Pleistocene and Holocene Epochs marking the end of the last ice age.
10K/2.2	Extinction of the Woolly mammoth near the end of the Pleistocene
7K/1.5	Earliest Sumerian civilization in Mesopotamia.
5K/1.1	Development of writing, in Sumerian cuneiform.
4.6K/1	Transition to next chart.

Fourth Chart

At the one-yard-line of our twice-expanded football field, corresponding to the time of 4600 years ago, we have the entire recorded history of modern man crammed into this last yard of space. If we were to stretch our chart again, we could only attempt to summarize this enormous subject, the era of mankind. But this task has already been admirably accomplished by Ed Hull in a vastly more detailed fashion than we could ever hope to duplicate. We therefore refer the reader to the *Wall Chart of World History*.[11] Hull's work presents the entire recorded history of mankind, brilliantly summarized and illustrated as a flow of branching streams in time, which unfolds to a colorful, 14-foot-long display.

Our own fourth chart, and Figure 4, follow a slightly different format than our previous ones by listing the names and dates of the people and events mentioned later in this book. It may be viewed as an index in chronological order. Note that we have changed the time-line from the number-of-years-ago format to the dates of the Gregorian calendar.

Introduced in 1582, the Gregorian calendar starts counting with the year 1 AD at the birth of Christ. If we assume the present time as the year 2010, this places the upper edge of our chart, 4600 years ago, at 2590 BC.[12]

The timeline of human history is said to start at 4004 BC, according to Hull, which corresponds to the biblical creation in the Garden of Eden. This number is consistent with the conclusions of Ussher, from Note 4, below, and places the beginning of recorded human history at 6014 years ago. In another perspective, the Jewish calendar traces its history back to the creation, or to the first man, Adam, as related in Genesis. In September of 2010 the Jewish calendar began the year 5771, which would place the creation at 3760 BC. So we can see that agreement on the precise date is problematic.[13]

Date	Person or Event	Chapter
4004 BC	Genesis	1
2590 BC	Origin goal-line of Fig. 4	1
1652 – 1320 BC	Moses, Exodus (estimated era of)	9
1335 BC	Akhenaten (monotheism)	9
551 – 479 BC	Confucius	10
469 – 399 BC	Socrates	10
428 – 348 BC	Plato	10
412 – 323 BC	Diogenes	10
384 – 322 BC	Aristotle	10
106 – 43 BC	Cicero	10
100 – 44 BC	Julius Caesar	22
1 AD	Birth of Jesus Christ	1
354 – 430 AD	Augustine	10
1020	King Canute	11
1215	Magna Carta, King John	24
1225 – 1274	Aquinas	10
1265 – 1321	Dante	10
1398 – 1468	Johannes Gutenberg	30
1439	Invention of movable-type printing	30
1446 – 1506	Christopher Columbus	14
1469 – 1527	Niccolo Machiavelli	16
1473 - 1543	Copernicus	14
1491 – 1547	King Henry VIII	24
1532	*The Prince*	16
1564 – 1616	William Shakespeare	18
1564 - 1642	Galileo	14
1581 – 1686	James Ussher	1
1582	Gregorian calendar	1
1588 - 1679	Thomas Hobbes	2
1643 - 1727	Isaac Newton	14
1687	*Principia*	14
1723 - 1790	Adam Smith	13
1732 – 1799	George Washington	30
1755 – 1835	Chief Justice John Marshall	26

Date	Person or Event	Chapter
1766 – 1834	Thomas Malthus	28
1776	*Wealth of Nations*	13
1776	*Declaration of Independence*	17
1809 – 1882	Charles Darwin	1
1818 – 1883	Karl Marx	12
1848	*Communist Manifesto*	12
1859	*Origin of the Species*	1
1863 – 1952	George Santayana	30
1870 – 1924	Vladimir Lenin	12
1882 – 1945	Franklin D Roosevelt	17
1883 – 1950	Joseph Schumpeter	13
1887	Lord Acton (power corrupts)	11
1897	Legislating the value of pi	11
1917	Russian Revolutions	12
1933	The New Deal	17
1916 – 1994	Richard Nixon	22
1918 - 1996	Spiro Agnew	22
1946 -	William Clinton	22

We thus conclude our tour of Earth history, hoping our readers have an appreciation for the vastness represented by 4.6 billion years of time, and the relatively insignificant period we humans have resided on the planet, representing one-millionth of the total.

Notes:

[1] There may be simpler forms of life, but we select the amoeba as our starting point. The amoeba is a eukaryote, which is to say a single-cell containing a nucleus. The eukaryotes were preceded in the development of life forms by the bacteria and archaea, which are single-celled without a nucleus.

[2] For a thorough and fascinating account of the discovery of deoxyribo-nucleic acid, find a copy of the book *DNA*, by James D. Watson. See Watson.

[3] See Darwin.

[4] We are using the conclusions of science in our arguments here rather

than those of religion. But we don't wish to exclude any readers who hold strongly religious beliefs. This book can be read as a logical argument based on the ideas considered, without denigrating ideas based on other doctrines. So let's take a brief look at one of the doctrines promulgated by a seventeenth century cleric.

James Ussher, whose dates are 1581 to 1656, was a prominent churchman and a bishop in Ireland. In the 1650's he published a chronology of incidents in the Bible, and came to the conclusion that the year of creation, as described in the book of Genesis, was 4004 BC. This result was based on his study of the scriptures and other documents available to him, and represents a highly erudite estimate for his time. Many people today still adhere to this number, since they believe the bishop must have been divinely inspired. However, over the ages many other leaders from various regions, and from other religious persuasions, have made different conclusions based on their own studies and backgrounds.

Today we have a vast amount of scientific information that was not available to these earlier investigators, and we plan to use much of it to form our own conclusions. If we were to limit our discussion to the 6000 years Ussher would allow, we wouldn't have enough time for the forces of nature to have evolved all the life forms we wish to consider in this book.

[5] See MacKenzie for a thorough discussion of the formation of the Earth-Moon pair in his book, *The Big Splat.*

[6] See Dennett 1995. The details of this question about the spontaneous development of early life from the inorganic constituents of the primitive earth have been extensively analyzed in scientific literature. *Darwin's Dangerous Idea* contains an excruciatingly detailed, though eminently readable, discussion of the subject.

[7] The information in this first chart is derived from the book *Earth: Portrait of a Planet,* by Stephen Marshak. See Marshak.

[8] We use the abbreviations: "M" for mega, millions; "K" for kilo, thousands.

[9] The anthropological information in the second and third charts is derived from the *Human Origins Program* on the website of the Smithsonian Institution. See Smithsonian.

[10] Please refer to your local library or your favorite Internet search engine to obtain further details about the primates mentioned here without elaboration.

[11] See Hull.

[12] Calendar date conventions.

The traditional date notations of BC and AD come from the Christian tradition that, for many years, dominated in Western Civilization.

BC – before Christ

AD – anno Domini (in the year of the Lord)

More modern writers have substituted the notations of BCE and CE in order to be more sensitive to easily offended non-Christian readers.

CE – common era

CE – current era

CE – Christian era

BCE – before common era

BCE – before current era

BCE – before Christian era

In any case, the terminology refers to the same thing, that is, dates on the standardized Gregorian calendar.

When the author was growing up and learning to read in his particular schooling environment, the customary terminology was to use the BC/AD standard, so he has chosen to continue that tradition in this book. Of course, for the purposes of political correctness, any reader is welcome, even encouraged, to substitute the terminology she or he prefers.

[13] Although we insist that this book is based on facts from science, it is impossible to entirely ignore the traditions of religion that have become important influences in our culture of today. A simple example is the Gregorian calendar baseline selected for counting years.

CHAPTER TWO

100,000 YEARS AGO

NOW that we have taken a cursory look at the history of our planet, let's go back to visit a time before the advent of modern man. Jump into our time machine while we adjust the controls for 100,000 years ago. This date will give Earth a chance to have evolved most of the life forms that are present today, but without the complications of modern man.

During the Pleistocene Epoch, the time from 1.8 million to 11,000 years ago, global cooling alternated with warming periods for 20 to 30 cycles. The resulting ice ages caused glaciers to advance and recede over Canada and the northern U.S., Europe and Asia.[1]

As we travel back in time, we should look to visit a period between ice ages. When we get there, we will find a world covered with lush vegetation, except for the snowy, polar regions and some desert areas. Vast forests and grasslands cover most of the land masses. The land plants have been evolving for more than 400 million years and range from mosses and ferns to grasses, bushes and trees. Living in the midst of this vegetation we find insects of many types; worms, crawlers, hoppers, flyers. Birds populate the trees and skies, in many varieties. The land supports amphibians, reptiles, and mammals in increasing variety. The seas, covering two thirds of the planet, are teeming with life as well, with plankton, mollusks, jellyfish, eels, sharks, and many others. Life, of course, started out in the seas.

Early man was also on the scene by this time, but he certainly hadn't taken command of his environment. Our ancestors, modern Homo sapiens, evolved in Africa about 130 thousand years ago, long after the earliest genus Homo of some 2 million years ago.

At the time we will visit, 100,000 years ago, man is still a hunter-gatherer, at the mercy of the weather and other forces of nature. Life is hard for these cavemen (and women, and their children), who live much the same as any other wild animals. So we will avoid disturbing any of them.

Let's choose to re-materialize our time machine in a temperate climate, in a place that may some day be chosen for a national park. Observe on our past-o-scope this particularly attractive area to park our machine in a meadow next to a little stream at the edge of a forest. Since our time vehicle operates a lot like a helicopter, we should be able to place it on that spot without causing any damage to the environment.

Thump. A perfect landing!

Now that we have arrived, open the hatch and step out of vehicle into the sunshine. What a beautiful summer day it is in this idyllic place. Take a deep breath of the clean fresh air. Smell the pleasant aromas of the forest in the afternoon.

See the birds circling in the air, riding the afternoon thermals, keeping an eye out for their dinner. Hear the calls of other animals in the forest, alarmed by our arrival, giving their fellows the word to be cautious. Listen to the birds singing from the trees. Hear the burbling of the water in the creek, flowing around the rocks.

Look at the profusion of wild flowers blooming in this meadow. See how they are attended by bees, busy collecting nectar, and incidentally, pollinating the flowers. Feel the rich soil, like a sponge beneath your feet, nourishing the roots of the lush vegetation.

Look across the meadow at that big tree. Can you see the fox, or perhaps a proto-fox, sneaking out of the woods? He sees us, but knows we are far enough away to be no threat. He is stalking some small creature in the grass. Did you seem him dart after it? Looks like he's got his lunch.

So here we have Mother Nature in all her glory. We can appreciate this balanced ecology with a great diversity of plants and animals living together in the continuing cycles of life. It seems to be an ideal world existing in a time before the depredations of man. Wouldn't this place be a true paradise for an avid environmentalist?

Now let's stop to think for a moment how this perfect ecology came to be. It seems an idyllic garden on an earth, from not too long ago, without the disturbances of modern man. This profusion of life forms, all the plants and animals together, are interacting in a busy, complex fabric of life and death. Each individual, in concert with others of his species, has carved out a niche to survive in the ecology.

How did all these creatures come to this happy state? They all arrived at this point in history by every individual watching out for himself, acting only in his own, selfish, narrow self-interest, with no regard whatsoever for his neighbor.

Think about that one for a minute. A highly complex collection of life forms, in amazing diversity, blanketing the entire planet, forming an ideal ecology, that looks frighteningly similar to what you see today outside your window, was created by each individual, throughout history, watching out for himself alone.

Anarchy

This idyllic scene represents the anarchy of the natural world. Anarchy is the complete lack of government, because there are no people to establish one. Anarchy means that behavior is governed by the law of the jungle, where the rules are: kill or be killed, eat or be eaten.[2] Anarchy leads to survival of the fittest, and natural selection at its finest, where violence is the answer to every question.[3]

When you, as an animal, live in this kind of environment, you need to act for yourself, and do whatever you are capable of. If you have teeth and claws, use them. If you are fleet of foot, use that talent to flee the creatures that want you for dinner. If you find some tasty berries on a bush, go ahead and eat them. Don't bother asking permission first. If you are a carnivore, lie in wait for your victim to wander into range. Jump out quickly and kill him before he has the chance to flee. Don't worry about fairness or a human concept of justice. You are an animal trying to survive in the wild. Satisfying your hunger is the instinct you must obey. Nobody else is there to help you. You must take care of yourself, if you want to survive and propagate your kind. Only the strongest and fittest survive. The slow or less skilled in killing succumb to the more powerful, and become their dinner.

Welcome to the wild world of nature, where might makes right, and the ends justify the means. Violence rules the world.

The question of good versus evil always arises at this point in our discussion. We wish to know whether this law of the jungle, as practiced by the animals we see around us, is morally justifiable or not. At this point in the history of the planet, there is no way to tell. Remember that we are looking at a time before man has developed any civilization worthy of the title. Nobody with a brain large enough to appreciate the concepts of good and evil has bothered to consider the subject. For the present we must ignore the subject of justice. The world of animals is simply life as it is, without judgments.

So here we are standing around our time machine, admiring the beauties of nature on the earth of 100,000 years ago. Have you noticed all the flying insects buzzing around our ears? That's fairly irritating to our civilized tastes, but you need to expect that when you go out in the woods. It's a good thing we brought along our insect repellent. We certainly don't want to give up our modern conveniences. Speaking of which, we can't stay here for too long, because there are no hotels or grocery stores. Besides, some large animals may smell us, and come to investigate. We wouldn't want some Sabertooth tiger, or a similar creature, to decide we look like dinner.

Also, we ourselves would start to get hungry after four hours or so, and we don't want to start hunting or harvesting fruit, for fear of disturbing the past and changing history. We wouldn't want to get back to our own time and learn that our trip had altered our own civilization in some significant way. So let's pile back into the time machine and return to our own time, where we belong.[4]

Now that we are safely back to our familiar twenty-first century environment, we may go outside and find a world similar to the one we just visited, one where the anarchy of nature still holds sway. If you visit your local national park, or even a nearby state park, you can hike for a half-hour and get far enough away from the highway to be completely on your own in nature. The plants, birds, insects, rodents, and whatever larger animals you encounter, still live in the same type of environment we saw during our time travel. Their lives are generally solitary, brutal and short as they strive to survive in the hazardous conditions of their competitive world.[5] They try to scratch their livings from their wild environment using whatever skills their evolution has provided. They still exist in that narrow ecological niche they and their ancestors have been able to carve out of their environment.

Notes:

[1] See Marshak, *Earth,* Chapter 22, Section 8, "The Pleistocene Ice Ages," pp. 709-718.

[2] Loaded words warning: "Anarchy" is one of those loaded words that means different things to different people. It can mean confusion, disorder, formlessness, illegality, lawlessness or revolution. Anarchism in the political sense can mean liberty, where people may agree to develop their own sense of morality based on their individual beliefs. This may be considered a good thing, a happy state of affairs, where people have the freedom of political and economic self-rule. As a philosophical concept, anarchy can suggest liberty without the implication of disorder. However, for the purposes of this book, anarchy means the complete lack of a government order, as in the world of animals where every creature acts only for his own narrow self-interest with no regard for how his actions might affect the lives of others.

[3] See Darwin. This view of nature, of evolution by natural selection, was first described by Charles Darwin in his 1859 book, *Origin of the Species.* These concepts represent a giant leap forward in the scientific understanding of nature. The subjects of evolution and natural selection, where the animals compete for survival in an evolving environment, and related topics have been exhaustively described in the literature. See also Dennett, 1995, *Darwin's Dangerous Idea,* for a modern analysis of the entire subject.

[4] Full disclosure: The scene featuring the time machine is a fictional device used to illustrate the points about life on the early Earth. Time travel is actually impossible under the current scientific understanding of reality, and will remain so until the second law of thermodynamics is superseded by a more sophisticated explanation of the underlying principles.

[5] The quote about life being brutal and short comes from Thomas Hobbes, whose dates are 1588-1679. In his book, *Leviathan,* Chapter XIII, "On the Natural Condition of Mankind, as Concerning their Felicity, and Misery," while lamenting the sad state of mankind in the throes of warfare, the philosopher wrote "... and which is worst of all, continuall feare, and danger of violent death; And the life of man, solitary, poore, nasty, brutish, and short." See Hobbes.

CHAPTER THREE

THE MEANING OF LIFE

IN Chapter 1, we looked at the amoeba and mentioned that it is the simplest form of life we would consider in this book. What is the meaning of life for this most basic life form? This may seem to be a ridiculous question, but if we eventually wish to contemplate the meaning of life for humans, for ourselves, we should first consider much simpler cases.

This creature exists in nature, and has survived for millions of years, so we think this kind of success implies an underlying meaning to it all. We, as humans, realize that the term "meaning" has no meaning to the amoeba itself, or even to the community of amoebae.

We propose that the meaning of life for the amoeba is simply the struggle for survival and propagation of its kind, because that is what it spends all its time doing. This explanation for its behavior forms the baseline for the simple forms of life, and will continue up the tree of life as more complex forms develop.

Above the single-celled creature on the tree of life, we find multi-celled creatures, which represent a major step in the progress of evolution, but they add little to our understanding of life. But once multi-celled creatures evolved, cells began to become specialized, so as to perform different functions for the host organism. Think of a primitive worm with a mouth, a digestive tract, and an anus. It has become a food-processing organism, made up of different types of cells that perform their own functions in support of the creature. It has skin cells to isolate it from its environment. It has gut cells to extract nourishment from its food. It has some early form of muscle to move the food along inside its gut, and also to propel the creature in its search for more food. It eats things and casts off waste products.

What does the worm eat? It eats organic materials and other creatures of lower life forms it is able to digest. It converts food to energy to support its bodily functions. Thus, a food chain has developed in nature to support a primitive ecology. And this worm may yet become part of the food chain for some higher animal of the future.

What is the meaning of life for this worm? It is still the struggle for survival and propagation of its species, just like the earlier, less complex creature. The larger the community of worms becomes, the better chance they have to survive and advance together in the scheme of nature. One of the functions of the worm in its environment will be to provide food for some other animal, higher on the food chain in the ecology. But to become food for others is not a meaning of life, it is one of the hazards. The meaning of life is the struggle for survival, which includes avoiding becoming food. The worms must propagate their kind faster than they are consumed by enemies, otherwise they will become extinct.

Extinction is a major hazard in the web of life. Extinction has eliminated many millions of life forms from the game of life, but the larger ecology still seems to grow in complexity and diversification over the ages, despite the many threats to its continuation.

Plants

Moving along to another life form, let's look at the meaning of life for a plant. Take a fruit tree as an example. Life for a tree is pretty boring. It can't go anywhere, and it has no brain to use for worrying about its lot in the world. It is stuck in one spot by its roots fastened in the ground. It uses its roots to extract water and nutrients from the soil. It uses its leaves to gather sunlight and make food via photosynthesis. It grows new branches and puts on more leaves. It creates fruit and seeds to drop on the ground in the hope that it will propagate its kind, to create a grove or even a forest of trees. But, of course, it has no awareness of this "hope."

If an animal comes along to eat its leaves or fruit, it has no defense. It must stand there and take it. But it has developed the capability to re-grow its leaves and create more fruit. So a plant can serve a useful function in the ecology as food for other creatures, but it still must grow faster than it is consumed in order to survive. It also retains the trick of re-growing from its roots if all of its branches are severed or burned away. And the seeds it has sprinkled about its location can hide in the soil until the conditions of moisture and temperature stimulate germination, and thus the beginning of a new tree. The meaning of life for a plant is also its passive struggle for survival, wherever it happens to be located.

Mammals

Let us climb up the tree of life, ignoring thousands of other life forms, until we reach the birds and mammals. These creatures have evolved into organisms with hundreds of different cell types to define their various bodily functions. Bone, muscle, nerve, blood, gut, hair or feather, and cornea cells represent a small sample of the many types making up the creature. Birds and mammals have their cells organized into fabulously complex systems which allow them to fly over or run across or burrow under the surface of their world to find food and shelter, build nests and modify their surroundings to benefit themselves and their offspring.

They have developed brains, and a degree of awareness about their surroundings. Use of tools and perhaps a bit of creative thinking might be attributed to some of the more advanced specimens. An example would be a simian using a stick to probe an anthill to stir up more of the inhabitants for his lunch. Or think of a sea bird carrying a shellfish high in the air and dropping it on the rocks below to release the tasty morsel inside.

The behavior of all of these animals is directed towards feeding themselves, fighting off enemies, and propagating their offspring. And they use all the capabilities at their disposal. If they find berries on a bush, they eat them without asking permission. If they see another creature they want for food, they will try to kill it for dinner. When they are hungry, their motivation is to fill their bellies, and they use whatever tooth, beak or claw they have for the purpose, while taking care not to be killed themselves.[1]

For all the animals and plants living in the wild, it is a hard life out there. They must compete for survival in the anarchy of nature, against other creatures for the same resources.

Although birds and mammals are abundantly more sophisticated than the life forms discussed earlier, the meaning of life for them is, again, simply the struggle for survival.[2]

Deception

Do animals lie, cheat and steal? These are human concepts, so how could they apply to the life of animals? But note that lying, cheating and stealing are merely human versions of deception.

Deception is a powerful weapon in the arsenal of survival. Deception has been practiced by animal life long before humans appeared on the scene. If you are a predator, hide behind a rock until your dinner wanders past. Pretend you are not really there. Conversely, if you are prey, hide in the bushes as your predator skulks by. Pretend you are not there. Try to fool them.

If you are a turtle with a tongue that looks like a worm, open your jaws and wave that bait around in the current. When your prey swims past looking for dinner, it will come over to investigate that tasty looking morsel. Slam your jaws shut at the last moment and eat him whole.[3]

If you are a chameleon, change your color to match the surface you are resting on. Camouflage yourself against the background. Pretend you are not there so you may deceive those nasty birds that want to eat you.

Watch any nature show on TV. Read an article about wild animals in *National Geographic*. Observe the animals practicing deception against their predators and prey. Lying, cheating, and stealing food is a way of life in the animal world. Deception is a handy tool for use in the game of survival.

A given species may eventually reach its full potential in its environment, that niche it occupies in the ecology, and be unable to advance further. But the success it has achieved up to that point may be adequate to keep it going for many generations.

Eventually, evolution in a species may stumble upon a mutation that gives the life form an advantage over earlier versions. An example would be sharper eyesight in a bird of prey, or an improvement in muscle development that gives a rabbit the ability to run faster. In such a case, the new variety may eventually split-off to form a new branch on the tree of life and become a new species.

A mutation may also prove to cripple some useful function in the creature's make-up, and cause the carriers to die out. In which case, the original species would continue without the members sporting that unworthy mutation.

In this chapter we have focused on several of the life forms that exist today. The purpose is to illustrate that the urge for survival appears to be the major motivation for all forms of life. But mere survival seems like an over-simplification. Certainly there is more to the meaning of life than survival. Living things strive for growth, both in themselves and in their communities. They wish to dominate their environment and take over territory from other competing life forms. They use whatever talents and skills their species has developed over the ages. They use their teeth and claws, if they have them, or their fleetness of foot. They use their little brains to come up with new innovations in the continuing challenges of their environment. There seems to be some life force that drives advancement, that keeps things moving ahead. The branch of study known as "emergence" may shed some light on this question.

Emergence

The concept of life appears to be a violation of the second law of thermodynamics, which is one of the bedrock principles upon which science is built. This law states that nature moves towards ever increasing states of chaos, or that entropy increases.[4] Life, on the other hand, is a force towards organization and order that appears nearly everywhere we look. How do we reconcile these apparently conflicting features we observe in nature?

Emergence is a concept that has arisen in philosophy and science that tries to explain the mysterious development of order out of chaos in the universe. We see in nature many instances where higher levels of organization seem to spontaneously develop in systems of interacting parts. It may be thought of as patterns emerging in complex systems, and being reinforced by some unseen guiding principle.[5] Life is perhaps the ultimate manifestation of an emergent process.

The phenomena of emergence are under active study, but scientists have not yet had much luck in reducing emergence to a viable theory.

Someone might suggest that emergence is an example of miracles happening every day, but that would require the intervention of some higher intelligence. Miracles, being supernatural in origin, are not allowed as explanations in the scientific method.

Let us consider water as a simple example of a material that exhibits emergent behavior. Science has discovered that an individual water molecule is composed, at the most basic level, of two atoms of hydrogen and one of oxygen, H_2O. This stable molecule is held together by the covalent bonds between the atoms. Since we think we understand water at this basic level (or we could find a professor who thoroughly understands it and could explain it to us), we should be able to predict the various patterns that groups of water molecules can form into.

Consider a few of these patterns: Fog, steam, water vapor, cloud, thunderhead, droplet, mist, haze, condensate, drip, squirt, splash, sluice, drizzle, rain, rainstorm, deluge, puddle, pond, lake, ocean, trickle, rivulet, creek, stream, river, waterfall, ocean current, tide, ice, sleet, hail, snow, snowflake, snowdrift, snowstorm, avalanche, glacier, ice cap, blue ice, black ice, iceberg, frost on a window, frost on a pine tree, geyser, and even, perhaps, a rainbow.

All of these words describe emergent conditions of water, patterns that occur naturally. Is there anywhere a serious scientist who can claim he could have predicted all these water patterns if he had not seen them first? Could he have anticipated so many features of water from his total understanding of the water molecule? Not likely, but nature has created this astounding variety of patterns without a thought.

All matter in the world is composed of atoms. There are 88 different, naturally occurring atoms (elements) in existence (plus another 30 or so unstable or short-lived ones). Water, with all its wonderful array of patterns is made from merely two kinds of atoms. The rest of the world, the rest of the universe, is made from chemical combinations of atoms. The many patterns of water molecules are a trivial subset of the forms that all atoms can assume. So we may expect to find a vast array of emergent characteristics in the available combinations and permutations of matter in nature.

The most interesting emergent property of nature is Life. Life eventually developed into human civilization, which led to language and writing and books. And here we are, reading a book about life.

This mysterious life force propels creatures towards greater goals, for growth and advancement. But how does the life force work? Where does it come from? We can understand the concept by considering the alternatives to growth: stagnation and decline.

What happens to an individual creature if he fails to defend himself from his hostile environment? If he stops eating, or stops trying to avoid his natural enemies, he will soon find himself dead, joining the millions of other failed life forms in the graveyard of history. The eons are littered with the dead-ends of terminated life forms. Some of these unfortunate plants and creatures served as food for their predators, and some were preserved as fossils for us to study today. The bodies of others, lying in the dirt, were consumed by decay, broken down into constituent, non-organic molecules by the action of microbes. The second law of thermodynamics predominates over life in such a case.

If the individual creature dies before he has bred, his personal line dies out as well. If his fellow creatures, those of his same species, also give up, the species heads for extinction.

Now look around you. Every creature you see has survived in the competition for life. You simply don't see any more living examples of extinct species. Natural selection has eliminated them from the scene. Life is reserved for the living.

Survival is the most basic requirement of life. Every creature has the obligation, the duty, to strive after his own self-interest. It may be a stretch to imbue dumb creatures with the human concepts of obligation and duty, but we can see that these traits are inherent in the continuation of life. We can thus say that the struggles for survival and growth are the imperatives of life.

Does an individual squirrel, foraging for food in the treetops, need to be aware of her obligation to fight for survival? Of course not. The imperatives of life are built into her behavior. It has become instinctual and automatic. No awareness by the squirrel is required. It may be that the squirrel species is headed for a dead-end in the tree of life, but they have achieved a successful formula for survival in the world of today. The squirrel is well suited to its niche in the ecology, and will survive for a long time; at least until its forest environment disappears.

Notes:

[1] An interesting feature in the anarchic behavior of animals is that the killing is self-limiting. An animal only kills when it is hungry, and quits when it is satisfied. A tiger may attack and kill one gazelle from a herd, but then she stops to eat. When satisfied, the tiger leaves the remaining meat for the rest of her clan. Note that the tiger does not kill all the gazelles in the herd just for the fun of it. The herd represents a food resource, which the tigers access as needed, so the killing is self-limiting. The ecology contains feedback mechanisms to maintain balance in nature. Equilibrium is achieved among the various forces.

[2] See Dennett, 1991. An excellent perspective on the evolution of consciousness in pre-conscious creatures is offered by Daniel Dennett in his book, *Consciousness Explained,* Chapter 7, Section 2, pp. 173 to 182.

[3] Macrochelys temminckii, the Alligator Snapping Turtle of the lower Mississippi.

[4] See Seife for a very interesting, thorough explanation of the second law of thermodynamics along with information theory.

[5] See Corning for a review of the work that has been accomplished in the study of emergence.

CHAPTER FOUR

SOCIETY

NOW that we have looked at individual animals and their urge to survive, let us consider their family groups and communities.

As soon as an organism begins to reproduce, it forms into family groups or communities with common goals. The most fundamental goal for the group is to survive. The group must seek food, build nests, establish territory, defend itself from enemies, and expand into its environment to grow and propagate its kind. Although the family is still composed of individuals who do these things on their own, the collective provides the individuals with a supportive environment. A predator is less likely to attack a group than it is to ambush a lone individual who strays behind the herd.

Once a group is established as a going concern, the individuals begin to specialize into particular jobs, and they depend on the group interactions for their own survival. If a group is reduced in number below some critical size, the individuals will probably die-out without the support of their clan.

Ants

Consider an ant colony, a society of tiny creatures who have developed a civilization to benefit their own kind. They have divided the tasks of their society into various specialties. The queen and her attendants run the nursery where the eggs are created and cared for. This department provides new ants to grow the colony. Worker ants dig tunnels to accommodate the size of the colony population, and store food. Other workers go out in the surrounding wilds to search for leaves and other food to bring back to the nest for their comrades.

Ants have carved out a highly successful niche in the ecology. Some 9500 species have been identified, and all together they are said to compose

15 to 20 percent of the terrestrial animal biomass, exceeding even that of the vertebrates. In the tropics, where conditions are more favorable for them, ants probably account for 25 percent of the animal biomass.[1]

Lifelike

The ant colony as a collective unit takes on a kind of life of its own. We shall call this unit a "lifelike" form, to distinguish it from a true life form[2] A true life form, a biological creature, an individual ant for instance, is made up of groups of cells acting together to make up the total creature. Cells specialize into particular functions. Some cells form into mandibles for eating. Others become intestines to process food and turn it into sugars and other forms the ant can use in his bodily functions. Some are nerve cells to transmit signals to the muscle cells, etc. All the cells become organized into a division of labor society, each performing its own task, the collection of which compose the entire ant creature and give it its character. Individual cells are always dividing and producing new cells. Older cells die off to be replaced by newer cells, which take over the duties of the ones they replace. Thus, the individual ant, continues to exist in his boring little life, while he casts off old dead cells, and goes about his business over many cycles of cell replacements, before he himself dies.

Compare the ant, a true life form, to the ant colony, a lifelike form. In the colony, the individual ants are the cell analogs. The ants are divided into job specialties, a division of labor society, to keep the colony running. The queen takes care of reproduction, while the workers handle other tasks to keep the colony going. Sometimes a food-gatherer will die while out on a foraging expedition. She is, perhaps, consumed by an anteater in the neighborhood. But the queen replaces the lost worker from her supply of new ants. So the colony, the lifelike form, survives despite the loss of the individual ants, the cell analogs.

Of course the ant colony will not survive if too many of the individual ants are lost to the anteaters and other hazards in their environment. Just as the individual ant will die if she loses too many of her own cells, if for instance her entire abdomen is separated from the body.

The ant colony exhibits lifelike behavior. It grows and takes over new territory. It has the drive to dominate its environment. Some species of ants will raid neighboring colonies to kill the enemy ants and carry their eggs back to the home colony. The captured eggs are allowed to mature, and the resulting ants are pressed into service as slaves to help the capturing queen care for her own eggs.

Army ants swarm across the jungle, aggressively eating their way through any organic matter they encounter. When they are not on the march, they swarm around the queen, protecting her from any threats in the environment where they bivouac.

Each ant species has developed its own techniques for survival and growth. Some do the army ant trick; others stick with more peaceful solutions. All have discovered a niche in ecology that works for their particular colony.

So now we understand that life in the world is composed not only of true life forms, biological creatures, competing for survival in their ecological niches, but also of lifelike forms competing among other life forms and lifelike forms. This situation makes life more complicated, but also offers a greater diversity of options available to the ecology. A greater number of competitors are thus available to participate in the anarchy of the wild environment. The process of natural selection will cull the less fit from the game during the continuing, brutal competition for survival.

Motherhood

An important concept to appreciate in the process of natural selection is that certain behavior patterns are preserved while others are eliminated. Consider motherhood among mammals. A good mother cares for her offspring until they are old enough to fend for themselves. She feeds her babies and provides them with a warm nest. She protects them from predators and tries to train them in the ways of her species. She goes out into the wild world, at no small hazard to herself, to find food to bring back to her brood. This is a lot of work.

Altruism

Wouldn't it be easier for her just to be done with them once they are born? They cost her a lot of effort, when she could use the time for her own survival, gathering and hoarding food, or hiding from predators. But instead she performs the seemingly altruistic, selfless acts of motherhood, defending her pups and teaching them her techniques for surviving on their own.

These behavior patterns propagate because the alternatives become dead-ends under natural selection. The animals that chose the easy ways, of eating their own offspring for example, guarantee they won't propagate into the future, and thus became extinct. Natural selection has efficient methods for weeding out self-destructive behavior in its realm.

So this apparently altruistic behavior by the mother towards her youngsters is actually selfish behavior for her species. She gives up her short-term selfish behavior of serving herself alone, for the longer-term selfish behavior of serving her species. This is a basic example of cooperation among individuals within a species to advance the interests of the group, survival being a major goal. Actually, we should say survival is the result. The term "goal" implies an intention, a thinking-ahead with some future purpose in mind. Natural selection is a blind process with no plan for success of any particular outcome. The successful processes for survival propagate into the future; the unsuccessful ones for survival die out.

Pecking order

Another behavior pattern that has emerged among animals is that of the pecking order. This is how animals in a group, chickens in a flock for example, arrange themselves into a hierarchy. Each individual, presumably, would like to be the chief, and have the others in the group do her bidding. But in order to become the chief, the aspirant has to show she can dominate the other individuals. This is usually determined by violence, or by the threat of violence.

The top chicken (hen) can largely succeed by flapping her wings and squawking at the others. From previous encounters with this aggressive behavior, the lesser chickens will give way to Flapper and let her have first choice at the food pellets stacked in the corner.

Eventually, some other individual is likely to decide that she has had enough. The top chicken has become insufferable, what with her strutting about and forcing the rest of us to wait for dinner. We have to sit around, grooming our feathers, while Flapper takes her sweet time sorting through the food pellets. That food really belongs to all of us, and I'm not putting up with her bossy attitude any more.

Once the challenging chicken decides she is bigger or tougher, she will need to fight the top chicken with beak and claw. The victor will earn the top position, if the battle has not disabled her in some significant fashion. The other chickens in the flock will have their own selection conflicts, some of which are fairly benign, involving a little shoving, but without major battles. Eventually, every chicken knows her place.

An interesting feature of the pecking order is that once it is established, the members of the group remember their places and don't challenge the status quo, until a new chicken is introduced to the flock. Keeping the pecking order intact saves energy. Since the chickens know their places, a lot of unnecessary fighting is avoided, so they can spend more time eating and caring for their eggs.

All animals organize their groups into their own version of a pecking order. Think of the alpha male in a wolf pack, or the mighty antlered buck leading a herd of elk.

If you have any personal experience caring for animals, you have no doubt observed the formation of a pecking order, a hierarchy, among them.

It is important to note again that no judgments are to be offered about whether animal behavior is good or evil. Such judgment might come from outside or above, from us, but not from the animals themselves in their ecology. The beasts have no concept of good or evil, fairness or sportsman-ship. Their philosophy is: eat or be eaten; kill or be killed; might makes right; the ends justify the means; and violence is the ultimate arbiter. This is because they are not capable of making higher judgments. There simply is no morality to be attributed to animal behavior. The idea of rightness must await the advent of a creature with a brain capable of grasping the concept.

Notes:

[1] For more about ants, see Schultz.

[2] Since we, as humans, represent a biological life form, we have a certain proprietary interest in keeping the term "life" for ourselves, in a kind of self-important, conceited, territorial sense. We are willing to share the term "life" with other biological creatures, like birds, reptiles, fish, and

plants, since we can appreciate our common ancestry. But a society of
ants, a collective, being considered as an instance of "life" is too close
to the edge for some of us. So we will accommodate our persnickety
brothers and sisters by reserving the definition of "life" for biological
individuals. We will refer to the ant colony, the collective unit, as a "lifelike" form. The individual ants, true life forms, compose the colony,
a lifelike form. Note, however, that the definition for "life" we gave in
Chapter 1, an agent exhibiting directed behavior, applies as well to lifelike forms.

CHAPTER FIVE

MAN

NOW that we have seen animal life develop on Earth from the single celled creature (of 3.2 billion years ago), up through the dinosaurs (about 200 million years ago), and into the advent of early man (perhaps 2 million years ago), we can appreciate the harsh environment where our ancient forefathers had to compete for survival.

Brains

Early man was just like any other animal attempting to survive and prosper in the anarchy of nature. But man had an advantage over all the other creatures, a big brain. He developed the ability to contemplate his actions before he actually tried them, and to reflect upon their possible outcomes. He learned how to remember his mistakes, and try to do better the next time. He learned how to speak and communicate with his fellow humans. He could now tell others what he discovered, so all members of his tribe could share knowledge without each individual having to discover everything on his own.[1] The lessons of trial and error led to more successful ways of surviving.

Man started to invent new and better ways of doing old things. He discovered that a club made a better weapon than his fist. Someone improved the idea by tying a rock to the end of a stick, creating a stone ax. A sharpened stick worked better in some applications than the ax, and the spear became a useful tool for the hunter. Eventually, the concept of the bow and arrow arose in the mind of some inspired thinker. The lever and the wheel certainly fit into this list of significant inventions.

Some industrious person came up with the idea for stacking rocks to build a wall. A wall built to surround a flat area made a sturdy shelter, if only a roof was added. People learned that small sticks and grasses could be woven into baskets. Animal hides can be fashioned into clothing. Wet clay can be formed into bowls, and when heated by fire, the clay bowl transforms into a re-useable earthenware utensil. Certainly the control and use of fire was one of early man's most brilliant discoveries.

Where did all these ideas come from? Many were merely extensions of the techniques that animals had been using for centuries. Birds built nests that inspired baskets. Burrowing creatures dug tunnels in the ground, creating cozy places to hide and raise their young, so people discovered they could live in caves, too. Other ideas occurred to certain individuals using their superior intellect to create new inventions never seen before on the face of the earth.

Cooperation

The family unit is the most basic form of organization. Humans have the family instinct, just like any other animal. They get together to benefit from their mutual cooperation, to survive, and to propagate their kind. This means that adults will have children. In order for the children to survive, they need the support of their parents, until the kids are old enough and skilled enough to care for themselves, when they can go out into the world and behave as adults.

But the family unit has enemies. It must fight off the animals that want to feed on their children, or chase away the deer in the garden that want to eat their crops. Sometimes the family will be forced to fight the clan down the hill who want to take over their cropland. But after a few skirmishes the family leaders begin to discover that cooperation among different families is more to their mutual benefit than constant fighting. They can use reason and compromise to settle their disputes rather than violence. Just like the cooperation among members of the family is more productive for the group than the every-man-for-himself model, cooperation between the various families in a region will be more advantageous to everyone than warfare. Groups of families thus form into bands or tribes for their mutual benefit.

Civilization

The benefits of his superior intelligence eventually led Man toward civilization. He changed his organization from a simple, nomadic, hunter-gatherer family unit, to one where he could live in villages, supported by farming and animal herding. Men could begin to specialize into areas where the individuals could exercise their particular talents. They developed a division of labor society, much like the ants, except on a greater scale.

Of course, each group of people developed a pecking order. The early versions of this hierarchy were, no doubt, based on the biggest or strongest individual, then perhaps on the most successful hunter. Many men found they could enjoy wielding power over others. Competition for the position of chief became intense.

Power

The men who exercised power discovered they could form groups of confederates to concentrate their strength and help enforce their authority. Soon the most successful tribal chief could become king over a realm of several tribes.

What was the form of government for these early tribal chiefs? We should probably not yet award this arrangement the title of a monarchy, but it was a step above the anarchy of the wild. It was an outgrowth of the pecking order among animals, so we could call it the top-dog syndrome, but instead let's refer to it as a chiefdom.

How does this chief establish and maintain his authority? He exercises power through his strength, and the threat, if not actually the use, of force and violence. The chiefdom is still a might-makes-right society, only a short step above the anarchy of wild nature.

So now our primitive people have advanced to the point where they live in a group, or a small community, or a village, overseen by a chief who wields power over his subjects. The community will have agreed upon a set of rules for behavior that allow them to live peacefully with one another and perform their tasks within the framework of their pecking order. They will have thus developed a primitive culture.

The chief, as a living creature, is interested in his own survival, and is also concerned about the survival of his clan. His people work for him and do his bidding. He recognizes that certain individuals have skills that are superior to other individuals. He therefore surrounds himself with these more talented people and rewards them with more food and other benefits in return for their loyalty. Soon he has a set of advisors to assist him in the administration of his tribe. His assistants form a council that helps with promulgating rules of behavior for his subjects.[2]

Law

The council made rules to govern who does how much work, and when it gets done. They decided who gets to be a hunter, a warrior, a farmer, a shepherd, a spear maker, etc. And they were very careful to make rules about how to show proper respect to the chief, so that he would continue to be in charge. No doubt, it didn't take long before tributes to the chief (taxes) were firmly established. Such rules become the precursors of law.

The sequence in which all these developments occurred, probably did not follow the order they are presented here. But the fact is that they all arose in primitive societies and competed for prominence in the marketplace of ideas. They are all still with us today, guiding behavior in the complex world of human interaction.

Writing

After thousands of years of slowly advancing civilization, following the tribal model, some clever person started making marks of a particular shape on various objects, and decided these marks meant particular things. Other people soon realized the usefulness of this technique, and a form of writing developed. People no longer needed to remember all knowledge in their heads alone. They could write it down for future reference for themselves, or for the benefit of others. Counting became a useful method for keeping track of things. The use of numbers became the basis of mathematics, another amazing feat of the human mind. The earliest writing that has been discovered is the Sumerian cuneiform markings on clay tablets, which date from approximately 3000 BC.[3] Along with the clay tablets were found small clay disks with unique markings, which are thought to be counters. So the births of both writing and mathematics seem to have occurred alongside each other.

Notes:

[1] Loaded words warning: "Tribe" is one of those loaded words that can mean different things to different people. It might be used in a degrading manner to imply a primitive grouping of people or to insult some ethnic minority. For the purposes of this book the word tribe simply means a small group of people who get together for some purpose of mutual support, such as a family or a grouping of families who form a village or community of some sort. In modern industry the term "tribal knowledge" means an area of specialized information that is specific to a particular department in a company. The sales department would have tribal knowledge about which customers tend to buy the most products in January, while the engineering department wouldn't have the slightest idea. The production department knows all the details about how to assemble widgets, while accounting couldn't care less. In this book the word "tribe" carries no negative connotations.

[2] See Diamond. A thorough discussion of the relationships among people in bands, tribes, chiefdoms, and states may be found in *Guns, Germs, and Steel*, Chapter 14.

[3] Ibid. A very readable and informative historical account of writing may be found in *Guns, Germs and Steel*, Chapter 12.

CHAPTER SIX

PRIMITIVE RELIGION AND TRIBAL LEADERSHIP

IN the primitive society, which we presented in the previous chapter, the people respect their chief because he holds power over them. He and his council of advisors exercise authority over the individual citizens, and the common folk must seek permission when they wish to do something that is outside their normal daily routine.

Our chief is no dummy. He had to grow up in the harsh environment of his primitive world and survive to adulthood. He is one tough character who has out-competed the other contenders in his tribe for position of chief. He has a short temper, and does not tolerate much foolishness, except perhaps, from the very young children. But let us assume our chief is also a benevolent sort, who respects his subjects and appreciates their contributions to the good of his tribe. He realizes that his power rests on the cooperation of his people, and that the more successful they are in their lives, the better off he will be also. He exercises his power to promote the success of his tribe, as he best sees fit.

So people come to him to settle disputes and ask for favors. He has established a set of rules for behavior in his tribe, and tries to enforce them fairly. He knows he should be consistent in his judgments, so he has his council keep track of his decisions.

One day a farmer with bad news comes in to see the chief. It seems many days have passed since the last rains, and his crops are beginning to wilt. He is running himself ragged, carrying water, a bowl-full at a time, from the creek to his field. What can he do, the farmer wishes to know, to cause the rains to return to his fields?

The chief hasn't the slightest idea about how to make it rain, but he does not wish to seem unknowing or incompetent in front of this farmer, especially with his advisors listening. So the chief makes up a plausible story to explain the lack of rains.

The spirit in the clouds is not pleased with the way you have been tending your fields, the chief explains to the farmer. Each day, before you start your work, you must go to the center of the field which needs rain the most, stretch your arms towards the heavens, turn around three times, click your heels, and beseech the cloud god to deliver rain, and explain why the tribe should be blessed with his largess. Do this also at the end of your workday, and spend longer hours toiling in your fields so the cloud god will see you are sincere in your supplications. Report your progress on this task every day to my secretary of agriculture, who will monitor the results of your prayers. When you are successful in attracting rain from the cloud god, we will remember how you accomplished your victory for the next time it is needed.

This all makes perfect sense to the poor farmer, who knows the chief is vastly superior in knowledge than he is. The farmer also knows that the chief has a short temper, and does not tolerate foolishness. The farmer would expect the same attitude from the god of clouds. After all, it would be only natural for a cloud god who is displeased with the farmer to withhold the life giving rain. So the farmer does as he is instructed. With a little luck, the rains return, and the farmer succeeds with his harvest.

The chief finds himself invoking a new god whenever a situation arises where he has no clue as to what to do. A whole pantheon of gods is thus generated for the growing mythology of his culture. Somebody needs to keep track of all these gods, and how the tribe has dealt with them in the past, so a new position appears in the chief's cabinet of advisors. The chief assigns this new advisor the title of "Priest." Eventually, the post of priest grows into the career field of the priesthood, and the first bureaucracy is born.

The priest, having achieved a degree of power in his tribe, wishes to expand his authority, so he is diligent in developing new rules to control the villagers, and to please the chief. He expands upon the chief's idea of the gods. These supernatural beings wield the powers of nature, powers even beyond those of the chief. These almighty gods must be appeased, and the priest knows, as the gods' representative (not merely the chief's), the proper procedures.

While he's at it, the priest also comes up with rules for behavior that actually benefit the tribe. He tells the people to bring in enough food from their hunting and farming to support their families plus some for the tribe. Take care of the children, because they represent the future of the tribe. Don't hit your little brother. Don't kill your neighbor, since he is an asset to the community, just like you are. Share your wealth with the community, work for the common interest. Support your chief and his advisors, because the chief is primarily interested in promoting the welfare of the tribe.

Once these rituals and customs take hold in the tribe, they develop an amazing staying-power in the culture. They are passed along from father to son, and take on new features and requirements as the years go by. The villagers find themselves prospering in their environment, despite the fact that they are heaping all manner of abuse upon themselves in an effort to satisfy the vagaries of the various gods. Human sacrifice to the gods is one example of the more extreme rituals that developed in more than one primitive civilization.[1]

After a generation or two, the succeeding chiefs, who have been brought up in the tribe's culture, actually believe in the veracity of their religious practices. These practices have become traditional. The tribe's religion has become a lifelike form, growing, defending itself, extending its influence, and reproducing by splitting off new sects.

The early chief's original inspiration for blaming the misfortunes of his tribe on the gods may have started out as a handy ruse to deflect blame away from himself. But the law of unintended consequences transformed his simple idea into a lasting cultural phenomenon.

Why did these religious ideas take hold? Aside from the authority of the chief, people want to believe that the things they do actually accomplish their intended goals. The poor farmer, who danced in his field to inveigle the cloud god, soon had rain return to his crops. Hey, it worked! Let's keep it up.

The random successes with the rituals tend to be remembered, while the frequent failures are ignored. Maybe we just didn't click our heels loud enough, or perhaps we twirled in the wrong direction. We'll get it right the next time for sure.

People have a knack for fooling themselves, and for generating faulty belief systems.

Cargo Cults

A more modern version of this phenomenon is demonstrated by the cargo cults of the South Pacific. During World War II, the U.S. Army and Navy established numerous bases on various islands in support of the war effort. Many of the native peoples had never before seen such a wealth and variety of cargo as the GI's brought with them. The natives saw plentiful supplies of food, jeeps, guns, cigarettes, ships, airplanes, Coca-Cola and hundreds of other new and wonderful things. Naturally, they wanted to have such things for themselves, too, but did not understand the vast infra-structure of the civilization from which all that cargo came. So they started copying the things they saw the GI's doing. They built mock radio stations and assembled bamboo antennas. They cleared their own land for runways and lighted the edges with torches. They built their own docks and piers to accommodate ships. They made up uniforms that looked a lot like the ones the foreigners wore. They built a headquarters hut and outfitted it with an office including a desk and a clerk who sifted through stacks of paperwork. The natives figured these activities would soon attract ships and planes full of cargo for them. Alas, their wishes were never fulfilled.

Since their efforts consistently failed to attract any cargo, many of the cargo cults have faded from the scene. But the island of Tanna, in the South Pacific nation of Vanuatu, still has an active cult featuring a savior known as John Frum. He is said to wear a sparkling white uniform, and has promised to return with cargo for everyone. The origin of the name John Frum is not clear. Some people have speculated it is shortened form of John from America, others think it may come from the similar native word for broom, meaning John will sweep away the foreigners and bring a restoration of the former native ways. The white outfit is thought to mimic the formal U.S. Navy uniform. John Frum day is February 15, and visitors to Tanna may still attend the yearly celebrations, which have become a tourist attraction. Asked why the cult persists, even after 50 years of no sign from John Frum or his cargo, a believer pointed out that Christians have been waiting for more than 2000 years for their second coming.[2]

Good chief -- Bad chief

Returning to our generic chief from the early paragraphs of this chapter, we may assume our leader is a virtuous man, overall. He primarily wishes to promote the success of his tribe, not merely his own personal aggrandizement. He may be considered the administrator or the brains of the tribe; he is the controlling force of a lifelike unit. When this unit behaves in a fashion to promote its survival and growth, it is obeying the imperatives of life, and fostering its own advancement. The chief encourages his people to work for their own individual benefit, so that each individual will survive. Then the individuals will have the opportunity to devote some of their excess time to the needs of the tribe. This is the principle of production, where a man creates goods or services that he could sell to somebody else, or in this case, donate to his tribe. Each individual has some minimum needs for food and shelter merely to stay alive, his subsistence level. Once he has satisfied his subsistence needs, he can spend his excess time creating a profit, so to speak, generating wealth. We use the term "profit" here in the loosest sense of an excess of income over expenses, even though the concept of money has not yet arisen in the primitive society.

How will our tribesman spend this profit? He will first use it to support his spouse and children, his family unit. Then he may want to use it for leisure, but he lives in a tribe with other individuals, and the tribe has needs for his time and skills as well. The chief realizes that his men will slack off, and try to get away with doing less work, unless he keeps after them to carry their own weight in the tribe. With his limited number of villagers, the chief wants to be sure each man is contributing his share of the work, and that nobody is freeloading on the others. So the chief demands that each tribesman spend his profit for the advancement of the tribe. The more that individuals contribute their efforts to the common good, the more the tribe prospers, and the greater is their tribal wealth.

Now we will look at a neighboring tribe that is led by a bad chief. The bad chief is enamored by his own self-importance. His power is absolute, or so he believes, and he abuses his tribesmen and does not allow them to keep the minimum necessities the individuals require to survive. His greed benefits himself for a while, but it is not sustainable since he is over-taxing his tribe. This bad chief notices that his tribe is declining and needs to obtain more resources. He sees that the neighboring tribe is successful and prospering, so he decides to steal their stuff. A war breaks out between the two tribes. But our good chief has realized long before the first attack, that his tribe must be prepared to fight off threats from the environment. These threats include wild animals, bad weather, and hostile neighbors. He has trained his tribesmen in the arts of self-defense, so he triumphs over the attacking hoard. The bad chief is killed in the melee, and most of his former tribesmen are thrilled to be absorbed into the victorious tribe, led by a benevolent chief.

We can see from this example that the practices of successful tribes propagate into the future along with their flourishing civilization. Practices of the unsuccessful tribes die out along with their cruel leaders and underfed tribesmen. The principles of natural selection apply to cultures as well as to species of animals and plants.

Notes:

[1] A noteworthy historical excess regarding deference to the gods is illustrated by the Mayan civilization. These people flourished in Mexico during the period from 800 to 1000 AD, and enjoyed sporting events. If you visit the ruins of Chichen Itza in the Yucatan, you may view the arena where ancient sportsmen played a game similar to basketball. A stone hoop mounted high on a stone wall served as the goal where the players could score points by tossing the ball through the opening. Tour guides at Chichen Itza like to tell the story of how the captain of the *winning* team would be sacrificed to the gods. Certainly, the gods would be insulted if a mere loser was the one sacrificed in their honor. After all, who knows what terrible retribution the offended gods might take upon the disrespectful tribe. One might wonder how well motivated the individual players would have been to win.

[2] For more on cargo cults, see Raffaele.

CHAPTER SEVEN

GROWTH OF EARLY CIVILIZATION

NOW we should consider how this tribal model, the chiefdom, is different from the natural anarchy of animals in the wild. Is it fundamentally different, or is it merely part of the continuum, a natural next step in the evolution of nature?

The humans could just as well have continued on the same path that the animals had followed since time immemorial. Early humans gathered into family groups to raise their offspring. Family groups clustered together in herds to take advantage of their enhanced strength in numbers. The herds roamed over a wide area, exploiting their environment for gathering food from plant sources and for hunting the animals they could learn how to kill for meat. All of these techniques are the same ones the lower animals had employed before. But with their superior intelligence the humans invented weapons and hunting techniques that no previous animal had ever been capable of. They used clubs, spears, and stone axes. They teamed up to make a lot of noise to stampede a herd of buffalo into a box canyon where they would be easier to harvest. The people could speak and understand language. They used their big brains to invent villages and farming and animal domestication.

Throughout prehistory the lower animals had employed all the capabilities their evolution had provided them to carve survival from a hostile ecology. They used their tooth and claw and fleetness of foot, and whatever cleverness their little brains could provide. Likewise the humans used their bigger brains and superior tools to advance their own welfare in their hostile surroundings. They came to dominate the lower animals and use them for food. They began to reshape their world like no previous animal had ever done before. Just like the lower animals before him, mankind took advantage of his capabilities as he acquired them.

So we conclude that the transition from the animal model, where each creature uses his inherent capabilities, to the human model, where man uses his enhanced capabilities, is a natural consequence of evolution in brainpower, or intelligence.

We would expect that the principles of anarchy would continue to hold sway in this new society of humans. Anarchy is the principle of no government, every man for himself, the law of the jungle, kill or be killed, eat or be eaten, and might makes right. We do see a lot of anarchy in the history of primitive man, but we also see the rise and advancement of civilization, and a move away from strictly anarchic behavior.

In the family group we see a competition of cooperation versus strict individual selfishness. This applies to animal groupings as well as human families, and as we have seen before, the cooperative behavior is a result of natural selection. The family that destroys itself does not propagate any offspring into the future.

So the family groups of animals collect into herds, while the people collect into tribes. The pecking-order principle arranges the individuals into a hierarchy of leaders and followers. The herd or tribe is a lifelike unit that must compete against other herds and tribes for limited resources in nature. And the principles of natural selection help decide which behaviors of these units propagate into the future. Anarchy is a powerful force in this natural world of intense competition. Every creature and lifelike unit works to maximize its own self-interest. Everyone wants to be top dog. Each unit wants to concentrate power and wealth unto itself. But power-seeking is balanced against self-preservation and the avoidance of pain. Competition sorts the contestants into a hierarchy of stronger over weaker. But the human mind has a tendency to question the way things are, and wonder whether things could be done differently.

Human capabilities

Let us consider a few more of the superior capabilities that humans enjoy over their animal neighbors. Along with his additional intelligence comes the ability for man to contemplate his actions. He is capable of reflection and planning, so he may take care of details no previous creature ever could. Before he decides to commit some act he may reflect upon its consequences, and question whether to continue or not. He is the first creature capable of rational thought, of using logic to anticipate what will happen after what will happen next. He can reason, not only from A to B, but also from A to B to C. He can understand the advantages of cooperating with his fellows versus trying to make his own way without them. He can realize that his own self-interest is intertwined with the self-interest of the group. He can appreciate that cooperative teamwork can accomplish more than the individuals working independently. His rational self-interest is better served by joining a tribal group and turning over the affairs of the team to a powerful leader. The division of labor model, where each man works in his own specialty, creates greater production than every man doing everything for himself.

Chief selection

Who gets to be chief in the primitive society? At first it will be the toughest and meanest individual, the one who is strongest, or the biggest bully. But there will be other ambitious men in the tribe who are smarter. The men who use their brains as well as their brawn will be angling to take over. The tribesmen will want to follow the best leader, not necessarily the meanest. If the leader of the tribe is insufferable, groups will break off and go start a new tribe elsewhere. Or they will form a faction within the tribe and attempt to take over from the chief they disagree with. The smart individuals will reason from A to B to C and even to D. They will figure all the angles, whereas the less-bright chief may only reason from A to B and miss the ramifications of his ill-considered decisions. Competition in brainpower will help select the chief who eventually takes charge.

There are, of course, many variations on this theme. Very bad leaders may manage to run their tribes for a very long time. But over the long run, the more successful tribes will create the more successful civilizations, and these will grow, while the less successful tribes will whither and die.

Wealth

What do we see when we compare the tribal chieftain's domain with the earlier caveman's society? We see growth, a greater population, more huts to live in, a greater variety of weapons, a larger collection of tools, bowls and utensils, a more prosperous society. We see more wealth. And we see more per capita wealth.

Where did this wealth come from? It came from man's labor. The individual work each man performed, beyond his requirements for subsistence, resulted in production. He created goods or services that benefited himself or his tribesmen. The deer he killed on his hunting trip provided more meat than he and his family could eat by themselves before it spoiled, so he shared it with his tribe. When he built a fire to cook the meat, he cooked the whole animal, and shared this wealth with the community.

When he went into the woods to collect sticks he could use for clubs, he came back with more than just one for himself. He collected all he could carry back to the village. He shared his collection with his fellow tribesmen, so they would all be better armed than they had been before. The extra clubs and excess meat represent wealth to the tribe. This wealth was created by the labor of the individuals. The sticks in the woods were a natural resource provided by nature. The sticks did not become wealth until they were harvested by the human and fashioned into clubs. The wealth represented by the clubs became re-useable assets to the tribe. However, the wealth represented by the deer meat was consumed by the tribesmen in one feast. So we see that different varieties of wealth can either last for a time, like the clubs, or be consumed in a short while, like the food. But these items did not constitute wealth until they were harvested by the labor of the tribesmen. So the individual goes out to collect resources from nature, fashions them into useful assets, and thus creates wealth. Wealth is one of the results of growth, the advancement of civilization, the flourishing of life.

Production versus destruction

History is rife with examples of destruction and decline in civilization. In Chapter 6 we looked at a tribe led by a bad chief who kept all the riches for himself, and didn't permit the natural tendency of his people to grow and prosper. What else can cause the decline and fall of a healthy society? The forces of nature can overwhelm it. Excessive storms or earthquakes can destroy more property than the resilience of the tribe can recover. A stampede of wild elephants might rampage through the village. A forest fire ignited by a lightning strike would destroy man's habitations. But the primary threat of destruction is undoubtedly man himself, in the form of competing tribes. An attack by a more powerful army can destroy a village, and enslave the surviving civilians. The chief of a neighboring tribe might emphasize the strength of his army as the primary virtue of its culture. He would guide the use of his tribesmen's assets into strengthening his fighting power. When his army attacked any neighboring village, he would have the strength to take it over and convert its wealth to his own use. His own wealth is concentrated in weaponry and soldiers.

These aggressive and warlike societies are a frequent and recurring model for behavior throughout history. These customs make a certain kind of sense in a natural continuation of the anarchistic practices of the animal world. But does this model of constantly conflicting armies contribute to the advance of civilization and the flourishing of life, or does it confuse production with destruction?

We should note that warlike behavior is self-limiting in the big picture of life on the primitive planet. Destruction consumes production and wealth. War uses up resources by killing men and destroying property. It does not create wealth, it merely transfers it from one tribe to another, while destroying some of it in the process. In the primitive society, warfare can only extend as far as the aggressors can travel. They are necessarily limited to transportation by foot or horseback, so the zone of influence is going to be some small patch of territory, compared to the total surface of the Earth. The peoples who live elsewhere will be unaffected by the conflict, and may continue with their own production and growth.[1]

Man can use his many talents for the advancement of civilization or he can use his power towards its destruction. He has the choice to pursue production or engage in destruction, whether or not he appreciates the distinction.

Notes:

[1] The alert reader may have noticed that we introduced several animals in the discussion that may not have been actually accessible to the primitive man, such as deer, buffalo, elephant and horse. The idea here is to present examples and illustrations accessible to the modern reader, although descriptions of prehistoric events must remain speculative.

CHAPTER EIGHT

FEEDBACK

IN this chapter, let us take a brief detour from the problems of life and society to discuss some engineering concepts that may be helpful for understanding the interactions between people. The following information may seem fairly basic, but it should be useful to those readers who have not previously thought it over.

Engineering

We want to mention the engineering concepts of control loops, feedback, stability, and equilibrium. But first we should think about the purpose of an engineer. What does an engineer do? An engineer takes the discoveries of science and tries to incorporate them in the design of useful products. When science discovers a new material, it is the engineer's job to decide how to use it to improve an existing product, or to employ it in something altogether new. Wood and stone are common materials that have been available to mankind since the dawn of time. Engineers, or the primitive men who were the precursors of engineers, figured out how to build bridges from wood and stone, and often used combinations of these materials in the construction process.

A modern engineer would appreciate the fact that balsa wood is light and flimsy, but suitable for building model airplanes. Balsa would not be a good choice for making dining-room chairs, because it breaks too easily. Oak is a heavier, denser and stronger wood that makes an excellent choice for chairs, but would be too heavy for a practical airplane. The engineer appreciates these distinctions and goes into much deeper detail than these simple examples in his selection of materials.

When iron and steel appeared on the scene, engineers figured out how to

incorporate these new materials into the construction of bridges and buildings, making these structures taller and stronger than the earlier versions.
Engineers are always investigating details, trying to find ways to make small
improvements in products, and making trade-off decisions between cost
and quality. Occasionally, an engineer may even decide to write a book
about the challenges of Life.

Controls

A common need people have is to control their personal environments
for comfort and safety. Everyone wants to feel like he or she is in control of
his or her life. An engineer would describe this control process by using the
abstract concept of a control loop with a feedback mechanism, so that the
controller can keep track of his success in satisfying his needs.

An example of a heating control loop that everyone should be familiar
with is the furnace and thermostat system. Your house, no doubt, contains
one or more of these. Once you provide your input to the system by setting
the wall thermostat to 70 degrees Fahrenheit, the automatic system takes
over and maintains the air temperature in your house at the selected level.

Figure 5 shows a sample diagram of a gas fired, forced air heating
system.[1] When the temperature in the house, detected by the wall thermostat, falls below 70 degrees, the thermostat switches on the gas valve in the
furnace. Gas flowing to the burner mixes with air and is ignited by the pilot
light. The flame warms the inside of the heat exchanger and the products
of combustion go up the chimney to be exhausted to the outside. Once the
heat exchanger tubes get hot, as detected by another thermostat, a fan turns
on to blow air through the air side of the heat exchanger, and this warmed
air circulates through the house via heating ducts. When the warmed air in
the house brings the wall thermostat above 70 degrees, it shuts off the gas to
the burner, extinguishing the flame. Once the blower has cooled down the
heat exchanger, the fan shuts off and the system waits for the next command
from the wall thermostat.

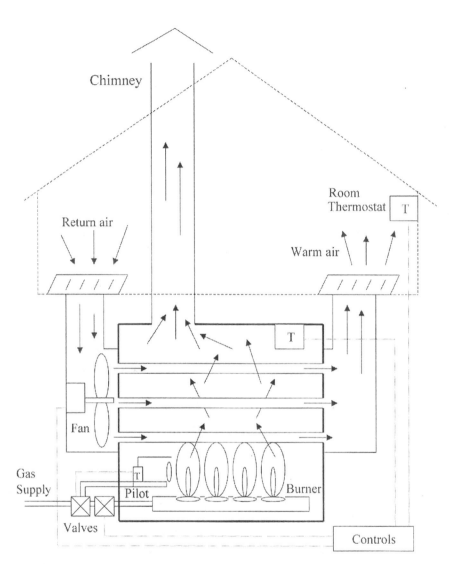

Figure 5. Gas fired, forced air furnace

There is, of course, a safety control loop in this system, which is the one for the pilot light. If the pilot light, which is a small flame that burns continuously, goes out for some reason, we would not want the gas to come on without being properly ignited in the burner box. So the pilot light loop will not allow the gas supply to come on unless the pilot is on first.

So we can see in this example of a furnace control loop, several smaller loops that go into making up the system. The furnace contains three control loops, the combination of which constitute the house heating system. The human who lives in the house may be considered an additional control loop, who decides what temperature to set the thermostat, depending on his own needs for comfort.

What happens to our heating system if someone leaves the front door to the house open in cold weather? The furnace does not have the capacity to heat the house to 70 degrees with the door open, so the furnace runs and runs, wasting the homeowner's money by attempting to warm up the county. We have thus defeated the control system by leaving the door open and exceeding its design limitations.

We could also fool the system by placing a blanket over the thermostat, so it cannot detect the air temperature inside the house. In this case, when the furnace starts heating the house, it would get no feedback from the thermostat when the house becomes warm enough, so it would keep running and running, making the house way too hot inside. This is called running the control system open-loop, which is considered a malfunction. For it to operate properly we need a closed loop, where the feedback information is available to the system.

Other ways to defeat the system would be to disconnect the electricity, so that the furnace blower can't function, and the thermostat electronics have no power. Or we could refuse to pay the gas bill so the power company shuts off our gas supply. These scenarios show methods of defeating the control system, or operating it outside of its design limits. But when all the system inputs are provided, and the feedback loop is unencumbered, the furnace and thermostat system will keep our house at a comfortable temperature automatically, which is the design goal of the system.

The furnace system is just one of the many control systems a home-owner uses to help regulate his everyday life. We can extrapolate this simple example of a control loop into whatever complexity we desire. The same principles apply, no matter what kind of system we wish to describe. We can think of your automobile as a collection of interrelated control loops. The car has a fuel system, a brake system, and a turn-signal system, among many others. Each operates independently, but collectively they provide an acceptable transport vehicle for your everyday needs. Even the functioning of the human body is likewise an extremely complex construction of bio-chemical control loops with their own feedback signals.

Stability

Another engineering concept we should appreciate is stability. If you try to stand a pencil vertically on its point, it will fall over, and probably roll off the table onto the floor. A pencil balancing on its point is unstable, but a pencil lying flat on the floor is in a stable condition. If you practice, you can learn to balance a pencil vertically on your hand, but it takes quick reflexes.

Similarly, a shopping cart being pushed forwards is stable, whereas a shopping cart going backwards is unstable. We are referring here to your typical cart as found in the neighborhood grocery store, the four-wheeled version with fixed-axle rear wheels and caster wheels on the front.

When you stand behind the cart, grasp the handle and push it forwards, the cart is simple to steer and guide in the direction you want to go. This is a fairly stable condition requiring small inputs from you, the operator. However, when you stand in front of the cart and push it backwards, it is much harder to control, requiring much larger inputs from the driver. This is a more unstable condition. While walking around in the store, you can successfully push the cart around either way, forwards being easier than backwards. But when you take the cart out to the parking lot and run with it, forwards will be the only stable condition. If you push it fast backwards, you will surely lose control of the situation. Although this is a simple, qualitative explanation of stability, it shows the idea for our purposes in this book.

The feedback system of the furnace example provides a stability point for room temperature at the 70 degree setting of the thermostat. It can be said to drive the error to zero. When the air is too cool, the thermostat turns on the furnace. When the room warms above 70 degrees, the thermostat turns off the furnace. It seeks an equilibrium air temperature of 70 degrees.

Equilibrium

A basic principle of hydraulics states that water seeks its own level. This demonstrates another case of nature seeking equilibrium. Consider two buckets, each half full of water, where a small hose connects them together at the bottom. Water may flow in either direction through the hose from one bucket to the other, so the equilibrium state is for the water level to be the same in both buckets. See Figure 6.

If somebody pours another quart of water into one bucket, the water level in that bucket will rise by the amount added. But since the buckets are connected by the hose, water will flow towards the less full bucket until the water levels are restored to equilibrium. This does not happen immediately because the hose leading between the buckets is narrow and restricts the flow. This same principle is what makes the surface of a pond or lake flat and level, in the absence of external forces, like high winds or boats racing around on the surface. We would say that water seeks its own level to restore equilibrium.

Reality

Scientists and engineers try to discover how and why things work the way they do. They want to come up with theories and applications to describe and use the principles that govern the natural world. We want to understand reality, and squeeze reliable information out of the apparent chaos of nature.

However, any scientific theory is really a mere approximation of reality. We never reach the ultimate answers, because there are always more details to be understood, no matter how deeply any question is analyzed. Nevertheless, we can get close enough to the truth in order to make plenty of useful objects for the comfort and convenience of mankind. Look around you. Do you see electric lights and other appliances, glass windows, wood and metal furniture, vehicles hurtling down the highway? All these products of your society were engineered from scientific discoveries.

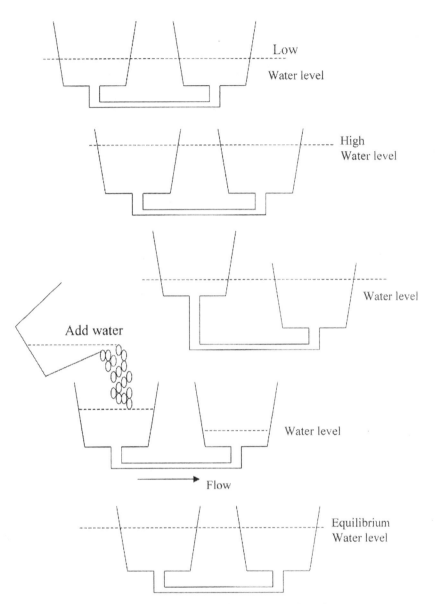

Figure 6. Water seeks its own level

So why is our understanding of nature only an approximation of reality? Because we need to simplify things in order to understand them. Consider a high school science class. When you were learning about Newton's laws of motion in high school physics, you saw a diagram of a hockey-puck sliding along a frictionless surface. We realize that a frictionless surface is an idealization to make the concepts of force and acceleration easier to understand. Later we can learn about how to account for friction in real-life machines. But then, what causes friction? Is it the lumpiness of two surfaces scraping together? What causes the lumpiness? Are the surfaces made out of molecules that are not perfectly smooth? What are the molecules made out of and how do they stick together? What happens if we add a lubricant to the system? Et cetera. Science attempts to answer all these questions, but there are always more detailed questions that may be considered.

An engineer needs to decide when to stop asking more and more detailed questions, and use the information he already has to go ahead and make the product. Future engineers may worry about improving the product for the next generation of customers.

TANSTAAFL

In Chapter 3 we mentioned the second law of thermodynamics, and stated that it is a bedrock principle of physics. It tells us that entropy increases, or in other words, that the universe tends inexorably toward a greater degree of disorder. These words are not very revealing without a deeper explanation.

Let us begin with the first law of thermodynamics, which states that energy can be neither created nor destroyed, but merely converted from one form into another. Energy comes in several forms including heat, chemical, mechanical, electrical, nuclear, or gravitational, and is also referred to as work.

When you burn gasoline to run the engine in your car, the chemical energy stored in the hydrocarbon molecules is converted to heat and mechanical energy, which works to push the vehicle down the road. Also a lot of heat energy is unavoidably generated and dumped overboard into the atmosphere through the radiator. The alternator mounted in the engine compartment converts some of the rotating mechanical energy from the engine into electrical energy to charge the battery. The battery converts the charging electrical energy into chemical energy for release later when discharging. Each of these conversions are accompanied by losses, that is, some of the energy is wasted in the process of conversion, mostly as heat.

This fact leads us to the second law of thermodynamics, which states that you can never breakeven in the conversion of energy from one form to another. Heat always flows from a hot place to a cold place, never in the other direction. We might say that nature seeks equilibrium, by cooling the hot places and thus warming the cold places. This represents an increase in entropy or a change to a more disordered state.

You can scramble an egg but you cannot unscramble it. You can't put Humpty-Dumpty back together again. You must pay for anything you want to do by expending more energy.

The refrigerator in your kitchen does indeed make the inside of the box cooler than the air in the kitchen, but it does so at the expense of making the air in the kitchen warmer than it would be without the refrigerator. You end up with more heat in the kitchen than you do cold inside the refrigerator (or you put more heat into the kitchen than you extract from the box). This is why the air conditioner in your house has a unit outside. In order to make it cooler inside, it must make it warmer outside, and you have to pay for the electricity to run it.

The second law of thermodynamics tells us that you cannot build a perpetual motion machine. In other words, you can't get something for nothing.[2] Thus the acronym at the beginning of this section: There Ain't No Such Thing As A Free Lunch.

Three-Body Problem

Before we get carried away by the infallibility of science and mathematics, we should again consider reality and the limitations to what we know for sure. A good example is the un-solvability of the three-body problem.

Sir Isaac Newton (1643 – 1727) in the year 1687 published his *Principia,* which answered the long-standing question of how to mathematically describe the motions of planets. He discovered that the force of gravity between any two objects is proportional to their masses, and inversely proportional to the square of the distance between them. This implies that a planet orbiting a much more massive object, such as the Earth around the Sun, will follow an elliptical path.

This is known as the two-body problem and has a fairly simple mathematical solution. If you know the masses, positions and velocities of the bodies, you may use Newton's Law to compute any future position and velocity of the two objects. You can also work the problem backwards to find the previous positions and velocities from the past.

However, if you add a third object to this orbital mechanics problem, such as adding the Moon to the Earth-Sun system, the mathematics becomes too complicated to solve completely. This is known as the three-body problem, or the simplest case of the n-body problems, which have no unique solutions. That is, you cannot accurately determine the positions of the objects far into the future. Details about this subject are, of course, way beyond the scope of this book, but we mention it to point out that some fairly simple seeming problems in math and science have not been thoroughly resolved.

Despite the mathematicians' consternation with this problem, there is no danger of the Sun–Earth–Moon orbits becoming unstable in the foreseeable future, so we need not worry about our future (in this respect) for many thousands of years.

This mysteriously insoluble three-body problem eventually led mathematicians into the area of inquiry known as chaos theory, which is the study of the behavior of dynamical systems that are sensitive to initial conditions. Prediction of the weather is a common example. This has also been referred to as the butterfly effect, where a butterfly flapping its wings somewhere in Mexico may influence the course of a hurricane in the Caribbean.

Such mathematical chaos is one of the reasons that an occasional comet or asteroid seems to come out of nowhere to threaten our planet with a possible collision. An object may be thus dislodged from its orbit in the Oort cloud to be sent careening through the inner part of the solar system.

Luckily for us, collision courses for large objects with our planet are extremely rare, typically occurring millions of years apart. A notable exception is evidenced by the Meteor Crater near Winslow, Arizona, which was formed by a 160-foot diameter, iron-nickel meteorite that struck the planet some 50,000 years ago.

A more recent example is the Tunguska event of June 1908. A cosmic visitor, probably 200 feet across, exploded in the air over Russia, knocking down trees like matchsticks in a 28-mile diameter circle.

On the other hand, many small orbiting objects encounter the atmosphere every day and burn up before striking the surface. Such meteors or falling stars may be seen in a clear sky every night.

Therefore we may conclude that our planet will eventually be struck by a large, extraterrestrial object, and suffer devastation to human civilization. Science may help us to observe the developing situation and predict the event shortly before it occurs, but we may be unable to prevent the disaster. However, we should not worry too much about our ultimate fate, because such an event is unlikely to occur until many millions of years in the future.

In this chapter we have strayed from the main purpose of this book to explore some background information from science and engineering. We have taken a brief look at some of the things that guide the engineer in pursuit of his goals, discussed the ideas of control loops, feedback, stability and equilibrium, bumped against the limits of reality and the constraints imposed by the second law of thermodynamics, and have seen that our civilization is subject to destruction by interplanetary chunks of rock. Let us return to the problems of life and society.

Notes:

[1] The fuel for our gas-fired furnace is natural gas, which is composed mostly of methane, or CH_4.

[2] See Seife for a thorough discussion of the second law of thermodynamics in his second chapter, "Demons."

CHAPTER NINE

COMMANDMENTS

SOMETIME during the murky prehistory of human civilization, religions seem to have taken over the job of making and enforcing rules of behavior, of governing morality, and of defining virtue and vice. The priesthood organized their precepts into teachings, doctrines and rituals, and imposed them on the people of their civilizations. A vast and powerful bureaucracy thus arose and became a lifelike form, competing in the marketplace of ideas, along with all the other life forms and lifelike forms.

Since this book is based on the precepts of science, we must not attribute any conclusions to the command of the gods, or even God, but we are permitted to consider the ideas attributed to God by the various religions. So let us discuss some small subset of religious teachings.

We need to temporarily set aside our personal beliefs regarding God and the doctrines of our own particular religion (if we have one). We wish to gain an unbiased understanding of the subject of religion in general, so let us consider how other people came to believe in their gods, from a strictly logical viewpoint.

We have speculated previously that an unnamed, generic chieftain in a prehistoric tribal setting may have invented the first god, the god of the clouds. When the chief was put on the spot by his farmer asking for more rain, the chief made up a story about the rain god.

After many generations, when religions had become firmly established among many tribes, vast collections of gods were understood to control many aspects of life for mankind.

From recorded history, we learn that the Greeks and Romans had their own great pantheons of gods. The following table shows a few of the Greek gods along with their Roman counterparts, and sphere of influence.[1]

Greek	Roman	Attributed duties
Zeus	Jupiter	chief god, sky, rain, thunderbolt.
Hera	Juno	goddess of marriage.
Poseidon	Neptune	god of the sea.
Hades	Pluto	god of the underworld, wealth, precious metals.
Athena	Minerva	the battle goddess, and of agriculture.
Apollo		the archer god, healer, light, truth.
Artemis	Diana	goddess of huntsmen.
Aphrodite	Venus	goddess of love and beauty.
Hermes	Mercury	god of commerce and the market.
Ares	Mars	god of war.
Hephaestus	Vulcan	god of fire.
Hestia	Vesta	virgin goddess of the hearth.

The people who prayed to these gods developed vast empires during the ascendancy of their cultures, and no one can doubt that they had successful civilizations for their times. No doubt, other tribes noticed their success and wondered about the influence of the many gods.

Conventional wisdom had long instructed that no man can serve two masters, much less many masters.[2] All of the different gods with all of their conflicting requirements became too difficult to keep track of. The priesthood was becoming overwhelmed with the magnitude of their task. So, in one small principality, the local king, along with his chief priest, decided to reorganize and simplify the way their society operated. They used their joint authority to declare that there is but one, and only one, true, All Mighty God. Over the subsequent years this concept caught on and eventually became entrenched in many cultures. Note that this doctrine persists, even to the present day.

To give an historical perspective, one of the earliest monotheistic kingdoms may have been that of Akhenaten, circa 1335 BC, the Pharaoh of the 18th Dynasty in Egypt. Akhenaten, formerly Amenhotep IV, worshiped the one god, the sun god Aten, and tried to convert his people to this belief. His queen was the beautiful and popular Nefertiti, who exercised an authority equivalent to the king's.[3]

Judaism is one of the oldest known monotheistic faiths, and Moses was one of the Hebrews' great chiefs who led his people out of bondage in Egypt to the Promised Land. The Exodus of Moses probably occurred some time during the period from 1652 to 1320 BC. Historians do not agree on the exact date, since the documentation of the times is not reliable. The Pharaoh of the Exodus may have been Ramesses II or perhaps Menephtah. Judaism traces its origins to the Genesis story, which is said to date from 4004 BC.[4]

After leaving Egypt, Moses found he was having problems with his flock. The people were behaving in a fashion that Moses knew was not conducive to a successful society. So Moses went to the mountain to contemplate his troubles and seek inspiration from God. When he returned he presented his people with Ten Commandments, intended to give them guidance for the conduct of their affairs and the flourishing of life in their community.

We quote from the Holy Bible, King James Version, Book of Deuteronomy, Chapter 5, Verses 1 through 24, as follows:

1   And Moses called all Israel, and said unto them, Hear, O Israel, the stat-
    utes and judgments which I speak in your ears this day, that ye may learn
    them, and keep, and do them.
2   The Lord our God made a covenant with us in Horeb.
3   The Lord made not this covenant with our fathers, but with us, even us,
    who are all of us here alive this day.
4   The Lord talked with you face to face in the mount out of the midst of
    the fire,
5   (I stood between the Lord and you at that time, to shew you the word of
    the Lord: for ye were afraid by reason of the fire, and went not up into
    the mount;) saying,
6   I am the Lord thy God, which brought thee out of the land of Egypt,
    from the house of bondage.
7   Thou shalt have none other gods before me.
8   Thou shalt not make thee any graven image, or any likeness of any thing
    that is in heaven above, or that is in the earth beneath, or that is in the
    waters beneath the earth:
9   Thou shalt not bow down thyself unto them, nor serve them: for I the

Lord thy God am a jealous God, visiting the iniquity of the fathers upon the children unto the third and fourth generation of them that hate me,

10   And shewing mercy unto thousands of them that love me and keep my commandments.

11   Thou shalt not take the name of the Lord thy God in vain: for the Lord will not hold him guiltless that taketh his name in vain.

12   Keep the sabbath day to sanctify it, as the Lord thy God hath commanded thee.

13   Six days thou shalt labor, and do all thy work:

14   But the seventh day is the sabbath of the Lord thy God: in it thou shalt not do any work, thou, nor thy son, nor thy daughter, nor thy manservant, nor thy maidservant, nor thine ox, nor thine ass, nor any of thy cattle, nor thy stranger that is within thy gates; that thy manservant and thy maidservant may rest as well as thou.

15   And remember that thou wast a servant in the land of Egypt, and that the Lord thy God brought thee out thence through a mighty hand and by a stretched out arm: therefore the Lord thy God commanded thee to keep the sabbath day.

16   Honor thy father and thy mother, as the Lord thy God hath commanded thee; that thy days may be prolonged, and that it may go well with thee, in the land which the Lord thy God giveth thee.

17   Thou shalt not kill.

18   Neither shalt thou commit adultery.

19   Neither shalt thou steal.

20   Neither shalt thou bear false witness against thy neighbour.

21   Neither shalt thou desire thy neighbour's wife, neither shalt thou covet thy neighbour's house, his field, or his manservant, or his maidservant, his ox, or his ass, or any thing that is thy neighbour's.

22   These words the Lord spake unto all your assembly in the mount out of the midst of the fire, of the cloud, and of the thick darkness, with a great voice: And he added no more. And he wrote them in two tables of stone, and delivered them unto me.

23   it came to pass, when ye heard the voice out of the midst of the darkness, (for the mountain did burn with fire,) that ye came near unto me, even all the heads of your tribes, and your elders;

24   And ye said, Behold, the Lord our God hath shewed us his glory and his greatness, and we have heard his voice out of the midst of the fire: we have seen this day that God doth talk with man, and he liveth.

Thus endeth the quoted scripture. Is this not an excellent example of writing from historic literature?

Let us summarize these Ten Commandments into the following list:

1   No other gods.
2   No graven images.
3   Do not take God's name in vain.
4   Observe the Sabbath day.
5   Honor your father and mother.
6   Do not kill.
7   Do not commit adultery.
8   Do not steal.
9   Do not bear false witness.
10 Do not covet your neighbor's wife nor property.

Now let us pretend for a moment that these commandments are not a part of our heritage as free citizens in Western Civilization. Let us say that we are really Ice Creatures from the South Pole, who come from an advanced technological society that lives deep in the fissures of the southern glaciers. We have emerged from our chilly environment in order to study the strange culture of the humans who seem to dominate the planet. Would we agree that these Ten Commandments constitute a reasonable guide to the behavior of citizens in an emerging civilization? Before we answer this question we should discuss the points raised.

Note that the first five commandments are administrative in nature. God is saying that He is the ultimate authority, and shall not be defied. The prohibition on other gods will keep the people from sliding back to their earlier practice of attributing godly responsibilities among many lesser gods.

A limitation on graven images keeps the people from praying to icons of the forbidden lesser gods.

To take God's name in vain would mean to treat Him in an irreverent or improper manner. To swear a promise upon the name of God and then not honor it would be a grievous transgression.

By observation of the Sabbath, the people are weekly reminded of their religious duties, from a priest or by holy scriptures.

To honor one's parents is an additional acknowledgement to obey the authority of one's elders.

The final five commandments are the rules for dealing with fellow citizens. Do not kill, because your neighbor is an asset to the community as well as you are, and the society always needs more workers that it has. Killing always arouses vengeance in those close to the victim, and encourages recrimination. Such behavior is self-perpetuating and abundantly disruptive in any society.

The prohibition of adultery is likewise intended to discourage strife among the people. Voluntary sexual intercourse between a married person and someone other than his or her lawful spouse, is bound to raise feelings of betrayal and injustice. The vengeance aroused in the breast of a sexually wronged individual is comparable to that felt by any victim of serious crime.

The policy against stealing is recognition by God of property rights among men. The possessions of another must not be taken without permission of the owner, or without a valid sales transaction.

Not to bear false witness means to tell the truth, and not to claim that your neighbor did something that you know he did not.

Not to covet your neighbor's wife nor property is closely related to the previous prohibitions of adultery and stealing. To covet means to desire something, which is a precursor to taking action, so a prohibition of the want is worth its own commandment.

Now, as Ice Creatures, living our lives as rational beings in a logical society, we understand that the last five commandments express valid advice, and even wisdom, for governing a community. The first five commandments deal with the power of authority, and although we do not recognize the existence of God, we appreciate the need for those in authority to prescribe reasonable rules of behavior. So we would wish to have the option to modify the first four commandments to better suit our own culture. But overall, we agree that the Ten Commandments constitute valid advice for any society.[5]

Regardless of whether we personally believe God exists or not, religions are a fact of life in the civilizations of today, and need to be taken into consideration by the readers of this book. Each religion is a lifelike creature, which competes among the thousands of other life forms and lifelike forms for influence and domination.

The major conclusions we should take from this chapter are that two principle commandments form the foundation of virtue. Thou shalt not kill, and thou shalt not steal, become the basis of behavior that nourishes the advance of Western Civilization. The prohibition against killing applies to your fellow man, the members of your own species. Killing plants and animals for food purposes is permitted, because a living man must eat in order to survive. This commandment is an early recognition of man's right to life. The prohibition against stealing is likewise an early recognition of man's right to own property, a precursor to the concept of liberty.

Notes:

[1] For extensive information about mythology, see Hamilton.

[2] "No servant can serve two masters," is quoted from the words of Jesus in Luke, Chapter 16, Verse 13. We presume that this truism was expressed by many previous bards.

[3] For more on Akhenaten, see Redford.

[4] For a summary of biblical history, see Hull.

[5] Full Disclosure: Actually, there is no advanced technological civilization of Ice Creatures living in the South Pole (that has yet been discovered).

CHAPTER TEN

GOOD AND EVIL

Virtue

ANOTHER subject that has come under the purview of religions is virtue. Many of the early philosophers spoke from a viewpoint of a particular religion, or subsequently had their ideas incorporated by religious doctrine. If the reader wishes to consult the works of individual philosophers, the Internet or any public library will have plenty of references to Socrates, Plato, Cicero, Diogenes, Aristotle, Augustine, Aquinas, Confucius and many others.

Consider the following list of virtues (in no particular order):

Charity	Kindness	Love	Politeness	Fidelity
Prudence	Temperance	Courage	Justice	Generosity
Compassion	Mercy	Gratitude	Humility	Simplicity
Tolerance	Purity	Gentleness	Faith	Humor
Success	Freedom	Goodness	Humanity	Piety
Excellence	Merit	Fairness	Service	Wisdom
Discipline	Restraint	Happiness	Fortitude	Hope

These are all certainly inspirational and feel-good words. Other writers have thoroughly expounded upon virtue, so we will not further belabor the subject here, other than to mention that various virtues have been selected for particular attention. These are subdivided into the "cardinal" and "theological" virtues. The four cardinal virtues are prudence, justice, temperance, and fortitude, and the three great theological virtues are faith, hope and love. These seven virtues have been thoroughly examined by Peter Gomes in his book, *The Good Life,* which should be available at your local library.[1]

The other side of the coin is represented by vices. Consider the following list (also in no particular order):

Waste	Fraud	Dishonesty	Lying	Infidelity
Betrayal	Perfidy	Treachery	Turpitude	Treason
Apostasy	Graft	Venality	Corruption	Thievery
Murder	Meanness	Falsity	Stupidity	Weakness
Apathy	Prejudice	Injustice	Cowardice	Cruelty
Addiction	Greed	Laziness	Ignorance	Malice

The vices have been famously detailed by Dante in his *Divine Comedy,* where he escorts his reader through the many levels of hell (the inferno), purgatory and paradise. He shows us, in his view, how punishments for each vice are served to sinners in the afterlife.[2] Other writers throughout history have selected a few of the more egregious vices to detail as the Seven Deadly Sins.[3] These are:

Lust, Gluttony, Greed, Sloth, Wrath, Envy, Pride.

These sins may be contrasted with their opposing virtues of:

Chastity, Temperance, Charity, Diligence, Forgiveness, Benevolence, Humility.

We might observe at this point that the achievement of a virtue requires more work than does a vice. A virtue results from diligent application of effort, either in thought beforehand, or in action, or both. A vice may be considered the easy way, without the hard work that the corresponding virtue would require. Certainly virtue demands more self-discipline.

Aristotle, in his *Nicomachean Ethics,* offers his opinion that a true virtue lies somewhere on a line of degree between the extremes of a particular trait. This mean (in the sense of an average or balance) is the desired state of virtue to be achieved. The virtue is not necessarily in the middle of the range, but may be skewed more towards one end or the other.[4]

```
Cowardice. . . . . . . . . . . . . . . . .Courage . . . . . . . . Foolhardiness
Vanity . . . . . . . . . Pride . . . . . . . . . . . . . . . . . . . . . . .Humility
Miserliness. . . . . . . . . . . . . . . . . . .Generosity. . . . . Prodigality
```

Note that the virtue, courage, is found between two vices, cowardice and foolhardiness, yet it is closer to foolhardiness. Proper pride, which may be considered a virtue, is located between vanity (a vice) and humility (a virtue), being closer to vanity. Generosity is considered closer to prodigality than it is to miserliness. It is clear that virtue requires a balance among conflicting forces. Moving too far from a virtue in either direction leads to a vice. It is no wonder that the philosophers have been wrestling with these concepts for centuries, and will continue their arguments unto eternity.

The problem that leads to disagreement, or at least to such lively discussion among the philosophers, is that most words do not have precise definitions. That is, how words are used in language may be subject to varying interpretations. Take the word "pride" for example. Pride is classed as one of the seven deadly sins, and when used as an excuse to belittle another's accomplishments, it is indeed a vice. But a man could say he is proud of his country, in a patriotic sense, because of the benefits it has bestowed upon its citizens. In this sense, pride is a virtue. Aristotle placed proper pride on a line between vanity and humility, and considered it a virtue. Vanity is a vice and humility is a virtue. But an excess of humility would also be a vice. When definitions may be so flexible, the same word can be used in different senses, both when stated by a speaker, and again when interpreted by a listener.

An exception to this word flexibility may be found in mathematics, where words are precisely defined to mean one and only one thing. Thus the definitions of the words for numbers yield relationships such as: two plus three equals five, which will always be true in every case. Logic, as expressed in language, also attempts to achieve this degree of perfection, but when an ill-defined word such as pride is used in an argument, a wide range of results may be expected.

Good versus Evil

A discussion of virtue and vice naturally leads us into the consideration of good versus evil. How do we distinguish good from evil and define where the line is that separates them? We could simply state that good is associated with virtue and evil with vice, but that would be too simplistic. What is the relationship that separates good from evil; when does one meld into the other? We might say that someone may be killed by kindness, which would convert a virtue into vice.[5]

We saw earlier how the behaviors of animals should not be judged as, or separated into good and bad, virtue and vice, good and evil, because the creatures do not have the thought processes to distinguish the difference. Animals operate on instinct, which has evolved during eons of natural selection. We might even say that natural selection has, in a crude fashion, encouraged virtue and discouraged vice among animals, by promoting productive behaviors that resulted in the flourishing of life, and punishing self-destructive behaviors with death.

Since the lower animals cannot truly understand why they act as they do, we conclude that the concepts of good and evil did not arise until we humans came into existence, with our superior brainpower. Therefore, good and evil apply only to the conduct of man's affairs.

Ethical questions

Before we get too deeply into our discussion of good versus evil, let us look at a few moral dilemmas that one commonly encounters in books about ethical concepts.

Let us speculate that you find yourself in the situation where you are working for the railroad and have a job in the switching yard. During your lunch break, you are walking across the tracks on your way to the cafeteria, when you see a runaway train car rolling down the track, heading for a group of five people working on the line. You see that if you change a nearby switch you can divert the car onto a siding, but if you do that the runaway car will hit one man working on the track over there.

Do you think quickly, throw the switch, and save the five while killing the one? Or do you freeze with horror, clamp one hand over your mouth, hyperventilate, and watch the tragedy proceed? Perhaps you could pull out your cell phone, dial 911, and calmly report the disaster to the authorities as it occurs.

Many people decide that throwing the switch is the proper answer to this dilemma, because it results in a less tragic outcome. Would it make a difference to your decision if the one to be killed is your best friend, and the other five are strangers? What if the one is your mother-in-law? What if you know all these workers as your friends and associates working for the railroad? Note also that under emergency conditions, you don't have much time to reflect upon all the ramifications of your action before you take it.

Let us expand this scenario by going to the Amazon jungle to stand beside a river where we see a group of five children playing in the water. Another lone teenager is standing in the water on the other side of the river fishing. You see a crocodile swimming towards them and have the ability to push a log into the river that will divert the croc towards the teen. But this time there is a very old man standing next to you on the bank that you could throw into the river in front of the croc. Are you justified in sacrificing the old man to save the young people in the river?

In a third situation, you are a doctor at a hospital where you have five patients who each need an organ transplant to survive, and they need these operations soon. You have the skill to perform the operations but no organs are available. A nurse tells you that a healthy young man has come to the hospital for a check-up, and he has all the organs necessary to accommodate all your patients. Is it OK to harvest the organs from the one to serve the five?

Before we declare the solutions to these ethical quandaries, let us go back to our discussion of good versus evil.

Power

"Money is the root of all evil," is an often misquoted aphorism. The actual quote is "For the love of money is the root of all evil," which comes from the Bible in the Book of Timothy, Chapter 6, Verse 10, where Paul is giving instructions on how to achieve righteousness. Although money and the love of it may be considered symptoms of evil, the actual source of evil is to be found in the unchecked desires of men.

Let us approach this problem by considering a few of the ideas we have mentioned in this book that illustrate goodness. Select the following virtuous words:

Survival, Cooperation, Production, Balance, Friendship, Peace.

Compare these words to the contrasting vicious words that show evil:

Death, Conflict, Destruction, Imbalance, Hatred, Strife.

Additionally, we must introduce the one word that controls the influence of one over the other: Power. Power, in this sense, is the exercise of might. In the world of animals, the rule is: might makes right. Each creature exercises his might for his own benefit. In civilized human society, each individual limits his use of personal might in order to cooperate with his group, and he cedes some of his power to the chief.

In a given tribe, cooperation among individuals is based on trust. Each individual in society trusts that his fellow tribesman will uphold his end of the bargain, and not misuse his power to cheat the other. This happy arrangement between citizens leads to the concept of rights.

A right is kind of contract between two individuals, or between a group and the individual, who both agree to treat each other with a certain amount of mutual respect. I agree that you have a right to exist and to pursue your chosen profession. You agree that I have a right to exist and to cooperate with the others in our community to the mutual benefit of all citizens. This is a description of rational self-interest.

Rights

Nearly everyone who reads this book will agree with the proposition that each citizen is entitled to life, liberty and the pursuit of happiness. These are rights, now justly considered basic human rights, that have arisen in the philosophy of Western Civilization.

Law is the codification of rights, privileges and responsibilities that are imposed upon, or agreed to by, the people in a society. Law is enforced by the power of the group over the individuals in the group, or by the chief of the group.

Now we have a stack of words to help define the obligations of people who gather together to form a successful society:

Virtue, Cooperation, Trust, Respect, Rights, Law.

And we have the one word that describes how people interact with one another as they exercise their individual power. The use of power is motivated by the individual's wants and desires. His use of power is tempered by his judgment, tolerance for pain, and drive for self-preservation. Goodness results from wisdom guiding the use of power. Evil results from the misuse of power. Goodness requires a balance of power between competing individuals, or between an individual competing with a group. Evil results when an imbalance of power encourages one party to violate a right of another. We may summarize the contest between good and evil with the following maxim. Evil may be avoided by restraint in the use of power. Or, from the other view: Goodness will be promoted by restraint in the use of power.

Examples

Let us look at a little story in which goodness prevails, and see how we could revise it to illustrate evil.

Abe owns a pick-up truck that he wants to sell. Since his rich uncle bought him a new one, he wants to get a few dollars for his old truck so he will have some money to buy gas for the new one. Abe places an ad in the newspaper to sell his old truck for $2400, an amount he considers a fair price.[6]

Bob wants to buy a pick-up truck so he can haul furniture around for his friends, who seem to move from one apartment to another on a frequent basis. Bob sees Abe's ad in the paper and goes to have a look at the subject truck. Bob kicks the tires and looks under the hood, takes it for a test drive, and decides this truck is just what he's looking for. Bob offers Abe $2000 for the truck. Abe says he couldn't possibly let it go for that. After all, he put a new set of tires on it a few months ago that cost him $400. He tells Bob the truck is in good shape, has been reliable transportation for years, and has only 94,000 miles on the odometer. A similar truck from a used car dealer would cost more like $3000.

Bob says he can go no higher than $2300. Abe really wants $2400, but decides he should sell it to this customer for $100 less, so he may avoid the hassle of having to deal with more prospective buyers. The deal is struck, money changes hands, and Bob drives away with his new vehicle.

Good. This is an example of an arms-length sales transaction between a willing seller and a willing buyer. Neither party is forced into doing anything against his will. A balance of power exists between the parties. If they could not agree on an acceptable price, they could both have walked away from the transaction, and gone on to deal with some other buyer or seller. Both compromised; Bob paid more than his original offer, Abe accepted less than his original price. An acceptable bargain was negotiated by both parties, with mutual respect for the rights of the other.

This simple scenario is fraught with opportunities for evil. If Abe knows that the transmission mounting-bracket is broken and doesn't disclose this fact, he is guilty of misrepresentation as to the condition of the truck. If Bob writes a bad check to pay for it, he is guilty of cheating Abe. Since this is a used vehicle story, the reader will surely have his own examples of evil that could lurk under the surface.

Now let's look at a small story about evil to see if we can find a way to change the evils into goods.

Charlie is hungry, but he has no money to buy dinner. He spent his last ten dollars for a bottle of wine yesterday. Charlie knows that a lot of people don't lock their doors in the evening and he is sometimes able to sneak in the back door for a few seconds, find something of value and leave before anyone knows he is there. Charlie has friends who will give him a little money for the things he steals. So Charlie finds an up-scale neighborhood where he hasn't been before, and walks down the street looking for a likely target. When a dog barks at him from someone's back porch, he keeps walking. Charlie does not want to attract any attention to his activity. From a back alley he sees a light in a kitchen, but nobody seems to be around. He sneaks up to look in the window and sees that, indeed, no one is there. He also sees a small microwave oven on the counter and knows he could sell one of those. He gently tries the back door, which opens noiselessly. What luck! He enters the kitchen to snatch the microwave, but instead he finds a woman's purse on the counter by the door. He grabs the purse and makes a hasty exit. A few blocks away, Charlie pauses under a lamppost to harvest the cash and credit cards from the purse. When he opens the purse it explodes in his hands.

Diane, the homeowner where Charlie lifted the purse, had been a victim of burglary before. She decided to booby trap an old purse so she could teach a lesson to the next thief who entered her premises. The charge she rigged in the purse was the size of a large firecracker; big enough to provide a nice surprise, but small enough not to cause major injury.

What are the evils in this story? Charlie has no respect for the property of others. Like an animal in the wild, he figures he is entitled to anything he can grab and run with, as long as he doesn't get caught by a meaner animal. The evil of stealing does not bother him, unless, of course, somebody takes something from him.

As far as converting Charlie from an evil thief to an upstanding citizen, we probably have a tough case. Charlie has, no doubt, a long history of minor crime. He has a support group willing to buy the fruits of his illegal activity. If Charlie wants to take Diane's lesson to heart, he will probably need professional help. He needs to learn to stop taking advantage of other people's weaknesses, to respect their property. He also needs gainful employment, so he must work on his alcohol problem as well as his honesty. Charlie is probably doomed to a life of being in trouble with the police. Perhaps his priest can help turn him around.

Diane, who is generally a law-abiding citizen, has also done an evil thing by building a mantrap. Explosive devices are against the law in most jurisdictions. An innocent bystander might as well have opened the purse for some reason. A child might try it, or a nosy neighbor visiting. Instead, Diane should have kept her back door locked, bought a watchdog, or invested in a burglar alarm. Taking the law into her own hands is discouraged by modern society. Diane may simply change her attitude towards evils perpetrated against her, by embracing forgiveness perhaps, to keep from planning vengeance against trespassers. Note, however, that Diane, as well as any living creature, has the right to self-defense. If she is physically attacked, she is perfectly justified in using her teeth, nails, fists, elbows, knives, or firearms to drive away her attacker. Calling the police is an advisable first step, but an emergency situation permits the use of one's animal responses for self-preservation. Evil is perpetrated by the one who initiates force against another. Responding to force with force is self-defense.

We could go on for hours with example stories about good and evil, but we trust our readers already understand the principles. The point to note is that any evil may be understood by analyzing the imbalance of power between the perpetrator and victim. Charlie chose to sneak around in the dark, taking things from unsuspecting victims. Diane hid a hazardous device in an attractive and innocent looking package. Both exercised their power of stealth to gain an unfair advantage over, and to deceive their victims. Conversely, when goodness prevails, we can observe the balance of power between the principals. In the transaction over the pick-up truck, the buyer and seller each respected the other's position. Neither threatened the other with harm or violence. They dealt with each other in mutual respect, and each man made his decision to buy or sell based on his personal feelings to satisfy his own desires. Each man exercised his own rational self-interest.

Many books about good and evil have been published over the last several years. One we have found that thoroughly covers many aspects of the topic is *The Science of Good and Evil,* by Michael Shermer.[7] He takes an interesting tour of morality from an evolutionary viewpoint, down the ages of history, and through the customs of different cultures. We recommend this book for anyone who wishes a deeper understanding of the features of morality that we have mentioned.

Answers

Now let us return to the moral dilemmas we considered earlier. Do we throw the switch on the railroad and kill the one while saving the five? We would probably be justified in taking this action, since it is a fairly clear choice of a greater benefit to a greater number of people. Probably, few people would fault us for freezing up and taking no action, given the requirement for fast thinking in an emotional situation. We are not personally responsible for those people being on the tracks in the rail yard. These employees know they have a more hazardous job than clerks in a grocery store, and should be covered by enough life insurance to care for their families in the event of a disaster.

We are definitely not justified in sacrificing the old man to the crocodile in favor of the kids in the river, because that would be violating the old man's right to life and liberty. Neither we nor the old man are responsible for the kids having chosen to swim in the crocodile's habitat. The children's mothers should have warned them against that kind of behavior. If the kids choose to ignore this advice, they are accepting the danger, whether they actually realize what they are doing or not.

If you are feeling particularly altruistic at that moment, you are free to jump in front of the croc yourself to save the kids. But you can't make that decision for the old man. If you tell him that he could throw himself into the river to save the kids, he could make his own decision. But then he might decide to push you in.

Likewise the doctor has no justification in sacrificing the healthy young man to save his five patients, because he would be violating the man's rights. The man has no relationship to the patients, and has no responsibility for their life-choices that caused their diseases, or the random germs that infected them.

When we understand that evil is caused by one man imposing his will upon another without the other's consent, we can more easily understand the answers to moral quandaries.

The root of evil is not to be found in money, but in the abuse of power by any individual human.

Notes:

[1] See Gomes.
[2] See Dante.
[3] See Schimmel.
[4] See Aristotle.
[5] How could anyone possibly be killed by kindness? Consider the example of a mother who wishes to provide a loving environment for her child, and protect her daughter from the evils that lurk at every hand. Only the finest things will be good enough for her youngster. The child is brought up in a healthy home with plenty to eat, and her mother guides her in virtuous habits among her family members, all of whom are similarly inclined. The child is not allowed to watch TV programs that depict violence, or see movies that show crude behavior between depraved characters. She is protected in her happy home, and insulated from evil. What happens to this over-protected girl when she is accepted at the college of her choice, and must now make her own decisions on how to conduct her life? Will she be prepared to deal with the typical male college student she will undoubtedly meet? Will she have the strength

of character to resist the temptations of tobacco, liquor, and other recre-
ational drugs? Will she trust that her new girlfriends in the dormitory
have the same wholesome concern for her well-being as her mother at
home? Does she harbor in her heart some latent rebelliousness against
her strict upbringing, as so many youth are wont? Alas, unprepared for
the real world, she is indirectly killed by the excessive kindness of her
mother. An overdose of goodness can lead to an overdose of evil.

[6] Abe, Bob, Charlie, and Diane are fictional characters used here to illustrate features of human behavior.

[7] See Shermer.

CHAPTER ELEVEN

FAIRNESS, SUMMARY, GOVERNMENT, LAW

Fairness

CHILDREN display an early appreciation for the concept of fairness. We have often heard the cry, "That's not fair!" when a youngster feels taken advantage of. The adult overseeing the welfare of the child usually responds with advice like: "The world is not fair, and the sooner you learn it the better." The adult wishes to educate the child by giving examples of minor evils so the child will learn to watch out for himself. Caution and alertness are virtues to possess in dealing with other people and the forces of nature.

Fairness is not only appreciated by children. Fairness is also understood, to a much deeper degree, by the adults who own and operate some of the largest and most successful businesses in America today. By a successful business we mean, in this case, a corporation that earns significant and consistent profits for its owners and shareholders year after year, by competing in the marketplace among other competent players. The example we have in mind is professional sports. Think Major League Baseball or the National Football League. These businesses put on the spectacle of competitive sports for the entertainment of many thousands of people, and in the process provide employment for many hundreds of others.

If we grant that the overriding motivation of professional sport is to win, perhaps even to win at all cost, where does fairness enter the picture? The game, let us choose baseball, is governed by a set of rules. The rules are consistent and set down in writing for all the players and other participants to agree upon before the game starts. The team hires umpires to observe the game as it unfolds and enforce the rules, to assure fairness equally to both sides of the contest. The job of umpire is a career field in sports that many people aspire to, as is the job of pitcher, outfielder or shortstop. So the umpires enforce fairness on the players within the rules of the game.

Now each team desires to win every game. Each team tries to hire the best players, mostly by offering a better salary than the competition. So the wealthiest organization should be able to pay the most to all the best players, and thus dominate the game.

Sorry, if this scenario were allowed to play out, one team would win all the games. It would be like the professional all-stars playing every game against the local high school team, no contest. All the sports fans would know who was going to win before the game was played, and they would stay home. They would not buy tickets. They would not show up to fill the stadium. They would not pay money to watch the games. Professional sports would thus die and become extinct.

What happens instead? All the team owners agree to a player draft at the beginning of each season. The teams alternate choosing the first choice players, then the second choice players, etc. This ensures that the teams remain competitive and interesting for the sports fans to watch. This is a voluntary exercise in fairness that allows the various teams to compete (may we say it?) on a level playing field. This fairness maintains a balance of power that encourages virtue and discourages evil.

We conclude that professional sports depend upon the concept of fairness for their very existence.

Note that a sports team is also a lifelike creature, an organization that acts like a life form, which competes for survival in its environment. The food of this team-creature is money. If it does not take in enough money, enough to earn a profit, it will die. The players and umpires on a team are the cell analogs to a life form, the team is the organism analog, and the league is the tribal analog. If an individual player cannot perform his task well enough, the team will cast him off and hire another player who can. This is similar to the biological creature casting off dead cells, and replacing them with new ones. The sports team competes for survival in its ecology, the economy of a modern society, along with all the other businesses trying to carve out a niche so they might continue to exist.

This sports team analogy is leading us into the concepts of capitalism, but we have several more subjects to cover before we consider the larger questions of a national economy.

Summary

Let us summarize the major points we have covered so far in this book. Our planet formed out of rocks and dust swirling in the primordial universe, attracted together by the force of gravity. After the new planet had orbited in the sunshine for one and a half billion years, simple life forms emerged on the surface. Each life form struggled for survival in its environment and attempted to propagate its species. Simple life forms progressed into more complex configurations, and the forces of evolution eventually produced a vast variety of life forms that settled into a balanced ecology of incredible diversity. The interactions between life forms also created lifelike forms that joined in the struggle for survival and dominance. Each and every plant and animal worked for itself alone to advance its own self-interest with no regard for any other creature in its environment.

The meaning of life is survival. The imperative of life is to strive for the flourishing of one's own species. Anarchy among animals is the law of the jungle, and represents neither good nor evil.

After three billion years of evolution, a large brained species arose that eventually created civilization, and used its intelligence to advance beyond the anarchistic basics that governed the animal world. Mankind invented philosophy and science, and discovered that virtue and vice also compete for dominance among the ideas and behaviors of man. Religions formed among men and gathered many followers by promulgating ideas that men found attractive. Religious doctrines and teachings dominated the culture of man for ages, and persist as powerful forces in civilized society today.

The pecking order principle separates individuals into a hierarchy. This leads to chiefs and kings and governments; the controlling individuals and groups who exercise power over others. The exercise of power among men generates the opportunity for evil, where evil is a violation of an individual's rights, either by another person or a group. The force of good is achieved when a balance of power exists between individuals and groups, where they can choose to cooperate and work together for their mutual benefit. The concept of fairness is related to the balance of power between competing individuals, or groups.

Anarchy among men creates evil. Evil is perpetrated by the one who initiates force against another. Cooperation among men results in goodness. Balance and equilibrium yield progress in obtaining the greatest good for the greatest number.

The example of fairness in professional sports demonstrates that mankind actually appreciates the concepts of cooperating for mutual benefit, while competing for domination in the struggle to win.

Government

Now let us consider the largest and most influential organizations of mankind: government. Government means power and control, and thus may be considered the seat of evil or the wellspring of goodness, depending on how power is implemented. Since mankind has tried many different forms of government, we should consider a few of them to see if we can decide which one is best in which situation.

Anarchy is the total lack of government. Anarchy means every man for himself, where might makes right, and the law of the jungle prevails, where violence reigns supreme. We have already considered anarchy as the mode among animals.

A chiefdom is the natural form of government for families, and groups of families or tribes.

A monarchy is a government or state where the supreme power is lodged in a single person, a king or queen. This person usually has some hereditary claim to the throne.

A dictatorship is run by a person who assumes absolute authority of a government, usually without consent of the people, and without any hereditary basis.

Autocracy is the term for uncontrolled or unlimited authority of one person over others, as in a monarchy where the ruler is especially domineering or tyrannical.

An aristocracy is a ruling class who are considered (mostly by themselves) to be superior to the common people. This elite class holds power and privileges not available to those they rule.

An oligarchy is a form of government where authority is vested in a few individuals, such as a particular family. This form of government may actually be the case in a dictatorship, monarchy or autocracy, since a dictator or king has a cabinet of advisors who help him implement his policies. Thus, power is wielded by a ruling group behind the figurehead.

A democracy is a form of government where power is vested in the people and exercised by them or by their elected agents in a free electoral system.

A republic is a government where the power comes from the citizens who are entitled to vote, and is exercised by the representatives chosen by them.

Much ink has been spilled in the battle about the differences between a democracy and a republic. Most people use the terms interchangeably, sometimes referring to the government of the U.S. as a democracy and other times as a republic.

Other folks insist that a republic is a much higher form of government than mere democracy. In a true democracy it is possible for a majority of voters to choose to abuse a minority. This is called the tyranny of the majority.

The Pledge of Allegiance, repeated daily by school children and less often by adults, refers to "the Republic" with no mention of democracy, which makes the distinction easy to remember. Certainly, the founders of the U.S. created a new form of republic that went far beyond anything the world had previously seen. The founders' inspired vision was based on their deep understanding of history and philosophy. They wisely feared the limitless capacity of mankind to sink back towards anarchy, so they designed a government to avoid those errors.

For the purposes of this book, we will further define our republic as a constitutionally limited government of the representative type, created by a written constitution, wherein the powers of the government are divided between three separate branches; executive, legislative and judicial, each with specific enumerated powers. The constitution may not be changed except by amendment, approval of which must be by a supermajority of the people.

Which of the listed forms of government is the best? From the standpoint of virtue and the avoidance of evil, the best one would be the one that spreads power the most widely, and avoids the concentration of power into one individual or one group. The best choice is clearly a constitutional republic. A dictatorship would be the worst. But note that any government may be corrupted or misused. Leadership must be exercised with wisdom. Power corrupts, and absolute power corrupts absolutely.[1]

The hazard in a democracy is the tyranny of a majority. The vulnerability of a minority should be protected from the majority by the granting of rights to all citizens. Take, for instance, a classroom where the teacher wants to reward her students for their hard work by passing out candy, but she doesn't have enough for every student to get one. The teacher also wants to demonstrate the concept of democracy, so she puts the candy question to a vote. Since the class happens to have more girls than boys, the majority decides that the girls will get all the candy, leaving the boys with nothing.

The teacher decides to intervene, since the classroom is not really a democracy, it is a chiefdom. The teacher is the chief, and we may assume she is a benevolent leader with the goal of education for her pupils. The teacher decides to distribute the candy equitably by drawing chances, a lottery. She points out to her students that their democracy needs to consider fairness, and use wisdom in what they decide, respecting the rights of every individual.

The tyranny of the majority also has the potential to destroy a democracy. When politicians learn that they may attract votes for themselves by passing laws that award the people with generous gifts from the public treasury, they will often take advantage of this technique. As more and more voters are attracted to the candidates who provide them with government freebies, the politicians are encouraged to make the electorate more dependent upon their largess. Thus taxes must be increased to support the government's rising expenses to pay for the entitlements. An increase in taxes removes some of the motivations for people to work hard to succeed in the economy. Thus economic output declines, forcing a further increase in taxes to support the government handouts, which results in a further decline in the forces that create wealth. Once these politicians have gained a majority of the voters, it will not be long until the economy cannot support the load of government spending. The economy may collapse, and transform the formerly healthy democracy into anarchy and dictatorship.

A study of history might reveal the following progression in the rise and fall of more than one civilization. A people who start out in bondage may discover some spiritual faith that leads them to courage. Their courage lights them the way to liberty, which results in abundance. When abundance becomes commonplace, the people drift into complacency, and then to apathy. Apathy leads to dependence, and the people soon fall back into bondage. The reader may find it instructive to judge where his own society may be found along this sequence.

Laws

Governments make laws to govern the behavior of its people. Governments can make good laws that benefit its people, or bad laws that harm its people, or laws that are impossible to enforce. Laws of man are decided by kings or legislators and are enforced by their systems of police, courts and armies.

Nature, on the other hand, comes with laws that are already built-in to reality, and are thus immutable. These laws govern the behavior of people, because an individual who violates a law of nature is not likely to survive the encounter. One who attempts to defy gravity, for example, may fall to his death. Man may discover the laws of nature, but he cannot legislate them.

Although the laws of man cannot alter the laws of nature, he will occasionally try to impose his will upon the cosmos. An example occurred in the Indiana legislature of 1897 when a bill was introduced to declare the value of pi to be 3.2. Pi, the ratio of the circumference of a circle to its diameter, is approximately 3.141592653, etc.[2] It is known to be an irrational number, that is, one that may not be represented as a ratio of two integers, although it is close to 22/7. The Indiana Assembly of representatives passed the measure to legislate the value of pi, but the Senate was astute enough to drop the bill.

Some men actually have an appreciation for their own limitations and will not even try to impose their will on Mother Nature. The powerful King Canute of Britain, around the year 1020 was so revered by his followers, they felt he had the power to hold back the sea and calm the waves if only he would issue the command. The king was confident enough in his authority to demonstrate his limitations in this regard. He had his throne carried to the edge of the sea at low tide and commanded the ocean to back away and not wet his royal robes. Of course, his effort had no effect.

The dampened king is said to have proclaimed: "Let all men know how empty and worthless is the power of kings, for there is none worthy of the name, but He whom heaven, earth, and sea obey by eternal laws."

Today, the popular expressions of "sweeping back the tide" or "standing against the tide" are used to represent any similar, hopeless effort.

Notes:

[1] This famous phrase is attributed to Lord Acton, a British historian, in 1887.

[2] See the Wikipedia article on Pi, which gives a thorough survey of the subject, on the Internet at en.wikipedia.org/wiki/pi.

CHAPTER TWELVE

SOCIAL ORGANIZATION

NOW that we have touched on the various forms of government, we should look at the larger systems of social and economic organization, which are overseen by government. We will consider three; feudalism, socialism, and capitalism.[1]

Feudalism

Feudalism is a system that was prominent in medieval Europe, but was never called "feudalism" by the people involved in it. The term came from later historians who looked back and needed a label for it. Feudalism was a structured class society where people were sorted into levels; kings, nobility or lords, knights, vassals and serfs. The king owned the land and parceled it out to his nobles. A grant of land was called a "fief" or "feud." The lords were subject to the rule of the king, and they provided him with taxes and the manpower for his armies. After death, the lord's property would pass to his eldest son, but could not be subdivided nor be sold off to knights nor vassals. The knights were able to lease portions of the land from their lord, and sub-lease it to other vassals. The vassals were the common people who were allowed to live on and work the land in return for fealty to the lord. The vassals depended upon the magnanimity of the lord for their every need. The serfs or peasants were an even lower class who struggled to scratch a living from the remains not already claimed by the upper classes. The lord was in charge of promulgating laws to manage his little empire, so the rules would be different from one lordship to another. The lord would be guided in administration of is domain by the culture he arose from, which would include predominately his religious precepts.

As modern people we can appreciate the relationships of this structured society where every man was aware of his obligations, both to his superiors and to his subordinates. We would, however, not wish to live under this type system, especially as vassals or serfs.

In the modern day, feudalism has faded in significance, although we might be able to find some societies where it is still practiced in some form. We are thus left with the two popular contenders for control of society, socialism and capitalism.

Socialism

If one searches the literature for information on socialism, one cannot find a definitive book that explains all the principles and presents all the arguments in favor of socialism in one place. There are certainly many articles and books that praise the concept and make claims for its benefits, but there seems to be no agreement on the way socialism should be organized and promulgated. Everyone has his own version with different details.

Nevertheless, consensus settles on the definition that socialism is the economic, social and political system wherein the means of production are owned by the state. The reasoning behind this arrangement is to reduce the inequalities between those who possess greater wealth and power, and those with less. Socialists see the world of man as a class struggle where one group of people exploits others unfairly to the benefit of the more powerful group. There is no doubt that this struggle goes on in society just as it does in the anarchism of animal life.

The socialist ideas were most famously promulgated by Karl Marx (1818-1883), the nineteenth century philosopher, political economist and revolutionary. As members of the Communist League in London, he and Friedrich Engles were commissioned to write the principles of their organization, and thus published in 1848 *The Manifesto of the Communist Party.* Their popular slogan became, "Working Men of All Countries, Unite!" or as is now more politically correct, "Workers of the World, Unite!"

Marx claimed that the history of the world represented a class struggle. Feudalism had led to the evils of capitalism, which would unavoidably be replaced by socialism, which would then mature into communism. One of the ultimate goals was the abolition of private property in land.[2]

In a later work, Marx wrote the defining slogan for socialism: From each according to his ability, to each according to his need.[3]

The writings of Vladimir Lenin (1870-1924) greatly expanded upon the socialist ideas of Marx. Lenin, who gained power as head of the Russian Soviet Socialist Republic after the Russian Revolutions of 1917, took the opportunity to implement socialist policies in his government. The history of the U.S.S.R. from that time to the present demonstrates that the brand of socialism practiced by the Russians failed to live up to its advertised potential. The worker's paradise and progress towards a socialist utopia simply did not develop as planned.

Socialism attempts to eliminate the stratification of society by equitably distributing wealth among all members. The workers who manufacture products should share equally in the proceeds of the sale. All products are distributed equitably among all citizens. As a result there should be no people left in poverty, and no people of great wealth. Everyone shares in the bounty of production and all people live happy and productive lives in their equitable society. Central planning determines what products people need and thus the system produces only the amount that is required so there is no over-production, thus no decline in prices (due to the law of supply and demand) and no waste.

This may appear to be a noble and desirable state of affairs, but it nearly always breaks down in practice. It depends upon the people in power having the integrity to equitably distribute wealth without favoritism, even among themselves. The people in power, the elite class, the central planning committee, the ones who make the decisions, must treat themselves as equals to the common laborers who empty their wastebaskets and sweep the streets. These leaders must decide who gets to ride in the chauffeur-driven limousines and who must take the bus to work, or even who shall walk. Do we see here even the slightest opportunity for favoritism, or enforced inequality? Who determines the abilities of the workers who produce products? Who decides the needs of the consumers who use the products? Certainly we could not allow the worker himself to decide what his abilities are, because he might claim a lesser capability than he actually possesses because he is lazy. Certainly we cannot allow the worker to decide his own needs because he will probably claim more than he really needs. So an overseer must be appointed to determine abilities, and another must be appointed to determine needs. This power, controlled by the overseer, certainly offers the opportunity to exercise evil in the form of favoritism. How is it decided which committee will take on the task of central planning and exercise this power? Do we not see another anarchy developing before our very eyes?

Let us use another classroom example to explore the logic of the socialist system at work. A teacher prepares to give her class a test on the material they have been studying for the past month. The students have several days warning before the test so they may study and be prepared. After they take the test and the teacher grades them, the scores on the test range from 52 to 98 on a 100 point scale.

But this is a class governed by socialism, not by merit, so that the scores must be redistributed to make things fair for everybody. After all, the guiding principle is: From each according to his ability, to each according to his need.

The teacher, therefore, takes points away from the higher scoring students and awards them to the lower scoring students, so that everyone comes out with a uniform score of 75. This seems so much more equitable.

When it comes time for the next exam, the same announcement is made so all students have plenty of time to study. But now the less able students realize that they don't need to study so hard, because they will be given points to bring them up to the average, no matter how poorly they do. The brighter students realize that they do not need to study so hard and do all that extra work, because the teacher is only going to take their hard earned points away to assure everybody will end up at the average score.

The result is that all the work stops getting done, and everybody cruises along knowing that "all will be provided for" by the beneficent teacher. Is there some fallacy in this socialist reasoning, or may we conclude that socialism encourages malingering and mediocrity?

This classroom illustration uses grades on a test as the measure of reward to the students. A similar analogy may be drawn in many other situations where the reward is money, food rations, housing, or any other form of remuneration. The sharing of wealth divorced from merit in the production of that wealth breeds contempt for the effort necessary to produce it.[4]

Where does the attractiveness of socialism come from? Why do so many people seem to think that there should be a way for the state to equally distribute the wealth, the bounty, or the resources, of a larger society among all its citizens, regardless of their individual contributions to the whole?

The family model of society seems to provide the answer. Consider a family composed of a father, a mother and four children. The father loves his wife and children and wishes to provide them with the best of everything to the best of his ability. The mother loves her husband and her children and works to give them a happy and healthy home. The children are learning how to become responsible citizens by listening to the guidance of their parents. The children love their parents because the kids depend upon them for their every need. Any conflicts that arise in this ideal family are wisely handled by the mother and father acting in their roles as coequal leaders.

Why cannot this happy family situation be extended to society as a whole, as the socialists seem to prefer? The problem is that love, the kind of love that exists in the family unit and keeps it together, does not extend very far beyond the family. The father must go out into the business world every day to compete with the other fathers who are working to advance the interests of their own lives, wives and children. This conflict or competition between families is another example of lifelike units struggling for survival in their environments. Of course, the fathers can compete for dominance in the workplace while respecting the human rights of the other fathers.[5]

So it appears that the socialist ideal of society as one big happy family, where all wealth is equitably shared among all citizens, distributed by one or more benevolent father-figures, is a hopeless concept in actual practice. What other social and economic system could possibly produce a healthy society and provide a distribution of wealth that is fair and equitable?

Notes:

[1]   Loaded words warning: The words "socialism" and "capitalism" carry a lot of baggage for many people. Everyone seems to have his own unique definition of, and attitude towards these words. In this book we try to carefully define them for our purposes, so please keep an open mind and follow along with our logic.

[2]   See Marx, 1846 *Communist Manifesto*.

[3]   See Marx, 1875 *Critique of the Gotha Program*.

[4]   For an exhaustive treatment of all aspects of socialism, see Von Mises, *Socialism*.

[5] We of course realize that women and mothers are also found successfully
competing at jobs in the workplace.

CHAPTER THIRTEEN

CAPITALISM

CAPITALISM explains everything. Capitalism explains wealth, where wealth comes from, how it is used and distributed. Capitalism gives a framework for understanding economics and the interactions of people in society. People who embrace capitalism appreciate that man is capable of producing products and services, and wish to facilitate those activities. Capitalism forms the system under which people compete in production for the rewards of profit. Such competition assures growth and an ever-increasing supply of material wealth along with the mechanisms that encourage improvements in quality, the increase in the productivity of labor, the reduction of prices, and the expansion of economic progress.

The following definition is quoted from the book *Capitalism* by George Reisman:

"Capitalism is a social system based on private ownership of the means of production. It is characterized by the pursuit of material self-interest under freedom and it rests on a foundation of the cultural influence of reason. Based on its foundations and essential nature, capitalism is further characterized by saving and capital accumulation, exchange and money, financial self-interest and the profit motive, the freedoms of economic competition and economic inequality, the price system, economic progress, and a harmony of the material self-interests of all the individuals who participate in it."[1]

These claims for the benefits of capitalism may seem unbelievable to anyone raised in today's society who accepts the opinions expressed in the popular press. The majority of journalists today would have you believe that capitalism is just another form of anarchy where any benefit gained by one man represents a loss by another man, and that capitalists and businessmen use their positions of wealth and power to unfairly exploit others, especially the workers who actually exert the labor in production.

However, a study of economics under capitalism demonstrates that one man's gain actually represents a gain for all men in his society. Adam Smith, whose dates are 1723 to 1790, was the first to recognize this principle, which he called the invisible hand.[2] He mentioned this subject in his 1776 book, *Wealth of Nations.* When men compete to produce products and services, based on their own rational self-interest, they are creating wealth; they are building something that did not exist before. This new wealth establishes a foundation upon which the owner may build more wealth. Some small portion of this foundation (wealth) unavoidably becomes a benefit to his society as well. It seems as though some invisible hand is guiding economic progress, even though the individuals are merely working for their own benefit. Many men working under this arrangement of rational self-interest contribute wealth to themselves, and some portion of it represents a growing wealth for their society. Ethical conduct, which we have previously concluded as being a part of each man's rational self-interest, guides men to respect the human rights of the men with whom they compete. We have seen this fact demonstrated by the example of professional sports, which hires umpires to enforce the rules (ethics) of the game.

Let us look at an example of competition in the truly anarchic realm of animals and compare it to the competition in the allegedly anarchic behavior of man.

Consider a community of lions that lives on the Okavango Delta in Botswana and feeds on a herd of Cape buffalo.[3] When a lioness kills a buffalo, the chief lion, depending on the pecking order established in the pride, gets first dibs on the carcass. When the chief has satisfied his hunger, the other lions get to feed, based on their standing in the lion hierarchy. After the carcass is consumed, there may be some lower ranking lions that did not get a share. These weaker lions must try to kill another buffalo if they wish to eat. So the wealth represented by the buffalo carcass is exploited first by the most powerful lion. What he takes (his gain) is a loss to the others in the pride. He will not share and share alike.

The lions are at the mercy of nature in providing the limited resource of food, the buffalo herd. If their environment suffers a drought, the buffalo herd will decline, and thus the lions will also suffer a decline in their food resource. When the weather and the flow of the river are more generous, the buffalo herd will flourish and thus will the lions. The lions have no way otherwise to manage the health and well-being of the buffalo, even though this represents their only food source. The animals are stuck in their limited natural environment with no way to improve upon their anarchistic life style. In an economic sense, the animals are consumers with no way to become producers.

What does man do in a similar situation? Man discovers he can feed off of sheep, so he builds a fence around a pasture to keep his animals safe from other predators. He provides his sheep with food and water, and an environment where they can breed and grow a larger herd. Man realizes his sheep have wool he can shave off and make into cloth to clothe himself, and make curtains for his wife's windows. Man finds he likes the taste of apples, so he saves some of his harvest from the one apple tree he discovered in the forest, and plants the seeds to make a grove of trees, and eventually an orchard.[4] Once he has more apples than he can eat himself, he can use the surplus to help feed his sheep, or he can sell his apples to other men who wish to buy them. Man, through his ingenuity and labor, creates wealth where no wealth existed before. He engages in production until he has more lamb chops and applesauce than he knows what to do with. This wealth becomes a benefit to his society. Under capitalism and freedom of competition, where the man owns the means of production, and is free to dispose of his property as he sees fit, he is motivated to continue working so he may create even more wealth, and trade it with other like-minded men for the fruits of their labor. Unlike the animals, man can become a producer as well as a consumer.

The man has an ability to use his labor to advance the flourishing of his species, whereas the lion may only exert his labor to carve a limited existence from the limited resources provided by an uncaring Mother Nature.

Note that the man will lose his motivation to work and create wealth if he is not permitted to benefit by it. If a man creates a large herd of sheep and an orchard of apple trees, and is then heavily taxed by his king, he may decide his labor is not worth the effort. Similarly if roving bands of thieves steal his fruit and run off with his lambs, he will have to divert some of his labor to hiding his wealth, and thus be unable to be as productive as he was before. The man needs security in his society. The benevolent king realizes this need for his subjects, and thus builds an army to protect his territory, and his farmers and shepherds, his wealth creators.

The socialists of today, who would have you believe that competition under capitalism is merely another exploitative form of anarchy, do not appreciate the actual situation. Reisman states the concept succinctly: "… under capitalism, competition is the diametric opposite of the law of the jungle: it is a competition of producers in the production of wealth, not of consumers in the consumption of wealth."[5]

To better understand capitalism, we should appreciate a few underlying concepts: economics and capitalism, division of labor, money, the price system, supply and demand, the need for profit, market forces and freedom of competition, and increases in the productivity of labor.

Economics and Capitalism.

Economics is the science of studying wealth in society. Economists look at the features of human interaction that appear to encourage the generation of wealth, and they attempt to understand the behaviors that detract from wealth. Economists study the laws and institutions that man has created to see what affects they have on the flow of money and the welfare of the people who live under the various systems mankind has devised. The subject of capitalism provides a framework of logical interactions that helps economists to understand and describe the behavior of people living and working in the societies of the past and present.

Division of Labor.

In the primitive world, every man had to produce everything he needed by himself. He had to build his own house, hunt for his food, and grow his own crops. His tribe may have developed a simple division of labor society, but each community was a self-sufficient group without the ability to trade with other communities, unless they lived within a day's walk. Modern man, on the other hand, must depend on his division of labor society, where his job is to perform one task, or at most a small number of tasks, and depend on others to provide the remaining products and services he needs to survive. Think how helpless a primitive man would be if he needed to replace the leaky drain pipe under his kitchen sink. Where would he get the metal or plastic to make it? How would he form it into a tube? Where would he find a wrench to disassemble the leaky pipe from the drain? The modern man, however, will just visit his local hardware store and buy the readymade materials for a few dollars. Or he could hire a plumber, if he didn't want to do the work himself. Capitalism depends on a healthy, division of labor society.

Money

If the primitive shepherd wanted to have something he could not make for himself, a bronze knife for example, he could trade one or more of his sheep for it. He lived in a barter economy. If he wanted a bushel of apples and his neighbor could accommodate him, he could trade a lamb for the apples. However, our shepherd thinks his lamb is worth five bushels of apples, but he cannot use five bushels before four of them would rot. So he wants to trade his lamb for one bushel of apples plus the labor of his neighbor's son for a few days. But the neighbor's son is visiting his uncle on the other side of the mountain this week. So these men who wanted to trade with each other would have to figure out some other mutually agreeable number of items to trade. The answer to this frequent dilemma is, of course, money. The benevolent king of the realm realized this need and issued copper coins to his subjects to enable commerce. Once a sufficient quantity of money came into circulation, trade flourished.

The Price System

Once people understood the concept of money, they could set prices for their wares and services based on the relative values. The king might proclaim that one coin represented the value of one loaf of bread, so the people would be guided in pricing all the other products in their society. The law of supply and demand soon made itself known when apples from the warmer climes across the sea became less expensive than locally grown apples, once the local apple season had passed. A particularly useful trading technique was discovered to be the auction, where buyers could gather to bid on items for sale by sellers. An auction is a fair method for determining the price of an item at a particular time and place, which allows for the forces of supply and demand to balance out in a marketplace. Capitalism depends on an unencumbered price system operating in a free market where buyers and sellers may interact with each other.

Profit

Profit is the excess of money left over after expenses are subtracted from the proceeds of a sale. A simple example is a storeowner who buys inventory for resale. Let us say our merchant buys a case of 100 widgets from his supplier for $200. His cost for each widget is $2. The merchant thinks he needs to sell his widgets for $3 apiece in order to make a profit and to remain competitive with the other merchants in his area who also sell widgets. The merchant needs to consider the demand for widgets in his market, how long they will stay on his shelves, and whether some other competing product would be a better fit for his customers. If our merchant learns he cannot earn a decent profit on his sale of widgets, he will no longer carry them. If his government makes laws that limit the price he can charge for widgets, he will have even less incentive to offer them in his store.

The wholesale cost of widgets is not the only expense of sale that enters the merchant's calculations. He must also consider some small part of the rent he pays for the business use of his premises, the cost of electricity to run his lights and equipment, and the wages he pays his employees. Note how the profession of accounting arose to keep track of all these details, income and expense, profit and loss.

Profit is necessary for the successful operation of business. Capitalism uses profit as the measure of success. Profit may be considered the "food" of business. An animal, a life form, must have food to survive. Without food it will starve to death. A business, a lifelike form, must have profit to survive. If a business is prevented from earning a profit, it will die.

Market Forces and Freedom of Competition

In order for capitalism to work properly as a system, it needs a free flow of information so that the markets may provide the necessary feedback to regulate the supply of goods and services, to accommodate supply and demand.

In a free market, the buyers have a choice of which vendors to patronize. If someone wishes to purchase apples, he may shop at whichever grocer he chooses. He is free to go down the street and buy apples from the vendor with a lower price. Free competition results in the lowest price that allows a producer to cover his costs and earn some small profit. Otherwise he has no motivation to continue his business, and will go into some other line of work that will provide him with a profit.

Free markets are self-regulating. If a vendor cannot sell his apples at his current price, he will lower the price until his customers see that they can buy from him at a lower price than his competition. If the vendor still has unsold inventory at the lower price, he will order less inventory from his suppliers the next time. On the other hand, if the vendor sells out his entire inventory quickly, he can raise his prices to slow his sales. All of the grocers in a region, acting in their rational self-interest by logically adjusting their prices, will reflect the wholesale prices charged by the apple growers. The lower limit to wholesale prices will be the growers' costs of production. The growers will thus compete to reduce their own costs of production to capture a larger share of the market.

If a government passes a law to limit the price of widgets, it would be similar to placing a stop on the thermostat in our furnace example. It would place an artificial limitation on the designed capability of the heating system. The government might proclaim that thermostats shall not be set higher than 65 degrees F, even though the homeowner desires to set it to 70. This law interferes with the designed capability of the heating system. The homeowner will make up for the lack of heat in his house by buying more sweaters and blankets, thus diverting the flow of money in the economy from the fuel suppliers to the textiles industry. Capitalism depends on free markets and the freedom to compete in them. The term laissez-faire capitalism is used to describe this concept where the government intervenes as little as possible in economic affairs.[6]

When a business provides products that no longer meet the needs of consumers, the business will decline and be replaced by others that do meet consumers' demands. The economist Joseph Schumpeter, whose dates are 1883 to 1950, recognized this process and called it creative destruction.[7] A free economy will destroy those businesses that do not meet its needs, and cannot adapt to evolving tastes. A free economy will also automatically create new businesses to serve the expanding needs of society.

Governments often attempt to prevent the decline of existing businesses by subsidizing certain industries or special interests. This interference becomes an encumbrance to the feedback loop that regulates supply and demand. An often-quoted example is the buggy-whip industry. In the old days, people needed buggy-whips for their horse-drawn carriages. Today, nobody needs buggy whips, so the industry has died out. If the government had decided to continue protecting this industry, so that at least one of the buggy-whip companies still existed, we can see how this would be a waste of resources and manpower. The facilities and employees devoted to the obsolete product could be better utilized in a modern industry, manufacturing products that current consumers demand.

When the citizens in an economy are permitted to act in their own rational self-interest, unencumbered by government interference, capitalism flourishes and provides the people with the most efficient economy, supplying them with the things they want, and not wasting effort on items they have no use for.

Productivity of Labor

We may attribute much in the advance of civilization to increases in the productivity of labor. As an example, let us say we have an industrious man who wishes to build a house, but first he needs to dig a hole in the ground to put in the foundation.

Primitive man did not have the advantages of modern tools, so he would need to dig the hole with his bare hands, or perhaps utilize a sharp stick he found in the forest. In order to dig the hole in a reasonable length of time, he would need to hire 100 men to dig using their bare hands and sticks. This employment of labor would be fairly expensive, depending on the wage rates of the workers.

Later in history, when technology had advanced enough to provide workers with shovels, the same size hole could be dug, in the same length of time, by ten men with shovels. This is an example of an increase in the productivity of labor, made possible by more advanced tools, invented by the cleverness of man during his march forward in civilization. The advent of shovels depended on the discovery of metals and the skills necessary to form metal into the appropriate shape.

Today our house builder would hire one man with a backhoe to dig the hole for his foundation. This increase in the productivity of labor by one man was provided by the advantages of civilization and the advance of technology. The advent of the backhoe depended upon the invention of the internal combustion engine and the supporting industries to manufacture various parts for the machine. The company that builds the backhoe has access to tires, oil filters, and hydraulic pumps thanks to increases in the productivity of labor in those industries as well.

We can see how progress in tools and machinery make individual workers more productive in their efforts. In today's economy, a division of labor system is required to support the many tasks necessary to build a backhoe, or any other sophisticated product. A single man simply does not have the time, knowledge and skills to build such a product himself. He must depend on many other workers, working in their own specialties, to achieve success in manufacturing sophisticated products.

Force of Nature

In Chapter 11 we mentioned briefly the differences between the laws of nature and the laws of man, where the former are immutable characteristics of reality, and the latter are subject to the whims of legislatures. We would now like to make the bold claim that capitalism is actually a force of nature that is evidenced by economic activity. Capitalism was not invented by mankind, but rather was discovered by him. Capitalism may be thought of as being similar to gravity. It is a force of nature that has always been a part of reality, and once it was discovered by man, became a useful explanation for why economic phenomena occur, and can be used to predict future results based on its principles.

Socialism, on the other hand, is a force of mankind that was invented by him, and is enforced by his laws and legislation. When socialism is overlaid upon capitalism, or is imposed upon the people's natural tendency to compete for their own rational self-interest, it interferes with the inherent feedback mechanisms of the economy and distorts the results that capitalism might otherwise achieve.

When pure capitalism would dictate that a particular business, which had outlived its usefulness, should be allowed to die, a socialist system might decide instead to subsidize it for a few more years, to protect the livelihoods of its owners and employees. Political expediency will never actually find a good time to declare it is time for a particular industry to die, because employees and business owners are voters, too.

Regardless of such interference, the forces of capitalism will ultimately destroy the business. The resources diverted for a time by the socialist system, will necessarily have been withdrawn from the larger economy, and will thus make the inevitable crash more harmful to the overall economy than it would have been if the business was allowed to fail earlier.

On a larger scale, this argument may be used to explain the collapse of the socialist system in the former U.S.S.R. The Russian society had achieved a kind of stable equilibrium, which struggled along for many years in competition with the western world. When it failed, millions of people in the vast Russian Empire were thrown back into the chaos of anarchy. It will be interesting to see what kinds of governments develop to replace the fallen regime. Anarchy will, no doubt, play a major role.

Socialist abuses of the economy in the U.S. may be charged with causing the Wall Street meltdown of 2008, when twenty years of irresponsible credit expansion could no longer be supported on its foundation of worthless collateral.

Are You Still With Us?

Now that we have declared capitalism to be ultimately desirable, and that capitalism should be the guiding system in the creation of wealth and well-being of society, we have probably lost half our audience. But note again that this book is written from an engineering perspective. We wish to give the reader a set of tools to observe and understand the world we see around us today. Capitalism, as a system, explains much of the behavior of people in society. Note also, as a reader with an unprecedented degree of liberty in a free society, you have the option, at your choice, to reject the ideas presented in this book and conduct your life as you see fit. The exercise of capitalism is available to the citizens of a free country, and is less available to the unfortunate people ruled by a dictatorship.

Natural selection is a concept we have referred to many places previously in this book. It is a blind sorting mechanism that tends to eliminate unsuccessful behaviors among animal species by driving to extinction faulty mutations or practices with self-destructive results. A similar analogy may be made in the competition between socialism and capitalism. If we look at the successes in recent civilizations regarding the production of wealth and the flourishing of a healthy economy, which ones stand out? The cultures that embraced capitalism grew and blossomed, the ones that favored socialism declined. Compare the United States, Japan post-WWII, and Hong Kong versus the former Soviet Union, Cuba, and North Korea. Q.E.D.[8]

Notes:

[1] See Reisman, p.19. Anyone who truly wishes to gain a deep understanding of capitalism should study Reisman's book. A reading of his first chapter, some 22 pages, provides an excellent overview of the entire subject and should be enough to stimulate an interest to learn more.

[2] See Smith. The invisible hand is mentioned in *Wealth of Nations*, Chapter 2 of Book IV, titled "Of Restraints Upon the Importation from Foreign Countries."

[3] See Joubert.

[4] Our Orchardman would also need to learn the techniques of propagating the more desirable trees by taking cuttings and making grafts to healthy root stock.

[5] See Reisman, p.434

[6] Laissez-faire: from the French for "allow to act."

[7] See Schumpeter. The concept of creative destruction is presented in the book *Capitalism, Socialism and Democracy*, Chapter VII, "The Process of Creative Destruction."

[8] The use of Q.E.D. here is intended to be mildly facetious.

CHAPTER FOURTEEN

MOTIVATION

WHY does an individual do what he chooses to do? What motivates our actions? We can separate the reasons into five broad classes: Survival, authority, habit, money, and sentiment.

Survival

A man will want to eat and seek shelter in order to survive. He will run away and hide out of fear. He will seek a mate to propagate his species. These are basic drives that all animals possess.

Authority

We do many things because a person of authority tells us to. Your mother told you to brush your teeth every day. Your teacher instructed you to do your math homework. A policeman made you turn left onto a detour when you wanted to go straight on the highway. A judge forced you to pay a fine for stealing pumpkins, with a threat of jail time.

Habit

Why do we eat oatmeal for breakfast every morning? Why do we always drive on the right side of the street? Why do we continue to smoke cigarettes? Because we have developed habits. Some habits start because an authority told us to do things that way. Other habits begin innocently when we unthinkingly sit in a classroom chair on the first day, and return to the same seat for the whole semester. A habit may also be established by a conscious decision, as when we decide to drive a certain route to work because it is the fastest or has the fewest stoplights. When we eat the same thing for breakfast, it removes one more decision we need to make every day and simplifies our life. Once we learn to drive on the right, and see that everyone else does the same thing, we agree that this is a healthy habit. Smoking cigarettes makes us dependent upon nicotine, so when we realize that smoking is unhealthy, we find it difficult to kick the habit.

Money

Why do we get up every morning and go to work when we would prefer to stay in bed and sleep off the hangover? Money. We wish to continue receiving that steady paycheck.

Sentiment

Sentiment is a much more nebulous concept that motivates our behavior at a more subtle level. We may think of it as earning feel-good points, or brownie points, or social capital. It is a hypothetical social currency that is associated with good will, fellowship, loyalty, sympathy, shared interest or group bonding. We do things because they are right, because we wish to make friends, earn the trust of others, and help people in need. We donate time and money to charity because it's good for them and thus good for us. We do it for the Glory of God or because our heart is in the right place.

Sentiment has no unit of measure. We can't declare this currency in dollars or miles per gallon, because its value is different for every individual. Some people detest money and embrace sentiment. Others feel money is their only measure of success and sentiment is for suckers. Most people fall on a line somewhere between these extremes.

Sentiment is easy to counterfeit. One may claim to embrace the same sentiment as another, but in reality be pretending to gain an advantage. A man may claim to have affection for kittens when he knows a woman shares this sentiment, when his actual motivation is sex. He wishes to gain the respect, trust and friendship of the woman to exploit her body. Just as with money, one must be alert for fraudulent behavior in the realm of sentiment. It is difficult to know what evil lurks in the hearts of men.

This line of reasoning may lead us back to the topics of virtue and vice which we discussed in an earlier chapter. As with any set of competing forces, one must be cautious when dealing with decisions based on sentiment, since it is so easily manipulated. Money, on the other hand, is more concretely defined and simpler to verify as genuine.

You may find it instructive to consider some of your own daily activities and analyze whether they are primarily motivated by survival, authority, habit, money, or sentiment.

Pleasure vs. Pain

We may further condense this section on motivation to the unpopular notion that people do things to get paid. Another way to consider this topic is to realize, whatever you do, you will be paid for it, either in pleasure or in pain. Naturally, we seek pleasure and avoid pain.

Money gives us pleasure; lack of money gives us pain. Seeing our children succeed in life gives us pleasure, regardless of the money involved. Seeing our children fail in life gives us pain, regardless of the money involved.

You may live to earn money, or you may live to earn sentimental points, or you may seek some combination of money and points. Regardless, you are seeking to maximize pleasure and minimize pain. This striving causes conflict and competition, both within the individual and between individuals.

If a man desires to have money, he can earn it by engaging in a legal business. He may learn that he can collect more money faster in an illegal business, but he must weigh the possibility that he will be punished by his society if he gets caught. He must balance his desire for pleasure against his aversion to pain. He should use wisdom in arriving at his decisions in life. He should seriously consider virtue over vice. He should consider his rational self-interest in cooperating with others in his society to achieve his goals in concert with the goals of his community.

Belief System

An individual can succeed in society while harboring a flawed belief system. Before the age of Christopher Columbus (1446-1506), most people probably believed the world was flat. This explanation seemed logical in the everyday observations of common people, and this belief caused no problems for them in the conduct of their lives. Some people with a more scientific frame of mind, however, observed that only the tops of approaching ships at sea appeared first, when far away. As the ship came closer, more of its lower parts became visible. This implied that the earth had some curvature when considered on a larger scale. Today we appreciate that our planet is mostly spherical, and incorporate this knowledge into our belief system.

Galileo, whose dates are 1564 to 1642, promulgated the theory that Earth and other planets revolve around the sun. From his observations of stars and planets with the aid of his telescope, Galileo became a believer of the sun-centered solar system that Copernicus (1473 – 1543) had proposed near the end of his career. The church (the authority over society at the time) had incorporated into doctrine the earlier Ptolemaic view of an Earth-centered universe. Thus the church persecuted Galileo for his audacity to support an alternate theory. He did not have the scientific freedom to challenge established dogma. Newton (1643 - 1727) published his *Principia* in 1687 describing the mathematical basis of elliptical orbits due to gravity. Today the sun-centered solar system is considered scientific fact.

One goal of science is to re-examine existing knowledge based on new discoveries. Science challenges current beliefs, and eventually replaces many of them with more logical or more complete explanations of observed phenomena. The new results are, in turn, subject to further refinement, as the knowledge base of mankind expands. The authoritarian enforcement of existing doctrines is always a powerful force in society, but scientific discoveries have a tendency to nudge popular ideas in the direction of truth.

Faulty Reasoning

Today we share our environment with many people who still believe in entirely discredited ideas. We could probably find some folks who still believe that the rain gods may be appeased by dancing in the fields. Newspapers still publish tables of astrological alignments to predict future events. Check your local listings. No doubt we could locate plenty of people in town who plan their activities based on such faulty reasoning. Some folks do live in a fantasy world.

But note that people with diverse belief systems can get along well in America today. They may live successful lives, and contribute their talents to the advancement of their families and communities. This despite the fact that some portion of their belief systems may be seriously flawed. The world is big enough to accommodate a great diversity of belief systems by individuals and groups. As long as these various life forms and lifelike forms respect the human rights of their fellow man, civilization can grow and prosper, and offer opportunities for people to live long, productive and satisfying lives.

If it makes no difference, this fact that people harbor some faulty beliefs, does that mean it is not important? It is more a matter of degree. Life is complicated and offers many routes through the maze of choice. Americans today are free to choose their belief system. They have freedom of religion, freedom of association, freedom of the press. Americans are free to arrange their personal affairs to suit their particular proclivities. They may set out on a path of production, or one of destruction. Some men may take the route of alcohol dependence or drug addiction. These men rarely succeed in life in the long run. A successful politician who has achieved high office may decide that he is above the laws that govern the lives of lesser men, and begin to practice aberrant sexual behavior. When these activities come to public attention, his promising career may be destroyed.

Many people merely stumble into their way of life without any fore-thought whatsoever. The purpose of education is to provide people with the tools necessary to make informed decisions in their choices in life. Many people fail to take advantage of this opportunity, despite the encouragement of their elders and instruction from a long history of wise men. Socrates (469 – 399 BC), the great thinker of the early Greeks concluded, "the unexamined life is not worth living."[1] How many school children today, how many college students, how many adult citizens of your country can honestly say they have examined their own lives with a goal of understanding and improvement in mind. As the rare individual who has read this far, you may compliment yourself in this regard.

Let us go a little further in analyzing whether it really makes a difference when an individual has a faulty belief system. It depends on how the beliefs are applied. If you want to have the leaky pipes in your kitchen repaired, would you call the doctor? If you hear a funny noise coming from your car's engine, would you take it to the plumber? If you were having terrible abdominal pains, would you go to visit your auto mechanic? People with faulty belief systems act in ways that waste time, money and effort, without achieving their desired results.

People may also have faulty beliefs within their realm of specialty. If you take your car to the auto mechanic and complain of a grinding noise when you apply the brakes, the mechanic might diagnose the problem as a worn out wheel bearing, then go ahead and replace it. When you get the car back and drive it home, you discover the car still has the same problem. The mechanic misdiagnosed worn out brake pads as a bearing problem. How many people have gone to the doctor with abdominal pains, to be sent home with a prescription for antacids, when they were actually suffering an appendicitis?

Everybody makes mistakes, and many people make mistakes in the practice of their professions. Most professionals will acknowledge their errors and try to correct any resulting damage. However, there are folks who will fraudulently represent themselves to practice professions for which they are not qualified. Occasionally, people actually get caught misrepresenting themselves in otherwise valid professional occupations. A fascinating example is illustrated by the book *Fashionable Nonsense,* by Alan Sokal and Jean Bricmont.[2]

Sokal, a professor of physics at New York University, observed that a number of writers in professional journals were making unsupported claims and coming to nonsensical conclusions. These writers were making seemingly erudite, scientific sounding remarks that had no bearing on the subjects they were describing. Sokal decided to make up a parody of his own, containing arguments he borrowed from already published works. While pretending that this work was a valid, serious article, he submitted his fabrication to a respected, professional, scholarly journal in the humanities and social sciences. After due consideration, the journal agreed to publish the article. Immediately upon publication, Sokal revealed his deception in order to demonstrate that one could actually perpetrate such a hoax through the professional literature. The main point being that he exposed the writers he was parodying as frauds by copying their style in an exercise of nonsense.

We conclude from this actual example that there really are professional people out there who may practice deception as a way of life, whether they realize what they are doing or not.

Words

While we are on the subject of fraud, we should briefly touch on the veracity of words, those little bunches of symbols that fill this book.

Words are used in language for communication. Words are used to impart information from the speaker to the listener, or from the writer to the reader. Words may be used to tell the truth, to tell lies, or to transmit some combination of truth and falsehood. Words may be intended to clarify the facts or to purposely obfuscate the truth. The words in this book are intended to present a picture of the world from the perspective of an engineer, containing certain insights and warnings about the many pitfalls to be encountered in life, and to make recommendations about the ways people should conduct their lives. These words are subject to the interpretation of the reader, and thus may not actually transmit the intentions of the writer. But such are the hazards of publication. We trust that more people will understand our explanations than will misinterpret what we are trying to say in our search for enlightenment.

Words can appear to impart profound inspiration when in reality they generate nonsense. Take the philosophical question: What happens when an irresistible force meets an immovable object? We could get into an animated discussion of this subject and spend hours arguing the various points. But it would be a waste of effort because the question is nonsense. By definition, an irresistible force cannot be successfully opposed. Also, an immovable object will not be affected by any attempt to displace it. So it is a logical inconsistency to ask this question in the first place. These are mutually exclusive concepts. The statements regarding an "irresistible force" or an "immovable object" are linguistic exaggerations for poetic effect, and would have no actual meaning in a scientific analysis.

Some words take on a shift in meaning over time. Take the word "unique." This was originally defined as meaning "one of a kind," an absolute word with only one meaning. Lately, it has taken on the sense of "unusual" or even "strange." One often hears some speaker saying that something is more unique than something else, which is logically inconsistent when it actually means one of a kind.

What causes words to creep towards new meanings? Ignorant people hear the word and assume it means something it does not, from the context of the sentence where it is used. Such a listener does not actually bother to look it up. Then he starts to use it in this altered meaning and other ignorant people hear it and also use it in the new way. Soon, so many people are misusing the word, it acquires the new meaning and gets into the next version of the dictionary. Many of us traditionalists find such bastardization inexcusable, but such is the evolution of language.

Sometimes statements seem to contain insightful revelations, but further inspection reveals contradiction. For example, you cannot tell which way a train was going by looking at its tracks. Is this an insightful remark, or is it just a joke? The statement is true, but it confuses two different definitions of the word "tracks." An animal leaves "tracks" as impressions of its feet as it walks across a muddy road. Since the bottoms of its feet make distinctive marks, one can tell which direction it was walking. A train's "tracks" are guide rails along which it may travel in either direction, so when one looks at these tracks, there is no way to tell which direction it was going, or even if any train has actually gone by. We might just as well say that you cannot tell which way a truck went by looking at the street, but such a remark would lead the listener to think that we are complete dullards.

What is the sound of one hand clapping? This philosophical question seems mysterious and possibly full of hidden meaning, but it is actually nonsense. The engineer or physicist would ask, "clapping against what?" For clapping to make a sound, two objects must make contact, surrounded by air or some other medium to propagate the sound wave. Don't be fooled by people pretending to be transcendental.

Puns and jokes make excellent use of the multiple meaning value of words, and can be very entertaining. But trying to explain a joke to somebody who didn't get it is a good way to lose the rest of your audience. But before we drop the subject, let's look at a couple of examples of funny nonsense.

Time flies like a bird, but fruit flies like a banana.

Groucho Marx.

Life is too important to be taken seriously.

Oscar Wilde.

Why was Cinderella such a poor basketball player?
Because she had a pumpkin for a coach.

Kenneth Jernigan.

A pun is the shortest distance between two straight lines.

Original source unknown.

(Yes, we know that four examples are more than a couple. It's so hard to stop when you're on a roll.)

The point of these last few paragraphs about words (other than the jokes) is to show that people may try to impress you with their words, or to win you over to their way of thinking. But words may be so variable, one must always be alert to the possibility that someone is trying to deceive you, or pull off some sort of scam. The more benign version of this practice is someone telling jokes or kidding around. Note that somebody playing a joke, when the victim does not know it is a joke, becomes a double joke.

We might expect commercial advertisers to engage in blatant puffery, word stretching and exaggeration, but Sokal has exposed a few of the well educated, professional writers, who should have known better, as being guilty of such deception. Sokal might be described as having played a joke on the unsuspecting publishers, who were not vigilant enough to detect the ruse.

Notes:

[1] See Socrates.
[2] See Sokal.

CHAPTER FIFTEEN

CHOICES

AN individual human, a life form, may join many groups, or life-like forms. These individuals and groups compete for survival and advancement in their environments. In America today, an individual may be affiliated with many interest-groups. He may be a Presbyterian, a Jew, a Hindu. One may join the Democrats, Republicans, or Libertarians. A man may choose to become a chiropractor, a grocer, a librarian, or a pilot. A woman may be a mother, a licensed driver, a merchant, or a corporate lawyer. Of course, many other choices are available to men and women.

An individual may join a combination of lifelike forms. One woman may be a Jewish mother, who owns a pickup truck, which she drives to the building she rents for her professional practice of ophthalmology.

A man may be a cook, who is a devout Presbyterian, lives in a restored historic building, votes for Republican candidates, and likes to play golf on weekends.

Did these people make wise decisions in their choices of religion, politics, possessions and career? Who is right? Are the Jews right? Are the Presbyterians right? Are the Democrats or the Republicans right? Can they all be right at the same time? Regardless of your personal opinion on these questions, the people of the United States have the freedom and liberty to choose the path in life they wish to follow. The point here is that a vast array of valid lifestyles are available to law-abiding citizens of America today. People in this environment may choose to carve a niche for them-selves to survive and prosper in their ecology, as long as they do not violate the laws of their society. People do have free will, and the ability to make choices in how the they wish to conduct their lives. Most people seem to choose productive careers that advance themselves and their families, and thereby civilization. Others may choose behaviors that prove self-destructive, and detract from their own well-being as well as from the advancement of mankind.

History demonstrates that freedom and liberty for individuals and their organizations in free countries promote success and the flourishing of life and wealth, to a much greater extent than the restrictive dictatorships and authoritarian governments of the world.

Children

Let us consider how our young people are influenced to choose the life style they will eventually follow. Beyond the motivations of their basic animal instincts, they select their paths in life from the cues they receive from parents, schools, peers, and the entertainment industry.

Consider Eric and Fred, two boys who live across the street from each other. Eric's father buys his family a new Chevrolet about the same time that Fred's father buys a new Toyota. Eric and Fred get together to boast about their good fortune.[1]

"My dad bought us a new Chevy," Eric says, with his nose in the air.

"Oh, yeah?" Fred retorts, "We got a Toyota, and my Dad says your car is a heap of junk. We spent a lot more for ours."

"Well, that was dumb. Why would you waste extra money for stuff you don't need? Besides, your car is red, and everybody knows that the police arrest more red cars than other colors."

"Just if they're going too fast. And who wants a blue car? That's so un-cool."

"Is not!" Eric objects. "My dad says we always buy American, so we're more patriotic. You're just supporting the foreigners who are trying to take away all our jobs."

"That's stupid. Everybody knows that half the parts on your car come from Japan anyways. When I'm old enough to drive, the girls are going to ride with me, 'cause my car is hot."

"No they won't."

"Yes they will."

"You are such an idiot," Eric says, slapping Fred on the side of the head.

"Don't hit me," Fred yells, punching Eric on the arm. "I'll kick your butt!"

Soon the boys are wrestling on the floor, attempting to settle their differences with violence.

We won't bother to discuss their arguments, since they were really playing the one-up game, merely trying to verbally out do the other.

Regardless of the merits of their arguments, when it comes time for the boys to acquire their own cars, Eric will likely favor a Chevrolet, while Fred will seek out the latest Toyota, based solely on copying their dads' examples. The reader may find it useful to reflect upon his own choice of a first car in light of his parents' earlier purchases.

Children are taught behavior, first by their parents, then by their teachers, starting in kindergarten. Keep your hands to yourself, don't hit your neighbor, stop fighting, say please and thank you, quiet down, don't play with your food. By the time they reach high school, most kids have been well socialized and can function as reasonable citizens in public. But they have also recently hit puberty and suffer from raging hormones. In this condition the boys are exposed to high school football, and the girls are encouraged to join the cheerleading team.

The boys are supposed to learn to channel their natural aggressive tendencies onto the sports field and to limit their violent behavior to that arena. Some boys miss the point and carry their aggression home to their families or into society.

The girls on the cheerleading team put on skimpy outfits, jump up and down, wave their pom-poms, and try to stimulate the crowd into a noisy display of support for the home team, along with martial music from the school band.

Do the young people receive mixed signals from this spectacle that might encourage them to misbehave in their relationships with others? Does this environment emphasize their animal passions or show them that they can accomplish more when they cooperate and work together as a team? Unless high school sports are accompanied by a healthy dose of adult leadership and guidance, the kids will learn to prefer their animalistic impulses.

Who is popular among the students in high school? Which kids are the ones looked up to as role models? Are they the studious types who obey the authority figures, study their lessons and do well in academic subjects? Or are they the rebellious sports stars who flout the rules and strut around arrogantly to impress the girls? Who are popular among the females? Are they the demure, ladylike, modest girls who like to have their homework done on time, or are they the raucous, bold ones who take charge and adopt the latest fashions?

Who are the heroes of young people today? What do they think is cool? What careers do they aspire to? Rock stars and sports heroes are high on the list. Rock stars stand on the stage, dance around, play loud music, holler at the top of their lungs (into amplifiers), and do outrageous things that their audience finds entertaining. They get paid big bucks for this behavior, because many people want to watch and listen to them. Thus, they are able to sell a lot of tickets to their performances.

Professional sports figures gather in arenas to compete against others in their chosen sport. They earn gigantic salaries for this behavior because they are the best at what they do, and people like to watch (and bet on) the spectacle. Thus, the teams are able to sell a lot of tickets to their performances.

What do young people see in these occupations that makes them want to emulate their heroes? Money, power, and the admiration of their peers. What could be more natural for motivating imitation?

We have over-generalized the high school environment here, and used the old, stereotyped male/female roles. But our point is to realize that a great number of choices are available in generating a life style to follow. We conclude that the education of young people should include a healthy portion of training in virtuous behavior, and plenty of examples of vice to avoid. Life is very complicated.

The entertainment industry constantly bombards us with opportunities to see the things we want to see, or to see the things advertisers think we want to see, and children are unavoidably exposed to the same onslaught of information. At any time of the day or night, one may find a show to watch on TV, see a movie, or watch a clip on the internet. Movies and other entertainment media often depict evil characters engaging in depraved acts, swinging swords and discharging firearms in irresponsible abandon. Adults who watch such shows should already appreciate that they are seeing fiction or drama, displayed for entertainment purposes, or to present the vicarious experiences of the unfortunate characters who get to suffer the consequences of their ill-advised behavior. The adult should recognize that the lessons illustrated by the characters should be considered against the background of reality. The adult might say to his friend, "Did you see the stupid things that character just did? I would never do something like that. This guy is certainly no role model."

A child, watching the same show, might think, "Wow, that looks like fun! I think I'll try it." The child has not yet acquired the life experience to make valid judgments regarding the things he sees. The "Monkey See - Monkey Do" syndrome is a powerful director of behavior in young people. Children need constant guidance from responsible adult guardians so that they may grow up to become responsible citizens.

Is it any wonder that children growing up in today's environment are confused about the way they should act in life? Are we really surprised that an occasional student will decide to take a weapon to his classroom and massacre his associates? He sees examples of this behavior in the news. If his judgment center has not been properly trained, he may commit terrible, tragic acts.

Returning to more acceptable behavior, if you pay attention to sports, and grow up in Pittsburgh, you will probably be a Steelers fan. If you're from Denver, you will definitely be a Broncos fan. Chicagoans follow the Bears. Sports fans generally follow their local teams first, and base their further choices on style, or performance in the stats. The reader my find it instructive to consider his own line of reasoning in selecting his favorite teams.

Some people are actually aware of the reasons why they make such choices; others just go with the first whim that strikes them. The easy and natural way to make decisions is to just go with the first idea that comes to mind. We refer to this simplistic decision-making technique as reasoning from A to B. Many people stop there.

I want it, so I grab it. This is the animalistic response, the childish response. The rational adult human should go a little further. He should reason from A to B to C, because he has the intelligence to understand the ramifications of his behavior. I want it, but I can't just grab it, because it belongs to someone else, and I respect the property rights of others. Stealing is not right, and I know how to reason from A to B to C to D.

Advertisers understand this feature of human behavior and try to capitalize on it by pounding people with incessant suggestions on what to buy, buy, buy. They wish to ingrain habits in the use of their products over those of the competition. How many advertising jingles come to mind when you stop to think about them? Note that slogans, both in advertising and in politics, are always shallow and simplistic. They are based on thinking merely from A to B, and thus are easy to remember. When a consumer makes an impulse buying decision, when he is simply thinking from A to B, he goes with his first reaction, which the advertiser has conditioned in his mind. But we, as readers of this book, and as responsible adult thinkers, realize that others will often try to trick us by taking advantage of our human weaknesses. But we are not fooled, because we can reason from A to F, and even to G, if necessary.

When someone gives you his pitch, offers you an opportunity to make a decision (to spend your money), consider the source. Is this man really trying to sell you something? Discover the motivation behind the message. Realize you have other choices. You will be a much happier consumer.

Notes:

[1] Eric and Fred are fictional characters used here to illustrate features of human behavior.

CHAPTER SIXTEEN

KILL OR BE KILLED

IN the animal world every creature must look out for himself. Each one lives in the brutal environment of natural selection and competes for survival with every other creature he encounters. He must eat or he will be eaten. He must kill or be killed. While staying alert to the hazards around him, he needs to be able to distinguish between friend and foe. Which animals are his friends? His own family and other members of his own species are his only friends. Which ones are his enemies? Just about everyone else. Sometimes, even members of his own species may become enemies, as when a different herd of his own kind (a lifelike form) is competing for the same feeding grounds.

Every other creature in his environment is predator, prey, or neutral. Consider the bunny. His predators are foxes, hawks and wolves. His prey is certain tasty plants and perhaps some insects. Neutral creatures in his environment are probably mice, songbirds and fish, although mice may compete for some of the same foods. As far as being a killer in the vast ecology around him, the bunny is not much of a threat. But it all depends on where your species falls in the food chain. Lions and tigers don't need to worry much about predators. Bunnies, mice and small birds need to be constantly on the alert.

At the cellular level, competition for survival goes on between microbes. In any organism the cells maintain a constant battle against viruses and bacteria. The organism fights off disease as a necessary function of survival, and this process continues at a subconscious, autonomous level, regardless of what activities the organism is engaged in. Only when a disease gains an upper hand against the creature, does the creature modify its behavior to combat the disease, such as when the fox returns to its cave to lick its wounds, or try to sleep it off, or when the man goes to see his doctor.

However, the creature has many friends among the microbes. The human gut, for instance, contains hundreds of friendly bacterial species that help him digest his food and fight off the bad bacteria that would afflict him with disease.

So every animal, including the human, is a vastly complex biological machine, a community of cells and microbes. The cells are organized into organ systems, connected by bone, skin and muscle, competing and cooperating to ultimately support the life of the organism.

Many separate human organisms will get together to form groups and organizations with common goals, such as clubs, religions, corporations and political parties. All of these groups are lifelike creatures, which compete for survival in the environment of their societies. Humans and their organizations, the life forms and lifelike forms, also have friends and enemies, which they must learn to identify.

Microbes attempt to survive, and in the process kill other microbes. Microbes may kill cells, plants, animals, or humans.

Cells attempt to survive, and in the process must kill microbes, other cells, plants, animals or humans.

Plants attempt to survive, and in the process may develop poisons that can kill prospective consumers, thus reducing the number of herbivorous enemies. Plants may kill other plants by shading them from the sunlight. Plants can kill animals and humans, although they must remain passive in their available behaviors, since they are mostly rooted in the ground.

Animals attempt to survive, and in the process kill plants and other animals in their search for food and dominance. Animals have been known to kill people.

All of this killing is perfectly justified in the delightful, anarchic, wild realm of Mother Nature, where the animals must fight to survive for their brutal existence. No consideration is given to fairness or morality. Virtue and vice do not apply because good and evil have not been defined in this world of violence, suffering and death. But life flourishes nevertheless, and a fabulously complex ecology has evolved to form an extremely diverse and fantastically beautiful blanket of life enveloping the planet Earth.

Add humanity to this mix. Humans attempt to survive, and in the process kill plants and animals, and even other humans. When viewed as just another animal, humans fit right in with the brutal realm of survival in nature.

Organizations formed by humans, lifelike forms, attempt to survive, and in the process may kill plants, animals, other humans and human organizations. Which of these life forms and lifelike forms have the capability to use judgment and wisdom in selecting the targets of their killing? Only the humans, and by extension, their organizations.

The humans have bigger brains than the other animals, and the capability to use reason in their everyday activities. They can use a greater degree of intelligence in deciding who is a friend and who is a foe. They get to decide which resources in their environment should be consumed and which should be preserved. They make decisions regarding the creation of wealth, whether to be productive or destructive. They can decide which animals to domesticate for food, to press into service for labor or transportation, or to keep for companionship. They can select which plants should be encouraged to grow as crops and which ones should be destroyed because they are poisonous. Mankind gets to figure out which insects should be cultured as beneficial to mankind, and which ones should be eliminated. Dung beetles were revered in ancient Egypt for their ability to convert animal waste to fertilizer.[1] Tsetse flies are subject to elimination because they spread disease in animals and people.

Humans have the power to decide which of their fellows are to be freemen and which ones shall become slaves. Western Civilization has advanced to the point where human slavery is considered evil. Basic human rights have gained a central position in the ethical thinking of some advanced civilizations. Life, liberty, and the pursuit of happiness are extended to the citizens of the United States.

In this book we have reviewed the development of life on Earth, emphasized the role that virtue should play in the behaviors of men, and encouraged it as the primary wellspring of civilization and the flourishing of human life.

But now we must recognize that all is not rosy in his advanced civilization. Mankind has enemies that wish to destroy him. Mankind arose from the natural processes of the Earth and Mother Nature. Mankind is subject to the same anarchistic hazards as the other animals. Tigers and wolves make no distinction between bunnies and men when it comes time to feed. If it smells tasty, and he has the power to kill it for dinner, why would he consider human rights or bunny rights when he has no concept of either idea?

As well as wild animals, some men have no regard for your rights nor the ethical ideas of your civilization. These men are not your friends. These men are your enemies. In order to survive, as is your personal obligation in your role as a living creature, you need to distinguish your friends from your enemies.

To your friends and fellow citizens you act as a lady or a gentleman. You respect the human rights of the people you meet in society, trusting that they share your civilized attitude towards others. You assume that they share the same rules of behavior that you have spent your life learning and practicing. When a man knows that he acts in his own rational self-interest, he expects others in his society to reciprocate.

But what if you must deal with an enemy? As is the case with any living creature, it is your imperative to survive and exercise your instinctual self-defense mechanism. Kill or be killed.

As a member of society, however, you have implicitly given up your option of exercising violence, and transferred it to the police powers of your community, and the legal system of the courts. So, when you are confronted by an enemy, you should first call the police. Nevertheless, in an emergency situation, such as when a drug-crazed miscreant kicks in your front door and threatens your life, you are justified in undertaking lethal force against him. Many jurisdictions actually recognize your right to self-defense as legally protected behavior. Unfortunately, others do not. Check your local laws.[2]

Speaking of criminals, what is it that makes some particular act a crime? The rule of law. When the legislature wishes to establish a rule of behavior for society, it adds a law to the statute books, which the police are authorized to enforce. Laws should be based on the fundamental Thou-Shalt-Not's, regarding stealing and killing. Or even more basically, to prohibit the initiation of force against a fellow citizen.

How does society, a lifelike form, deal with criminals? It puts them in jail, or puts them to death. Either way they are eliminated from causing further destruction in society, either temporarily, while they are incarcerated, or permanently with the other option.

What is different about a criminal from a law-abiding citizen? The criminal does not respect the laws imposed by his society, whether or not he understands the concept. A criminal may possess the necessary thought processes to select right from wrong, but he chooses to ignore his conscience. It may be possible for an individual to be incapable of complying with the norms of society because of some defect in his psychological makeup. But more often he merely chooses to ignore the laws, and he will attempt to deceive the judge by claiming insanity, or some other specious excuse.

At a more basic level, a criminal may just be a man who never developed his humane characteristics. He failed to learn the self-discipline necessary to control unbridled self-gratification.

A criminal reasons only from A to B. He has no conscience. He justifies his actions as does an animal. If he sees something he wants, and no one is there to stop him, he takes it. He has not developed enough self-control to inform his psyche that stealing or violence is not acceptable behavior. He has ignored or chosen to reject the guidance of his teachers and authority figures in his earlier life. A man does have free will and can choose among many options in life. One may choose to emphasize virtue or vice in his conduct, or flit randomly from one to the other according to his whim of the moment.

Is a society, a lifelike form, justified in attempting to remove criminals from its midst? A similar question would be to ask if a man, a life form, is justified in activating his immune system to fight off disease.

The laws a society chooses to enforce determine what kind of environment it will offer its people. A king or legislature may enact bad laws or good laws. The laws may give a certain class of people all the power, and oppress another class of people. We have discovered earlier that an imbalance of power facilitates the growth of evil. A society may create laws that make criminals out of normal, law-abiding folks who merely wish to get along in life, obey the rules, and attempt to carve some small niche for themselves in society. Such laws are bad laws. Legislatures and lawgivers must act in good faith to create fair laws that encourage the productive characteristics of citizens, and discourage destructive behaviors and abuse of power.

Wisdom is required in the selection of competent legislators and leaders who gain positions of power. Is this easy? No, it is very difficult. Among the complicated interactions of life forms and lifelike forms, competing to survive in life, advancement of the civilization requires wisdom and good judgment from a large number of people, all at the same time, especially during political campaigns.

This is why a prosperous civilization took such a long time to develop on Earth, and it is why we do not advance faster in the present state of affairs. Superstitions and faulty belief systems hamper the advance of those of us who understand the big picture. In our magnanimity, we wish to drag along with us the rest of humanity, to benefit even those who do not appreciate our enlightened views.

The founders of the United Sates of America, the men who wrote the Constitution, were inspired leaders who created the greatest nation the Earth has ever known. They appreciated the virtues of freedom and liberty, and the ability of law-abiding free men to interact in a society where they might practice their own rational self-interest, and thus benefit all citizens. Observe that the ultimate purpose of the Constitution is to protect you, the citizen, from the power of the government.

Once we accept the concept that an individual, as a life form, is justified in acting in his own self-defense, it follows by extension that his family, his tribe, his kingdom, and his nation are also entitled to self-defense. Survival is the imperative of any life form or lifelike form.

If we consider one of the largest lifelike forms, a nation, we might ask how a president should act in executing the obligations of his high office? He is the leader of a nation, a large, lifelike creature that struggles to survive among other nations, all of which compete for power and dominance. When the president deals with his fellow citizens, his legislature, and his allies in foreign countries, he is dealing with friends, and should act in the rational self-interest of his country, while respecting the rights of his citizens and the rights of allied countries. However, when dealing with his enemies, the countries that are clearly hostile to the welfare of his nation, he should be harsh, ruthless, deceptive. He should use the powers of his nation to eliminate the threat of the enemy. But the president needs to wisely utilize the political process to achieve his ends, so that the enemy does not realize it is being snookered. Wisdom in dealing with friends, and wisdom in dealing with enemies, are two different animals. Wisdom requires a careful balance between truth and deceit.

A good president will realize that there are always barbarians at the gate who wish to take over (steal) the riches of his nation. He should not be so naive as to think he can appease enemies by treating them as though they are friends who need a little counseling. A president needs the courage to exercise his power in a fashion that protects his nation. A good president will also realize that there are enemies within who wish to destroy his nation, just like a cancer might destroy the body of a biological creature. Dealing with the enemies within is even more difficult for a president than dealing with the more easily defined enemies without. Life for a man who takes on the mantle of power is fraught with hazard. Life is complicated enough for a normal citizen. The leader of a nation needs wise advisors to assist in the affairs of state. A man who takes up the reins of power, must be prepared for assaults from every quarter. A president should prepare himself with the realization that the exercise of power brings one constantly to the threshold of evil.

Machiavelli

Niccolo Machiavelli, whose dates are 1469 to 1527, was an Italian political philosopher who is most famous for his book *The Prince,* published in 1532.[3] The book offers advice on how a ruler might control his realm, and advises on the actions necessary to perpetuate power. This work is responsible for the pejorative term "Machiavellian" coming into common usage, which implies placing political expediency above morality. *The Prince* has been used as a guidebook for several of the world's most egregious despots, and has thus acquired a distasteful reputation in the popular culture.

Machiavelli was an astute observer of history and the behavior of past princes. He also saw clearly the state of affairs during his own lifetime and wrote his analysis of the management behavior of the men he saw in power. He did not promote the practice of evil, but described how many rulers had used their power, both in just and evil ways. He described those princes who obtained power over their realms by way of heredity, by force of arms, by conquest in a foreign land, or other means. He observed in a highly perceptive fashion how these leaders acted during their reigns, either as

just arbiters in the affairs of men, or as tyrants. He saw which techniques
worked to inspire loyalty in the subjects, and which methods produced
discontent among the nobles or common man. In this process, he admired
the successful rulers and showed how others sowed their own destruction
through abuse of power.

Here is a quote from *The Prince,* Chapter XXI, "How a Prince Should
Conduct Himself so as to Gain Renown," which shows Machiavelli's general
philosophy:

"Never let any Government imagine that it can choose perfectly
safe courses; rather let it expect to have to take very doubtful ones,
because it is found in ordinary affairs that one never seeks to avoid
one trouble without running into another; but prudence consists
in knowing how to distinguish the character of troubles, and for
choice to take the lesser evil.

A prince ought also to show himself a patron of ability, and to
honour the proficient in every art. At the same time he should
encourage his citizens to practise their callings peaceably, both in
commerce and agriculture, and in every other following, so that the
one should not be deterred from improving his possessions for fear
lest they be taken away from him or another from opening up trade
for fear of taxes; but the prince ought to offer rewards to whoever
wishes to do these things and designs in any way to honour his city
or state."

These are not the remarks of a man who promulgates evil and believes
in anarchy as the ultimate justice for mankind, wherein might-makes-right
takes the central role, and the ends justify the means.

In our view, Machiavelli has been unjustly maligned by historical
commentators, because of their failure to distinguish between the ways a
leader should treat his friends versus the behavior he directs toward foreign
enemies who seek to kill him or to usurp his nation.

Let us consider simplified examples of creatures striving to survive in
their ecology, and build up to the situation where Machiavelli found himself
commenting on behavior he observed among the rulers of his day.

An animal is kind and gentle with its mate and offspring. Think of a mother raccoon taking care of her pups. That same mother is also a ferocious fighter when it comes to defending her den from an invading terrier. This animal that lives in the anarchy of nature watches our out for herself and for her own kind.

A man in a primitive world acts similarly to his animal counterparts. He is cooperative with his family and fellow tribesmen, because they share common interests. But he becomes a fierce warrior when his territory is invaded by a foreign tribe intent on destruction of his village. He fights for survival so that he might live successfully in some niche of his environment. This behavior must be considered ethical conduct in the primitive realm where he exists.

When a man lives in a civilized society he acts in a friendly manner with his fellow citizens, he respects the rights of his neighbors, and he refrains from practicing violence against other people. He follows the laws and rules of his society, because he has relinquished his option to take the law into his own hands. He trusts the local police and court system to handle the use of force against lawbreakers. These are the moral and ethical principles he follows in his ecology.

The leader of a nation, a prince (in Machiavelli's terminology), must act as the leader of a lifelike creature, his nation, which must compete against other nations in an anarchistic realm. He must be ruthless against his enemies so that his nation will survive and prosper in this environment. When dealing with his fellow countrymen, who follow the laws of his society, he is a benevolent ruler. These are the principles that Machiavelli expounded in *The Prince*.

Note that in the era when Machiavelli wrote the world was a collection of city states, or principalities, or nations, all of which competed for dominance and territorial control in an anarchistic environment. The various nations had not agreed to operate with a common set of laws under which they would all be held accountable. Therefore governments constantly grappled in an anarchistic free-for-all.

A man may deal with his fellow citizens in a moral and ethical manner only when all citizens have agreed to abide by the same set of laws and rules of behavior, when the people have awarded themselves rights that apply uniformly to everyone. Otherwise everyone is fighting for survival in an anarchistic realm, just like the animals in nature.

When the governments of many nations can finally agree to a set of laws that apply to all nations consistently, then nations will begin to deal with each other in an ethical and moral fashion. Until that time, governments will continue to grapple, as they do today, in their customary anarchistic free-for-all.

When viewed under the illumination provided by these paragraphs, Machiavelli's principles may be seen to rest on eminently logical foundations. We may summarize this overall concept with the maxim: "To a gentleman be a gentleman, to a scoundrel be a scoundrel."

The Just War

Any nation must be prepared for the possibility of war. If a nation chooses to go to war, does this necessarily imply evil? If a nation is attacked by a foreign power, is it not justified in defending its homeland with its armies? If a nation sees that an enemy nation is preparing for war against it, would it not be advisable to make a pre-emptive strike before the hostile neighbor can build excess strength for its inevitable invasion? These questions raise thorny and controversial issues, which are beyond the scope of this book, and have been thoroughly debated elsewhere. We will not belabor them here, other than to mention that the concept of a just war has been defined and treated by philosophers as noteworthy as Cicero, Augustine and Aquinas. We mention it here for those readers who may not have encountered this subject before, or those who wish to investigate further at their local library.

On balance, war sets-back civilization. War destroys property and kills people. Property represents wealth, and people are the assets of civilization who create wealth. When people or property are destroyed, civilization suffers. Peace promotes the flourishing of life and the advance of civilization. War is hell, but the victorious side determines the character of the subsequent civilization.

Notes:

[1] The sacred scarab of ancient Egypt, Scarabaeus sacer.

[2] The Castle Doctrine is an American legal concept that recognizes that "a
     man's home is his castle." He is entitled to defend himself and his family
     against housebreakers, using deadly force if necessary. This has also been
     referred to as the "make my day" or the "stand your ground" law. In
     some jurisdictions the law requires a victim to retreat under any threat,
     in order to avoid engaging in lethal force. The castle doctrine protects a
     person who acts in self-defense from being charged as a criminal, or from
     being sued by a burglar or a burglar's family for assault or injury upon
     the burglar.

[3] Note that *The Prince,* Machiavelli's magnum opus, was not published
     until after his death. This fact suggests that Machiavelli knew it would
     be controversial, and he would be persecuted by his enemies if he went
     public during his lifetime. This demonstrates that Machiavelli was not
     only smart, but also wise. See Machiavelli.

CHAPTER SEVENTEEN

INDEPENDENCE

IN this chapter we wish to summarize a few of the forces and principles we have discussed thus far and draw some conclusions from history.

Summary

Self-organizing structures arise in complex systems where the forces of nature, including energy and the elements of matter, are free to interact.

Life arose spontaneously on the primitive Earth as a result of such emergent processes.

Life evolved over the ages to create a vast variety of successful life forms. An amazing diversity of plants and animals eventually blanketed the planet.

Human beings are the result of continuing evolution in the animal kingdom. The human brain is the distinguishing feature that gives mankind his advantage over the other creatures.

The most basic meaning of life is the struggle for survival. This struggle results in competition between species for food and territory. All species are forced to interact with competitors in their environments. Each species attempts to carve a niche in the ecology where it might survive and prosper.

The law of the jungle prevails in the primitive world of life in nature. The principles of eat or be eaten, kill or be killed, might makes right, survival of the fittest, and natural selection, govern the affairs of existence. Violence is the arbiter of every question.

Once humans appeared on the scene, they began using their superior brainpower to out-compete the other animals in the environment. Humans fit right in with the anarchic behavior of the animal kingdom, and figured out clever new ways to use violence for their personal advantage. Adapting the principles of might makes right to their own benefit, humans soon dominated their realm.

Men formed into tribal groups and competed against rival tribes for domination over the resources in their respective neighborhoods. Intertribal warfare became the primary activity of civilizations for thousands of years.

Gradually, the more educated individuals, or the more clever ones, used conspiracy and treachery to wrest power from the merely strong. Eventually, men who actually used their reasoning power began to realize that cooperation with their fellows served their mutual interests better than continual warfare.

Early religious leaders discerned the two primary rules for a successful society: 1) Do not kill, because each of your fellow men is an asset of civilization and thus deserves a right to life, and 2) Do not steal, because each person has a right to own property.

Sometime along the way, mankind discovered the concepts of virtue and vice. The benevolent leaders among men, who were interested in peace and harmony, encouraged their people to embrace virtue and shun vice. But this enlightened concept had to compete against the deeply ingrained tendency towards violence and the maintenance of established power.

The history of mankind is filled with brief episodes of advancement in civilization. During these times the arts and sciences flourished, mankind built great structures, established universities and libraries, expanded trade among far-flung peoples. Overall, these enlightened peoples cooperated to enhance their mutual benefit, so that their civilizations grew and advanced.

Interspersed with these transient successes were periods of descent into destruction, warfare and decline. The outsiders would observe with envy the accumulating wealth of the successful cities, and decide that they could harvest such treasure with their armies. The fat and happy citizens of the advanced culture would become complacent in their plenty, and neglect to maintain their military defenses. They became easy prey for the armies of barbarians who lived for plunder and violence.[1]

Enlightenment

How could our civilization have survived these repeated setbacks to arrive at our current level of advancement? Some unnamed principle among the biases in nature seems to favor the slow advance of civilization, versus its destruction and decay. Regardless of the many advances and retreats in the fortunes of various civilizations, the overall sweep of history suggests some tendency towards survival and growth. For the purposes of this book, we will postulate that the survival of civilization is the meaning of its existence. We have concluded earlier that the meaning of life is survival, no matter which biological life form we considered. Similarly, a civilization, which may be considered a lifelike form, strives for survival. We may think of this life force, striving ever-upwards, as an emergent process among the intricate relationships of a complex system. Adam Smith was the first to remark upon this life force in the subject of economics and called it the invisible hand.[2]

As civilizations evolved over the centuries, the advance of science and technology eventually brought about the industrial revolution. Increases in the productivity of labor enabled prosperity to benefit vastly greater numbers of people. Cities grew in population as people saw better opportunities for themselves among the teeming masses in manufacturing jobs versus their traditional agrarian life style.

A significant number of citizens in various countries became fed up with the tyranny of the powerful classes in their kingdoms. They learned there was a new country across the sea where they could live unfettered by the restrictions of the established authoritarian governments. Many of these people sought religious freedom, others wished to escape famine, or the squalor of life in overcrowded cities. The ones who survived the perilous journey to the New World found a vast and primitive land where they would be required to fight the forces of nature. But in this new realm, far from their former countries, they were spared the additional load of fighting the forces of an oppressive king. These hardy folk eventually succeeded in creating a prosperous civilization along the new frontier.

When the king of the old country observed the growing success of the new colonies, he wished to exert his power over these upstarts, and to tax their newfound wealth. In his arrogance as The King, he felt he was entitled to it.

The colonists, however, wished to remain independent, and challenged the king's authority to tax their wealth. Using slogans like, "No Taxation without Representation," and "Don't Tread on Me," they resisted the various power grabs imposed by the foreign government.

Several leaders among the colonists got together and declared their independence from the king, citing what they believed to be their unalienable rights, and swore their allegiance to the new country.

The king, upset by these traitorous rebels, sent his armies to the new colonies to quash the rebellion. The king's forces met resistance from a number of ragtag militias.

The resulting war eventually turned in favor of the colonists, and the king withdrew his forces. The colonists went on to establish a new government based on a classless society. Individual freedom and the liberty to earn one's own living through hard work established the tone of the new country. The constitution guaranteed the people a list of freedoms, a Bill of Rights, that the new government would not be allowed to deny its citizens.[3,4] Observe again that the purpose of the Constitution is to protect the citizens from the power of the government. This fact was thoroughly understood by the founders, the men who had recently fought to throw off the tyranny of the king.

For nearly 150 years, the citizens of the United States had the opportunity to practice unfettered capitalism, the like of which had never before been seen on the planet. As a result, these ambitious people created the most successful, wealthy and prosperous civilization ever, while the rest of the world suffered under the paroxysms of self-imposed socialism.

It wasn't until 1933, when Franklin D. Roosevelt introduced his New Deal, that the forces of socialist reforms gained a significant foothold in the government of the United States, retarding the progress of capitalism.

Independence

Since we mentioned the Declaration of Independence, and most people don't often have a chance to read through it, here is our printed version. We have taken the liberty of placing linefeeds and tabs after each listed injustice to make the document more readable. We realize that many readers prefer the original, handwritten version, so please feel free to seek out a local retailer who might provide you with a vellum reproduction, suitable for framing. Or you may order one from us, while supplies last.[5]

While reading through this historic document, imagine yourself in the place of a colonist of the time, suffering under the tyranny of the distant monarch, and subject to the many edicts of the imperious king. A realization of what life was like at the time puts the proper perspective on the freedoms we in the United States take for granted today.

The Declaration of Independence of the United States of America

IN CONGRESS, July 4, 1776

The unanimous Declaration of the thirteen united States of America

When in the Course of human events, it becomes necessary for one people to dissolve the political bands which have connected them with another, and to assume, among the Powers of the earth, the separate and equal station to which the Laws of Nature and of Nature's God entitle them, a decent respect to the opinions of mankind requires that they should declare the causes which impel them to the separation.

We hold these truths to be self-evident, that all men are created equal, that they are endowed by their Creator with certain unalienable Rights, that among these are Life, Liberty, and the pursuit of Happiness. That to secure these rights, Governments are instituted among Men, deriving their just powers from the consent of the governed, That whenever any Form of Government becomes destructive of these ends, it is the Right of the People to alter or to abolish it, and to institute new Government, laying its foundation on such principles and organizing its powers in such form, as to them shall seem most likely to effect their Safety and Happiness. Prudence, indeed, will dictate that Governments long established should not be changed for light and transient causes; and accordingly all experience hath shewn, that mankind are more disposed to suffer, while evils are sufferable, than to right themselves by abolishing the forms to which they are accustomed. But when a long train of abuses and usurpations, pursuing invariably the same Object evinces a design to reduce them under absolute Despotism, it is their right, it is their duty, to throw off such Government, and to provide new Guards for their future security. -- Such has been the patient sufferance of these Colonies; and such is now the necessity which constrains them to alter their former Systems of Government. The history of the present King of Great Britain is a history of repeated injuries and usurpations, all having in direct object the establishment of an absolute Tyranny over these States. To prove this, let Facts be submitted to a candid world.

He has refused his Assent to Laws, the most wholesome and necessary for the public good.

He has forbidden his Governors to pass Laws of immediate and pressing importance, unless suspended in their operation till his Assent should be obtained; and when so suspended, he has utterly neglected to attend to them.

He has refused to pass other Laws for the accommodation of large districts of people, unless those people would relinquish the right of Representation in the Legislature, a right inestimable to them and formidable to tyrants only.

He has called together legislative bodies at places unusual, uncomfortable, and distant from the depository of their Public Records, for the sole purpose of fatiguing them into compliance with his measures.

He has dissolved Representative Houses repeatedly, for opposing with manly firmness his invasions on the rights of the people.

He has refused for a long time, after such dissolutions, to cause others to be elected; whereby the Legislative Powers, incapable of Annihilation, have returned to the People at large for their exercise; the State remaining in the mean time exposed to all the dangers of invasion from without, and convulsions within.

He has endeavoured to prevent the population of these States; for that purpose obstructing the Laws of Naturalization of Foreigners; refusing to pass others to encourage their migration hither, and raising the conditions of new Appropriations of Lands.

He has obstructed the Administration of Justice, by refusing his Assent to Laws for establishing Judiciary Powers.

He has made judges dependent on his Will alone, for the tenure of their offices, and the amount and payment of their salaries.

He has erected a multitude of New Offices, and sent hither swarms of Officers to harass our People, and eat out their substance.

He has kept among us, in times of peace, Standing Armies without the Consent of our legislatures.

He has affected to render the Military independent of and superior to the Civil Power.

He has combined with others to subject us to a jurisdiction foreign to our constitution, and unacknowledged by our laws; giving his Assent to their Acts of pretended legislation:

For quartering large bodies of armed troops among us:

For protecting them, by a mock Trial, from Punishment for any Murders which they should commit on the Inhabitants of these States:

For cutting off our Trade with all parts of the world:

For imposing taxes on us without our Consent:

For depriving us, in many cases, of the benefits of Trial by Jury:

For transporting us beyond Seas to be tried for pretended offences:

For abolishing the free System of English Laws in a neighbouring Province, establishing therein an Arbitrary government, and enlarging its Boundaries so as to render it at once an example and fit instrument for introducing the same absolute rule into these Colonies:

For taking away our Charters, abolishing our most valuable Laws, and altering fundamentally the Forms of our Governments:

For suspending our own Legislatures, and declaring themselves invested with Power to legislate for us in all cases whatsoever.

He has abdicated Government here, by declaring us out of his Protection and waging War against us.

He has plundered our seas, ravaged our Coasts, burnt our towns, and destroyed the lives of our people.

He is at this time transporting large armies of foreign mercenaries to compleat the works of death, desolation and tyranny, already begun with circumstances of Cruelty & perfidy scarcely paralleled in the most barbarous ages, and totally unworthy of the Head of a civilized nation.

He has constrained our fellow Citizens taken Captive on the high Seas to bear Arms against their Country, to become the executioners of their friends and Brethren, or to fall themselves by their Hands.

He has excited domestic insurrections amongst us, and has endeavoured to bring on the inhabitants of our frontiers, the merciless Indian Savages, whose known rule of warfare, is an undistinguished destruction of all ages, sexes and conditions.

In every stage of these Oppressions We have Petitioned for Redress in the most humble terms: Our repeated Petitions have been answered only by repeated injury. A Prince, whose character is thus marked by every act which may define a Tyrant, is unfit to be the ruler of a free People.

Nor have We been wanting in attention to our Brittish brethren. We have warned them from time to time of attempts by their legislature to extend an unwarrantable jurisdiction over us. We have reminded them of the circumstances of our emigration and settlement here. We have appealed to their native justice and magnanimity, and we have conjured them by the ties of our common kindred to disavow these usurpations, which would inevitably interrupt our connections and correspondence. They too have been deaf to the voice of justice and of consanguinity. We must, therefore, acquiesce in the necessity, which denounces our Separation, and hold them, as we hold the rest of mankind, Enemies in War, in Peace Friends.

We, therefore, the Representatives of the United States of America, in General Congress, Assembled, appealing to the Supreme Judge of the world for the rectitude of our intentions, do, in the Name, and by the Authority of the good People of these Colonies, solemnly publish and declare, That these United Colonies are, and of Right ought to be Free and Independent States; that they are Absolved from all Allegiance to the British Crown, and that all political connection between them and the State of Great Britain, is and ought to be totally dissolved; and that as Free and Independent States, they have full Power to levy War, conclude Peace, contract Alliances, establish Commerce, and to do all other Acts and Things which Independent States may of right do. And for the support of this Declaration, with a firm reliance on the Protection of Divine

Providence, we mutually pledge to each other our Lives, our Fortunes and our sacred Honor.

Notes:

[1] World history is a vast subject with thousands of books available on every conceivable approach to the subject. If you are looking for an interesting place to start, we would recommend *Civilization, a Personal View* by Kenneth Clark. This book, and companion DVD television series of 13 episodes, presents the sweep of Western Civilization from the fall of the Roman Empire into the modern day. See Clark.
Another excellent book we can recommend is *The Black Death,* by Robert Gottfried, which gives a clear account of what life was really like for people of the Middle Ages. See Gottfried.

[2] See Smith.

[3] Many fine books have been written about the founders of The United States and the history of their times. One book we can highly recommend, which develops a thorough analysis of the various founders' thinking and philosophies on government, is *The 5000 Year Leap,* by W. Cleon Skousen. This book explains the twenty-eight principles of freedom the founders expressed in the Declaration of Independence and Constitution, and employed to establish the new government. See Skousen.

[4] See the Constitution of the United States.

[5] A reproduction of the original Declaration of Independence, on a sheet of vellum, suitable for framing, 14 x 16 inches, rolled for mailing, is available for less than $5.00 plus shipping, while supplies last. (Price subject to change, of course, due to availability and ever-changing market forces.) See our website for current details: www.johndwaterman.com/declaration.

CHAPTER EIGHTEEN

LIFESTYLE

NOW that we have covered the basics of where man comes from, how he differs from the lower animals, and how he may choose to differentiate between good and evil, it is time to have a look at the way man deals with situations he encounters in life. We will take the concepts developed earlier and apply them to the situations that affect the affairs of mankind to see if we can make distinctions and select preferable behaviors from his many options.

Let us look at two different men and compare their choices in life-style. They will both be law-abiding citizens who are able to function in society and carve out a niche to survive in their ecology.

Gus will be our self-reliant character with the pioneer spirit. He has a self-motivated, can-do attitude, and strives to succeed at whatever he tries. He works hard and tries to benefit himself and his family.

Hank, on the other hand, will be our less motivated, more dependent character who has a tendency to go with the flow and get buffeted by the random forces around him.[1]

Gus sets aside money for emergencies. No matter how little he earns in his early years he puts ten percent of his discretionary income in a savings account. He forbids himself from using this money for entertainment or luxuries, reserving it only for living expenses as a last resort. He takes to heart the old Aesop tale from childhood about the ant and the grasshopper, where the ant works hard all summer and sets aside assets for the winter, while the grasshopper plays all summer long and suffers starvation in the winter.

Hank spends all his money as soon as he earns it. Although he tries to budget his expenses so he will still have enough money to buy food on the last day before his next paycheck, he finds he often needs to borrow money at the last minute from his brother, or his girlfriend, or his drinking buddies. He is also not very reliable in assuring these loans are paid back promptly.

Gus keeps himself clean and well groomed. He washes his hands several times a day, bathes and washes his hair on a regular basis. He believes the advice his mother gave him as he was growing up, and the instructions on behavior he received in school from the time he was in kindergarten. Thus he avoids sickness and disease by keeping germs and microbes outside his body. He does not have sex with strangers, and particularly shuns prostitutes.

Hank is less meticulous with his personal grooming. He will put off doing the laundry until he has worn the same shirt for several days, and a coworker makes a remark about his body odor. He finds he frequently catches cold, and seems to get the flu when it's in season. He is not particularly selective in choosing sex partners and figures that girls like to have fun as much as he does.

Gus pays his bills when they arrive in the mail. He makes sure he has the money to pay his mortgage on time. He seldom carries a balance on his credit card, realizing that he can save the finance charges by keeping up to date with his expenses. Gus knows that the companies that send him bills are actually extending him credit in the trust they will be paid promptly.

Hank resents the companies that send him bills. He feels they are just greedy and overcharge for their services in the first place. If they want to be paid, they can just get in line with everyone else. Hank carries a balance from month to month on his credit card, and tries to get by with paying the minimum amount due, thus accepting finance charges.

When Gus notices that his expenditures are threatening to overtake his level of income, he looks for ways to reduce his expenses, or to take on some new job to supplement his income.

Hank cannot bear to cut back his level of consumption. He figures things will work out, because they always have in the past. His brother seems to come to his rescue at the last minute, or a charity or some government program may offer some temporary welfare.

Gus pays his taxes in a timely manner, not because he prefers to, but because he knows he must conform to the forces in his society. The government imposes obligations on him, which he ultimately has no power to resist. But he also knows he has a wide latitude to arrange his personal affairs to maximize his chances for success in dealing with the factors he does have power to change.

Hank puts off filing his income tax until the last minute, and goes for the extension every year. He knows he is a small fish, and the IRS prefers to go after the big guys who owe a lot more than he does.

When it comes time to retire, Gus has money in the bank and a healthy balance in his 401k account. He can live comfortably without depending on his children, or government handouts, to support him in his old age.

When Hank gets too old to work, he doesn't have enough saved up to provide for his declining years. He must depend on government programs to provide for his needs. He must live off the charity of his brother or his neighbors in order to buy food, housing and medical care.

Throughout his life, Gus carries his own weight, and then some. He goes beyond earning enough to cover his bare necessities, and creates an excess. This wealth benefits himself and becomes the foundation upon which he builds more wealth, both for himself and his society. The benefit to his society is the result of the invisible hand of commerce. Gus is a producer as well as a consumer. He practices the virtues and contributes to the growth of his civilization.

Hank just gets by, and barely caries his own weight. He is happy to freeload on the success of others, and live on the edge between survival and growth. Hank does not rise above the common vices to which humans are subject, but he does not sink into criminality.

Which one of these fictional characters is a better citizen? Who contributes more to the flourishing of human life and the growth of his civilization? Both men are offered the same opportunities by their society. They both are brought up under the same conditions, and have access to the same free public schools through high school graduation. Both are exposed to the same opportunities for advancement. Gus handles his life decisions with forethought and responsibility, while Hank ignores his opportunities to make wiser decisions. These are individual choices on the part of the two men exercising their free will. It boils down to their attitudes toward life. One continuously chooses to strive towards success, the other does not. The results of their choices are reflected in the success of their lives. Certainly, we may conclude that Gus should be our role model, and Hank may be used as an example of one who makes less wise decisions.

Self Assessment

Now comes the hard part, where the reader is advised to consider his own behavior in light of the concepts we have discussed so far. In this book we are attempting to build a logical construct of ideas that the reader may use as tools for understanding the world he finds around him. If this may be considered a self-help book, we may apply these ideas to our own behaviors and see if we need to improve in some fashion. So go ahead and ask yourself: Am I like Gus, who wants to be independent and take care of himself, or am I more like Hank, who depends too much on others for his existence? Everyone has features from both personality types, and everybody can work on improving his performance in life.

Are we in danger of losing some of our audience again, because some folks may feel that they are being criticized, put-down or insulted by the opinions on behavior discussed in this book? If you have read this far, we may assume that you are receptive to suggestions for modifying your behavior in order to improve your success in life.

Please note that an insult only works if the target takes the bait. We would advise you to not take any perceived criticism personally, but rather view it as advice offered in the spirit of friendship.

If you feel you are being criticized, you don't want to allow other people (or this book) to manipulate you into a position of weakness. The idea here is to understand the interactions among people to see who is the aggressor, who is trying to influence your behavior for his own benefit in conflict with your own. Remember, as a law-abiding citizen, you are entitled to your own life, liberty and pursuit of happiness. But as a living creature you are always competing with others, even when the competition is not obvious.

It Ain't Easy

Note how easy it is to be caught in the trap of spending all your money as soon as you get your hands on it. One of Murphy's Laws states that your expenditures rise to consume all of your income, regardless of how much you earn, even if your salary keeps ahead of inflation.[2] Credit card offers come in the mail regularly. How tempting it is to solve your current money problems with a little borrowing against the certainty of better times in the future.

Realize that each individual has the choice to exercise his self-discipline, to spend less today in order to set aside assets for the future. The secret is to avoid the temptations of credit. Shakespeare advised a long time ago, around the year 1600, "Neither a borrower nor a lender be."[3] But in today's world cheap credit permeates society. Of course, it is the rare individual who has the ability to buy his house outright from the balance in his checking account. So he takes out a mortgage to borrow the money. But he must have the capability to afford the monthly payments from current income. Otherwise he should not sign up for the mortgage in the first place. The mortgage is a contract to repay the loan, so when the borrower cannot meet his obligation, the bank or finance company will repossess the house and evict the unfortunate (irresponsible) borrower.

Also, few people are able to purchase their cars outright from the balance in their savings account, and must therefore borrow the cash. But an auto loan follows the same basic rules as the mortgage, so similar penalties for default apply.

Credit cards represent a more manageable form of debt, which can be reduced or eliminated with the exercise of self-control. If you carry a balance from month to month on your credit cards, you are doing something wrong, and need to reassess your financial discipline. If your need for credit increases over time, you should probably seek financial counseling.

You're OK

Another technique for understanding the interactions among people is described in the book *I'm OK, You're OK,* by Thomas Harris. This popular book from the 1970's promulgated a psychological concept called Transactional Analysis.[4] The title of the book reveals the secret to the technique. Four combinations are possible in this universe of OK vs. not-OK.

1. I'm OK, You're OK.
2. I'm OK, You're not OK.
3. I'm not OK, You're OK.
4. I'm not OK, You're not OK.

The first combination implies a balance of power and cooperation between two individuals. This idea may be illustrated by two mature adults dealing with each other in a friendly fashion, or in an arms-length business transaction, where each one respects the rights of the other.

The second combination implies that I am better than you are, so you must do what I say. I have power over you because you are not as smart, or as capable as I am, so I may dominate you and direct your life. A benign example of this situation is the parent to child interaction, where the parent, the more powerful individual, truly has the best interest of the child at heart. A more hostile example would be where a dictator decides how to spend the money of a citizen without the citizen's consent. Evil may easily arise in such a case.

The third combination implies that you are better than I am, and thus I must bend to your desires. The benign example of this situation is the child obeying the rules of the parent. A less desirable situation would be where a woman continues to live under an abusive relationship with a dominant man because she doesn't understand that she deserves better treatment. Evil is a likely consequence in this scenario.

The fourth combination, where both sides act without regard for the rights of others or even of themselves, guarantees conflict and evil.

Nearly any interaction between two individuals, or between groups, can be analyzed, and better understood, by using the viewpoint of the "I'm OK, You're OK" technique.

Gas Pains

Let's take a look at a young person who makes a discovery about politeness and how it conflicts with a particular, necessary, biological function.

Ike, as an eleven-year-old, was a smart kid who liked to make friends and socialize with his classmates. He wanted to do the right thing, and take his mother's advice about how to behave in public. One day he was visiting a friend's house where he and three of his buddies were sitting around the dining room table playing a board game. While shuffling the cards, Ike felt an urge to go to the bathroom, but he was having so much fun with his friends he decided to suppress it and continue playing. After a while he developed intestinal pains, and thought he might pass a little gas while sitting in his chair. But he knew that would not be polite, and his friends would make remarks if he made a smell, so he held it in to avoid embarrassment. His private distress led to considerable discomfort, but he had

decided he could put up with a little pain to continue being polite in deference to his friends.

After a while he began to feel ill, so he finally excused himself from the
party and walked home. On the way to his house he vomited on the side-
walk, and suddenly realized that his body had been giving him clues about
his necessary functions. When he prevented his body from discharging the
gas pressure in a simple fashion, it took an involuntary override to achieve
relief. This realization taught him a lesson about the foundations of social
courtesy. Although it is important to be polite and avoid offending the
people around you, it is also important to take care of your personal needs.
One may politely excuse oneself from a social setting to take care of personal
necessities. Although his "friends" might have made snide remarks about
him interrupting the game to go to the bathroom, they would be the impo-
lite ones for mentioning the subject.

Pain can be instructive. Pain means you need to do something to relieve
it. Pain will often be the first clue that some action is necessary. Sometimes
a little social pain needs to be suffered to relieve physical pain. One should
become aware of the tradeoffs that are available under his personal control.

Note that Ike might have misinterpreted the messages his body gave
him. He could have concluded that his intestinal pain was a punishment
from the gods for having offended one of them. But Ike already had a few
years experience with his body, and knew that a visit to the toilet would reliably relieve such intestinal distress. He might have decided that his vomiting
on the way home was retribution against him for having salted his little
sister's glass of milk yesterday. But Ike was astute enough to put cause and
effect together and arrive at the correct conclusion about his body's clues.

The True Gentleman

After discussing a youngster who was worried about being polite, we
should conclude our chapter on lifestyle with an inspirational message
about an ideal model of polite behavior. The Baltimore Sun ran a contest in
1909 to see whom among their readers could write the best description of
the ideal gentleman. The winner submitted the following:

THE TRUE GENTLEMAN

The True Gentleman is the man whose conduct proceeds from good will and an acute sense of propriety, and whose self-control is equal to all emergencies; who does not make the poor man conscious of his poverty, the obscure man of his obscurity, or any man of his inferiority or deformity; who is himself humbled if necessity compels him to humble another; who does not flatter wealth, cringe before power, or boast of his own possessions or achievements; who speaks with frankness but always with sincerity and sympathy; whose deed follows his word; who thinks of the rights and feelings of others, rather than his own; and who appears well in any company, a man with whom honor is sacred and virtue safe.

John Walter Wayland

Notes:

[1] Gus, Hank, and Ike are fictional characters used here to illustrate features of human behavior.
[2] The most fundamental Murphy's Law is: "Anything that can go wrong, will go wrong." See Bloch for a compilation of Murphy's Laws.
[3] William Shakespeare, *Hamlet,* Act 1, Scene 3, where Polonius gives advice to his son, Laertes.
[4] See Harris.

CHAPTER NINETEEN

FANTASY THEME-PARK SYNDROME

A cat and a mouse can never keep house.[1]

Grimm

ONE problem that comes with civilization is that people become insulated from the realities of the natural world. We are referring here to the anarchistic brutality in attitude of the wild animals.

This problem is a subset of a faulty belief system, which we refer to as the Theme-Park Fantasy Syndrome. The only exposure many people get to real animals is their pets and their neighbor's pets, which are domesticated, and thus are friendly and dependent upon their masters for food, care and shelter. When people go out to the woods and encounter wild animals, they subconsciously expect the critters to be as friendly as the domesticated versions they are used to.

Children are taken to petting zoos where they meet bunnies, goats and sheep. Here they can hug the nice, warm, fluffy animals and learn to appreciate how these gentle creatures deserve to be praised and cared for. They hear that they should respect the rights of animals and not be cruel to these beneficial creatures that should be preserved for the continuation of God's plan. Note however, that no visitors to the zoo are permitted in the cages with mature tigers, wolves, gorillas, or rattlesnakes, because of liability concerns from the zoo's lawyers.

When people watch TV or go to a fantasy theme-park, the vast majority of animals they see are cartoon creatures like Donald Duck who know how to talk funny and act in ridiculous ways for entertainment purposes. Or they meet mechanical mockups of bears or sharks that look remarkably lifelike, and scare folks by growling fiercely or leaping towards them, but which never actually get close enough to bite the customers. Children learn they can trust teddy bears and learn happy songs from frogs and pigs and purple dinosaurs. These wonderful learning experiences are of no help when a person meets an actual wild animal in the real forest. Every child is immersed in the fantasy culture, but it is the rare youngster who learns how to deal with real animals. A visit to a farm, or a lecture from the forest ranger, is the only exposure many young people get to real animal behavior.

Take two examples from the thousands of stories rangers tell at the national parks. A father and his seven-year-old daughter were visiting Rocky Mountain National Park. Despite the warnings not to feed the animals, they decided it would be a fun thing to take a picture of the child feeding a deer. The kid held out her hand with some corn for the animal, and the deer obligingly nibbled the offering. Wasn't that cute! When the corn was gone, the deer still wanted some more, so it pawed at the child with its sharp hoof and sliced open her arm. Oops, this wild animal had apparently missed the training class on how to politely deal with human visitors to the park.

A man visiting Yellowstone National Park wanted to get a picture of himself posing next to a buffalo, patting the nice animal on the head. The irritated beast used its horns to gore the man and toss him into the air. His wife with the video camera captured the entire event.

If you go to Rocky Mountain National Park, on any day, you can see this common behavior of people. Folks from all walks of life, from many different countries, chase after the wild animals with their cameras, oblivious to the hazards these beasts present to their safety, and also oblivious to the stress it places on the animals. Some folks get their photos. Others occasionally learn a harsh lesson from a mighty antlered elk or a massive bighorn sheep.

If you visit Yellowstone National Park, you will be instructed not to feed the bears. The ranger will tell you "a fed bear is a dead bear." Once a bear learns that people will give him free groceries, he will continue to pursue them for their generous contributions to his feeding program. He will stop seeking food from his natural environment, as he should, and become dependent on humans for his food. Soon he will become aggressive towards humans and will eventually injure somebody. Then the rangers will have to shoot him, because he cannot be retrained back to his more natural habits.

The ultimate example of the Theme-Park Fantasy Syndrome was

illustrated by Timothy Treadwell. As a devoted environmentalist, this man went to Alaska to live among the grizzly bears. He wished to learn about their ways, to promote their well-being and conservation. He spent 13 years of summers at various camps in bear country, living and interacting with the bears' society. He never carried a weapon, and during the last few years, decided he didn't even need "bear spray," a variety of pepper spray, to repel any belligerent animals.

In October 2003, while he and his girlfriend were preparing to depart their campground for the season, one of the bears ate them for dinner. The 2005 documentary film *Grizzly Man,* by Werner Herzog, offers a unique glimpse into the life and death of Mr. Treadwell.[2]

We, as rational human beings, need to realize that wild animals still live in the anarchy of nature. Their only concerns are finding food, defending themselves from perceived threats and breeding new members for the herd. The animals do not know how to read. Their mothers did not teach them anything about vehicles hurtling down the highway. They do not watch television, so they don't have the slightest idea that they should surrender when a policeman yells at them to freeze. They do not speak your language. They do not understand one word you say to them. An animal has no concept of that weapon you are carrying, and will feel absolutely no compunction against attacking you. If you choose to stand your ground with your rifle, you better be prepared to fire when that tiger buffalo moose elephant bear charges.

Wild animals may seem to be stupid when it comes to dealing with the world of humans. How many songbirds would be spared from windshield impacts if they could only learn the simple concept to fly across the highway at a minimum en route altitude of fifteen feet. But that would presume understanding the concept of distance, or altitude, or highway. Alas, these ideas are beyond the capability of their little birdbrains.

However, animals are pretty smart when it comes to surviving in the wild. They do fine living outdoors in all kinds of weather. They know how to live off the land as hunter-gatherers. They learn from their mothers when to hide, and how to stalk other animals they might pursue for food. They form herds for their common defense and to propagate their kind.

Most humans, if left alone in the wild, will simply die off after a few days. They will starve to death, or poison themselves by eating inappropriate vegetation. They will get too hot, or too cold, or become exhausted. Perhaps a wild animal will find them to be a tasty treat. You can read about such incidents several times a year in your local newspaper.

Wild animals are happiest when you leave them alone in their natural habitat. Likewise, you are happiest when the wild animals leave you alone in your civilization.

Many animals have learned to avoid humans just like they avoid other animals. Foxes have the intelligence to keep away from people.

Other critters may consider you a threat, if they find you in their realm. They may decide you smell like a tasty tidbit for lunch, and try to kill you.

Lions and tigers are fairly arrogant and have little fear of man. They are high on the food chain and are used to getting their way in the jungle. When you go into their territory, they may decide to avoid you. If they are big enough they might merely ignore you, but if you irritate them they will try to kill you. For the animal, this represents legal behavior. When you are in his territory, he is in charge.

Conversely, if the wild animal wanders into your territory, you will kill him. How many people allow rattlesnakes to live in their bedrooms? How many people tolerate an infestation of cockroaches in the kitchen? When they invade your home you kill them. This is considered to be legally protected behavior. When wild animals and humans come into contact, killing results, just like in the anarchic realm of the natural world.

As wise readers of this book, at least we can avoid the errors committed by people afflicted with the Theme-Park Fantasy Syndrome.

Animal Rights

If we agree that the wide diversity of animal species on our planet should be preserved, the topic of animal rights arises. The legal concept of rights is derived from the logical conclusion that people should be fair with their fellow creatures. When the term "fellow creatures" is limited to one's own species, the result is human rights, justice, a balance of power, and the rule of law.

However, when the concept of rights is extended to animals, a logical inconsistency soon develops.

Plants and animals represent a food resource for humans. Some animals are used as beasts of burden, as a pack mule, or for their muscle power, as an ox pulls a plow. Plants and animals are property that may be owned by individuals. A farmer may own the fruit trees in the orchard on his land. He may own his herd of cattle, or a barn full of chickens. The owner of this property has the right to sell it to his neighbors, or consume it himself as food, or to dispose of it in whatever way he deems fit.

When an animal is granted rights, that interferes with the human's property rights. What right could we grant to a horse, say, if we decided we should be nicer to horses? How about the right to life? That would mean the farmer is not allowed to kill his horse, even if it gets old and sick. The farmer would have to pay for the horse's food until it died of natural causes. The farmer could not sell his old sick horse because it would have no market value. With these restrictions, the farmer would quickly decide to get out of the horse ownership business, and so would everyone else who might have considered it before. The result would be that nobody would own horses any more, and eventually the only horses would be in the wild.

This same scenario applies to any animal that is granted "rights." Dogs and cats are common beneficiaries of people who wish that we should be kinder to unwanted animals. Many cities now have "no-kill" animal shelters for such unfortunate beasts. They are supported by charitable organizations of animal lovers, and by taxpayers in some jurisdictions.

Many people bemoan the sad state of affairs in the realm of county animal control agencies. Stray dogs and cats rounded up from communities are eventually euthanized, when loving homes cannot be found for them. Thus have developed programs for spaying and neutering household pets.

Animal herds need to be managed for the welfare of humans. Market forces regulate the numbers of domesticated animals that are raised for food (cattle, chickens) and for entertainment (racehorses). Wild animal herds are managed by wildlife organizations by licensing of hunters and regulation of hunting seasons. International treaties attempt to regulate fishing in the oceans to prevent the extinction of fishes used for human food. Non-game wildlife species remain on their own in the old-fashioned, anarchistic environment of natural selection.

When animals are granted "rights," it interferes with natural feedback mechanisms in the economy and also in the wild. For instance, hunting is not allowed in national parks. As a result the elk herds in Rocky Mountain

National Park have flourished to the point where they are destroying the natural beauty of the park's forests, particularly by decimating stands of willow and aspen.[3]

Of course, humans who wish that animals should not be abused will make laws and regulations to prevent cruelty to animals, but the granting of rights to animals leads to unreasonable restrictions on human behavior. Granting rights to animals leads to self-destructive human behavior, which is contrary to the human's basic imperative for survival of his own species.

Man cannot grant rights to his food, or he would not be able to eat it, and thus he would die. Note that there is no "nice" way to kill another creature. Killing is the ultimate definition of not-nice. A man, unlike some animals, must first kill his food before he eats it. However, there are humane techniques for killing our food, without inflicting torture in the process. We can be nice to animals, and give them a happy place to live, but if we wish to survive and flourish, we cannot grant them rights equivalent to our own.

Plant Rights

Some people have actually proposed that the dignity of plant life should be preserved, and in order to protect it, laws should be added to the statute books. Language to this effect already appears in the Constitution of Switzerland, Article 78. This is the document that forms the foundation for law in that country. The next step, for granting rights to plants, is within reach.

Plants do not have brains. Plants do not have nervous systems. Plants do not care whether or not some animal stomping through the forest tramples them blindly underfoot, or decides to eat their leaves. Plants are indifferent to the birds that eat their berries. Plants may become the property of humans, who may burn them in the fireplace for warmth, or convert their fibers into paper for books. For a human to grant plants rights that limit the human's exploitation of the plant's resources is ludicrous. If the human restricts his use of plants to preserve the dignity of plants, he is acting towards his own self-destruction, contrary to his imperative for survival.

One might argue that plants are life forms and all life is sacred, therefore plants should be protected.

Brief timeout. "Sacred" is a word from the realm of religion, and thus is restricted from use in this book. The word "revered" will be considered a suitable substitute. End timeout.

One might argue that plants are life forms and all life is revered, therefore plants should be protected. Wrong. It is a fallacy that all life should be revered. A cancer tumor is a life form. Cancer cells should be killed to preserve the life of the human host. Flying insects are a life form. No one would logically suggest that you should limit your car's velocity to five miles-per-hour so as to prevent these hapless bugs from splattering the windshield. The bacteria that cause tuberculosis are a life form, but that does not mean that they are welcome in your lungs. Mold, a life form, is not permitted to colonize the rim of your bathtub. You rub it out with basin-tub-and-tile cleaner. Mold is dirt. Warm, fuzzy bear cubs are not granted the right to attend kindergarten along with four-year-old humans, because they don't share the intellectual capacity to learn about keeping their hands (claws and teeth) to themselves. Any form of life does not automatically deserve the right to exist, merely because it is life. Parasites, infestations and disease are life forms that should be destroyed. Human life, on the other hand, is the only reason you exist. Therefore human life should be protected by human laws, as long as the humans can agree to live by a set of rules about cooperating with each other.

Animals and plants live in the anarchy of Mother Nature, and are not smart enough to be promoted into the realm of humans, where citizens are required to use good judgment in cooperating with others to promote the advancement of civilization. With rights come responsibilities, and any creature unable to comprehend his responsibilities has no right to rights.

We agree that plants may become the property of some person, and the person's property rights in the plants should be protected by the humans' laws. But to grant a plant a right to dignity is absurd.

Machine rights

Here is one last example for emphasis. Many people love their cars as much as they love their pets. Some folks are torn with emotion when it comes time to retire that worn-out, though formerly reliable, loyal old vehicle. Perhaps we could grant these sad machines some rights to protect them from the ignominy of the scrap heap. A herd of Volkswagens has rights, too, you know. And you'll go to jail if we catch you kicking tires again.

If you read the editorial pages in your local newspaper, no doubt you have seen proposals as ridiculous.

Notes:

[1] Quote from *Cat and Mouse in Partnership* by the Brothers Grimm.
[2] See Herzog.
[3] See Rocky Mountain National Park.

CHAPTER TWENTY

ANTHROPOMORPHISM

ANTHROPOMORPHISM is the term scientists use to explain how people will ascribe human-like forms or attributes to non-humans. We can use this term as an explanation for why people are lured into the Theme-Park Fantasy Syndrome. Some people will assume that animals think about the world in the same ways that we humans do. This is a mistake because of the limited brainpower animals actually possess.

People like to say that their pets are as smart as their masters, and dogs especially are held up as examples of intelligence in the world of animals. But it is the rare dog that can learn the simple task of how to unwind his leash from around a tree, or a parking-meter post, when he walks past the opposite side from his master. It seems like such a simple concept to the dog owner, but it is usually beyond the mental ability of the dog. So the person walking the dog spends a lot of time following the dog around trees, or unwinding the leash, rather than vice versa.

An excellent example of how animals think was illustrated on the popular TV show *America's Funniest Videos,* or *AFV* on the ABC Network. A contestant sent in a video that showed how his dog would not go through the storm door even though the glass had been removed.

The homeowner had trained his dog to wait at the front door until he opened it to allow the dog outside. But for Halloween, the homeowner removed the glass panel from his storm door to make it easier to hand out candy to the trick-or-treaters.

When the dog saw his master step through the glassless doorframe, the dog still waited until his master opened the empty doorframe before he would go outside.

In the other direction, when the master stepped through the empty doorframe into the house, the dog still waited outside until the master again opened the empty doorframe before the dog would go inside.

This behavior is very funny for the humans to watch, but we can understand the dog's point of view if we analyze how the dog failed to make the connections in his mind about the larger concepts of "door" and "glass."

The dog reasons only from A to B. I must wait for my master to swing that barrier thing out of the way before I go outside. The dog never bothers to think about the larger concepts of "aluminum door frame" or "removable glass panel." Such ideas are probably beyond the intellectual capacity of the doggie brain. So we are amused by the antics of the funny dog because the concept "storm-door" seems so obvious to us.

We don't wish to pick on dogs too much since they are much loved and revered pets, but unbiased observations can lead to the conclusion that these highly intelligent animals are sadly deficient in brainpower when compared to humans. The author has personally observed a jogger out running around the neighborhood, followed dutifully by his loyal doggie. In fact, the dog was following so closely that it would be kicked in the chops by the heel of its master's right foot at every second step. The simple solution to this obviously unpleasant experience would be for the dog to move to the right by a few inches, or to follow his master a little less closely. Perhaps the master might be motivated to retrain his loyal mascot so as to avoid the pummeling.

Dogs provide their masters with attention, loyalty and love, so they earn a prominent place in the owner's heart. One might even say that the dog is smart enough to make his master think he is smarter than he really is. This is a very clever strategy, which was encouraged and preserved by the blind processes of evolution. The dogs that cozied up to their masters won favored treatment and were thus encouraged to breed and propagate along with the humans. The dogs that remained un-friendly to men were killed off, or shunned back to the wild to fend for themselves in a more hostile environment.

Attributing a humanistic point of view to an animal is a mistake, but anthropomorphism is pervasive in our society. Cartoons show our children an endless stream of talking animals. Children's TV shows display intelligent puppets and imaginary talking creatures of all kinds. Computer graphics create characters, in the shape of anything, which are presented with intelligence equivalent to the human. So it is natural for us to anthropomorphize any real creature we encounter, even though it has no basis in reality.

Anthropomorphism also provides the explanation for many of the beliefs of primitive man. Early peoples needed a way to understand the world around them, so they made up stories about spirits who controlled the forces of nature. Such spirits are understood to be motivated by the same emotions that affect a man, because a man can understand why his father, chief, or king might be angry with his sons, tribesmen, or subjects who disobey his orders. Why did that storm arise and send a flood to destroy our village? Clearly, the sea god was angry with the way we failed to honor his wonderfulness, so he punished us with destruction. We must therefore sacrifice another virgin in his salty waters to show that we are serious about our dedication to his authority. We must demonstrate our abject obeisance to his magnificent power, so he won't send us another such disaster. Since these beliefs and the related stories are handed down from one generation to the next, from our elders who are clearly more educated and smarter than we will ever be, they must be right. So we will perpetuate and even expand upon the rituals, making them harder on ourselves so the gods cannot help but realize that we are sincere.

Of course, none of that dancing, clicking of heels and sacrificing of virgins had the slightest affect on the weather, or any other phenomena attributed to the gods.

The stories from Greek and Roman mythology can be better appreciated when viewed in the light of men anthropomorphizing the gods' motivations. When man's behavior is then viewed as a reflection of the things the gods do, the men do not feel so bad about their own shortcomings. So the ancient bards made up stories about gods misbehaving like men do, then the readers of these tales, men, learn lessons from the gods, thus closing another never ending circle, one more bubble in the complex foam of life.

Note that today's stories about Superman, and other super-heroes, are the modern analog of Roman or Greek mythology. Fortunately, most children who learn about good vs. bad from these tales later realize the stories are fictional.

CHAPTER TWENTY-ONE

HOLLYWOOD SYNDROME

THE entertainment industry knows that flash and sizzle are the most important things in the world. Flash gets your attention, like a strobe light on a school bus. Sizzle is unusual; it tells you things are hot, like the steak served to you still cooking on a hot metal platter in your favorite restaurant. In your ordinary life you don't get a lot of flash and sizzle, so Hollywood steps in to fill the void. Hollywood understands advertising, so they want to grab you by the collar, shake you up, get in your face, cram their message down your throat. And you put up with it because they have treated you this way all your life and you accept this as normal behavior from them.

Hollywood is a lifelike form composed of a collection of businesses that make movies and TV shows. Each of these businesses strives to exist in its environment, therefore each one needs to make a profit to survive and prosper. They all compete for dominance in their ecology, and they keep score by way of the ratings industry. The ratings tell them how many people are watching. The fight to become top dog in the ratings is intense. If your show does not rate highly, it will be cancelled, regardless of its artistic merit or educational value. To grab high scores in the ratings, Hollywood goes for flash and sizzle. Everything they produce needs to be new, something you have not seen before. If you have seen it before, you will become bored and stop paying attention. Every new show must out-do the previous ones.

What then do we get from Hollywood? We get sex, violence and crime. Hollywood serves up entertainment about the things that are forbidden to us in our ordinary, boring, everyday lives. After a long day in the real world, where we need to be polite to our fellow workers, do the things our boss tells us to do, serve our customers with a smile, and yield the right-of-way to strangers on the drive home, we want to relax and watch funny characters on TV. These characters may handle their problems with an abandon we are not allowed to engage in ourselves.

So we see explosions and fire, war, crime, destruction and treachery. We get to watch warriors swinging their swords at hoards of marauding barbarians, we see machineguns mowing down rows of enemy soldiers, and we see our usually timid neighbors deciding to take the law into their own hands. All the while, of course, we realize that we are watching fiction, a made-up world, presented for our enjoyment by an accommodating entertainment industry.

After all, how believable is it to watch a ten-minute fist fight between James Bond and his evil opponent? When our hero eventually triumphs by beating the bad guy into unconsciousness, he will brush himself off and then calmly walk away, without a bruise on his face, or a wrinkle in his neatly pressed tuxedo. Wouldn't he actually be totally exhausted, and need a few days in the hospital to recover? Maybe not. Some guys are really tough.

The soap opera is a popular type of show that appeals to many viewers, although others of us fail to see the attraction in this type of entertainment. Some soap opera fans do not appreciate that the drama is actually fiction, which deals with characters in a fantasy world where they make bad choices in the conduct of their lives, and thus suffer the consequences. The viewers have the opportunity to vicariously experience the failings of these characters and thus learn some of the harsh realities of life. But some viewers will actually go so far as to model their own lives on the characters they see in these dramas. This is generally a mistake, wherein the victim, the misled viewer, adopts a faulty belief system. Perhaps you know a person like this.

Another irritating feature of the Hollywood Syndrome is the laugh track. Everyone has seen the TV shows where every line spoken is followed by a brief recording of an audience laughing. This regardless of whether the line was funny or not. We may consider the laugh track as a mutation that seems to persist in this species, but doesn't seem to be sufficiently self-destructive to have died out during recent generations. If enough viewers were to write to the producers complaining about this irritating practice, the laugh track might fade from the scene.

In real life, some people provide their own laugh track. Perhaps you have met somebody who follows every statement with a nervous little laugh.

Such people have a psychological need to take the edge off their statements, seeking approval from their listeners. Such folks could probably benefit from a little assertiveness training to improve their self-image. Hollywood's use of the laugh track implies a hidden agenda to make you think you are being entertained when you would be better served to switch off the television, and do something constructive.

If a naïve person were to pretend that Hollywood does not provide merely entertainment, but actually instruction in how to behave, that misguided individual would absorb the following beliefs:

1) Corporate executives are money-grubbing criminals who are out to exploit their customers at every opportunity, and by extension, anyone who works for a corporation is similarly inclined.
2) The only honorable professions belong to newspaper reporters, lawyers, doctors, and detectives, not necessarily in that order. These are the only honest people who selflessly spend their time helping others, and wish to make the world a better place.
3) Practically everyone else is a corrupt, selfish lowlife who wants to steal money or property from unsuspecting innocents.
4) Anyone motivated by earning profits is an evil creep to be shunned.
5) Altruism and helping those less fortunate than oneself is the only valid reason for existing.

However, when we look below the surface of such Hollywood clichés, we realize that these simplistic assumptions are false. For example, look at your own life, and place it on the imaginary stage of a Hollywood production. If you work for a corporation, is your boss a criminal who tries to take things from you and from your employer? How about your subordinates in the business? Do they try to cheat and steal from the people they deal with? Look at your own personal motivations. Do you try to misrepresent yourself and cheat your employer and customers in your own job? Or do you do your best to serve your customers by providing the things they want to buy from you? You are honest in your dealings with your associates to advance the goals of your employer. You have acquired the skills necessary to perform your job in an acceptable manner. You serve your customers to the best of your ability in order to keep them as your customers. Your job could not be performed by just anyone off the street, because you have specialized knowledge and skills you have learned through your education, experience and hard work.

Change your perspective to the side of the customer, and look at the businesses you deal with every day. How often does your bank make an arithmetic error on your checking account statement? How long would you allow them to continue as your bank if they started making such mistakes? You would move your money to a more reliable bank.

Does your grocery store stock fresh milk and vegetables, or rancid butter and rotten fruit? How long would you continue to buy groceries from a dysfunctional store? If you are not satisfied with the service you receive from some vendor, you merely move your business to one of their competitors. This is capitalism in action, with all its self-regulating feedback loops, providing efficient service to the economy, operating automatically without any guidance or interference from the government.

All businesses are in business to serve customers, and these customers are ultimately individual people, like you and me. Customers buy things from the business because it offers a product to the customer more cheaply than the customer can make it for himself. To survive, the business must offer its product at a reasonable price, yet it must also earn a profit. Competition between businesses drives prices down to the point where prices are barely above production costs, thus minimizing profits. This conclusion may seem inconceivable, given the popular view of capitalism, but true capitalism, when allowed to function in a free market, will drive down prices to the minimum sustainable level.

Hollywood, with all its glamour, flash and sizzle, is really just another business, which must earn a profit to survive. It is composed of corporations that try to serve their customers better than the ones competing with them. Every trick they use to get you to watch their programming is intended to transfer your money out of your pocket and into theirs. Advertisers depend for their success on this same principle. Don't let them fool you with their preaching about how you need to sacrifice your own well-being to the greater good for your fellow man. They will take their cut before any benefits find their way to the oppressed and downtrodden of society.

After all the pushing of altruism as the ideal model of virtue, we find that Hollywood does not practice what it preaches. Hollywood must sell its product to the public, feed the hungry audience with the fare the executives think the populace wishes to consume, and earn a profit.

We might even hazard to say that Hollywood is a prime example of Sturgeon's Law: Ninety percent of "everything" is crap.[1]

Back in the early days of television, the 1950's for example, people would commonly lament that even with six channels available, they couldn't find anything they wanted to watch. As the industry grew and technology advanced, cable TV was able to supply many more channels than broadcast TV. At that time people would complain they had fifty channels, but nothing to watch. Nowadays we have expanded cable and satellite TV offering over 300 channels, and some folks are heard to say they still can't find anything worthwhile to watch.

What seems to be the problem? As the technology advanced making more channels available, businesses rushed in to take advantage of the market. Along with the competent artists, a lot of hacks and wannabees slapped together programming without skill or artistic merit. Too much mediocre work got published along with the occasional gems, and all those hundreds of time slots, all day long, had to be filled with continuous video.

Remember that our children are constantly exposed to the products of Hollywood. Do the kids also receive a counterbalancing perspective of reality from responsible adults? Will they become educated entirely by what they see on TV, and adopt a faulty belief system like our naïve viewer described above? Is it any wonder, in this environment, that some youth choose rebellion, disrespect, hedonism and vice over virtue and gentlemanly or ladylike conduct?

Avoid buying into the Hollywood Syndrome. Resist becoming a patsy for their sales pitches. Refuse to embrace their faulty belief systems. Don't become another victim of distorted reality. Hollywood presents stories for entertainment, not role models for acceptable behavior.

Now that we have finished trashing Hollywood, we would like to acknowledge that nearly everybody goes to the movies once in a while, and most folks watch TV on a daily basis. We consumers are free to choose among the products of the entertainment industry. Nobody forces us to go to the movies or watch TV; we choose to do it because we want to.

Market forces determine which shows succeed, and will guide the producers to make the kinds of shows that people want to see. Capitalism gives the people what they want. People who want junk get to buy junk. People who want quality will demand products that meet their specifications. So the kind of stuff Hollywood delivers is merely a reflection of what the viewing public wants.

But we have just spent a few pages denigrating the products of Hollywood. So either we are wrong, or TV viewers want to watch stuff that is bad for them. The answer to this apparent discrepancy lies in a psychological need of the human animal.

We like to experience some situations, especially dangerous ones, vicariously, rather than in person. It is so much safer to watch the bad-guy characters in a movie shoot at the good-guy characters, than it is to have real bad-guys shooting at us with real bullets. In real life you don't stick around to watch when the gunfire begins, you run like hell.

We will gladly go to the movies to see fiery airplane crashes, but when we read in the news that a particular airline had a plane crash for some unexplained reason, we airline customers promptly stop flying with that airline. This results in a financial decline for the airline in question, if not its bankruptcy. Real plane crashes are bad for airlines. Phony plane crashes are good for Hollywood.

The distinction, for us mature individuals, is that we can tell reality from fiction. Unfortunately, this distinction can be hard for children who are still learning how to interpret the things they experience in the real world. Kids are more susceptible to the Monkey See - Monkey Do syndrome, than are adults who have already learned right from wrong, reality from fantasy, truth from fiction.

So the answer to the Hollywood Syndrome is education, or shall we say, the acquisition of wisdom. Once an individual graduates from grade school, or high school, or college, he is not done with his education. Life experiences that follow are also important educational experiences that should be incorporated into one's store of knowledge. Reading this book about an engineer's perspective on the lessons of life is a good addition to your ongoing self-education. It seems a shame that your efforts to learn new things will not earn you college credits.

Now that all of us are intelligent, responsible adults with highly developed and mature senses of reality, we should use our wisdom to help the children learn right from wrong. Show them how to distinguish reality from fantasy, and point out the many big-bad-wolves out there who want to sell them shoddy goods, fraudulent services and faulty ideas, all for inflated prices.

Not only the children need such guidance. Many of your fellow adult citizens have need of additional education. Help your fellow man avoid the insidious traps of the Hollywood Syndrome.

Notes:

[1] During an interview in the 1950's, science fiction author Theodore Sturgeon needed to defend his genre as a valid literary art form against complaints from literary critics. He made the point that a lot of junk is published alongside the competent work in any field, and came up with his now famous aphorism. Sturgeon's Law is included as one of Murphy's Laws. See Bloch.

CHAPTER TWENTY-TWO

A. HACK

IN this chapter we have collected a few notes for political speeches. They come from the personal musings of a fictitious candidate we will call A. Hack. Some editing may be required before he could actually come out and say all these things in public.

Greetings, my fellow Americans! My name is A. Hack and I want to be your mayor. I'm running for Congress as your Representative in this district. I am seeking the office of Senator from our fine state. If you vote for me as President of the United States, we will take back the country from our current incompetent administration and recover the America we all want and expect. Together we will move forward to a future of prosperity and comfort where all of our people have the opportunity to excel in their chosen lifestyle. Relics of the past, like suffering and want, shall be permanently banished from the lexicon of our culture. As citizens of America, we are the chosen people, and we shall not fail in our resolve to achieve greatness in our every endeavor.

Yes, friends, remember my name: A. Hack. You will be hearing a lot more from me during the following weeks and months as we set out on our quest for a better America.

By way of introduction, my full name is Aloysius Hack. That's pronounced Al-O-Wish-Us, and comes from the Latin for "famous warrior." The most well-known person in history with this name was probably Saint Aloysius Gonzaga from Italy. But our younger voters may be more familiar with my name from the Sesame Street character, Aloysius Snuffleupagus. He is such a friendly, trustworthy, cuddly character, just like me! Since Aloysius is such an uncommon name, and there are a lot of rude people in our society who would make fun of me because of my unusual name, I have decided to use just my initial. Yes, good people, I am A. Hack. Actually I would prefer to be called Abe. Abe Hack, for Abraham, you know. Like in Abe Lincoln who is so well associated in our national consciousness with title of "Honest Abe." He has such a favorable reputation; I would like to ride along with that. It sounds so good. Those of us in politics know that everything we say must sound good, even though there may be no real meaning in our words.

The name Abraham comes from the Hebrew for "father of the people." The most famous Abraham was probably the one in the Bible, the leader of the early Jews, but his fame has been overshadowed in our country by Abraham Lincoln, our great humanitarian president who freed the slaves. Honest Abe, that's who I want to seem like. Honest Abe Hack. I must do my best to plant that association in the minds of voters. Honest Abe. Honest A. Hack.

Yes, ladies and gentlemen, Honest A. Hack, famous warrior, father of the people, is the candidate who is on your side. I must strive to implant this association in the minds of voters everywhere. Incessant repetition of this message will eventually make it so. Honest A. Hack has only your best interests at heart. Vote for me, vote for me, vote for me. Together we can change the world for the better. There really can be hope for the future, with me as your leader.

Now, gentle voter, why would I choose to go into politics? Why would I expose myself to the unremitting criticism of political opponents? As soon as anyone announces his candidacy, the loyal opposition jumps upon anything he says, subjects him to ridicule and derision, calls him a liar and a crook, and does their best to destroy his reputation through character assassination. Regardless of my sincerity and good intentions, despite my past victories and accomplishments, the opposition will not relent one iota, or back off from their incessant disagreement with my views and policies. But I realize that this is just the way politics works, and the majority agrees with me and my ideals. We are right, and furthermore, we are in the right.

So that is why I chose politics for my career. Because I want to help people. I want to make a difference. I want the world to be a better place for you and your children. I hereby dedicate my life to working for the advancement of downtrodden and oppressed people in all walks of life. America can reclaim her former greatness with me on the job. I want to fight poverty. I want to encourage brotherhood (and sisterhood, of course) among men and women everywhere. I want the weakest and most disadvantaged people, the vulnerable ones, to have a chance in our society. In my America, everyone will achieve the life to which he or she aspires. I want to solve the social ills of our society today and work on the problems of tomorrow before they become a threat to our very existence. Everyone should have affordable housing. Healthcare must be accessible to all, regardless of their station in life. We must stimulate the economy so that opportunities for advancement are available for anyone who has the ambition to succeed.

We need a safer, more caring environment. We should extend our family values to all peoples of our communities. We must be aware of our responsibilities to prevent the rape of our valuable resources, the exploitation of our irreplaceable treasures, and the pollution of our clean air and waters. We must save the planet from global warming and develop alternative energy sources so we may break our addiction to foreign oil. We must encourage international fellowship, since all nations share our one fragile planet, and it is in the best interests of all humanity to preserve our common resources. We need to create jobs in the new industries that will arise due to our grand plan for the coming generations. You, as a voter in America, deserve a better life, with less government intrusion in your affairs, lower taxes, and greater opportunities to realize your aspirations for your families and communities. We will eliminate unnecessary and obsolete government programs, and will discard those ideas that have been demonstrated to be wasteful of our time and effort.

My administration will work tirelessly to achieve these goals for the future of our people and the advancement of our civilization. With your help, we can make the world a better place for all citizens, regardless of race, color, religion, sex, age, national origin, handicap, disability, creed, income, intelligence, merit, aptitude, ability, body mass index, sexual preference or hair color. God bless America.

Whew. All that stuff sure sounds good. Do you suppose anybody actually believes any of it?

Some clues may be found in the above talking-points that indicate A. Hack may be exaggerating, or he may be engaging in deception by claiming to care more for your welfare than his own, or he may be merely an outright scammer, interested only in his own power and aggrandizement. One other possibility is that he is being entirely honest, and actually believes all the platitudes he advocates. If this is the actual case, we may conclude that he is hopelessly naive and therefore not qualified for the leadership position he seeks.

Let us look at a few of the things he says from a logical standpoint to see if they make any sense at all. He starts out by claiming to be one of us, a fellow American. He tells us his name and what office he is seeking. He claims to be on your side, and implies that your life will be better with him in charge. As yet we have no evidence that these things are true, other than his statements.

Then he tells us about his name, and plants in the listener's mind the ideas that he is honest and trustworthy. He invokes the record of Abe Lincoln to try to associate himself with a great leader. He admits that the things he says must sound good, even though they may not be entirely truthful. This provides a clue about the thought processes of any politician.

He claims he wants to suffer the indignities of political life to make the world a better place for you, the voter. He is willing to bear the hardships of life in public service in order to fight for your well-being in a harsh environment. Again, so far we have only his word on the subject. We might suspect that he has ambitions for the advancement of his own career.

Then he gives us a list of sound-good and feel-good issues that most folks wish could be realized in our society of today. Some people still believe that government has the ability to solve these problems by spending taxpayer money on well-intentioned programs. In most cases, this is like believing the fables told to children. It is another example of people adopting faulty belief systems. Note how A. Hack promises lower taxes along with his desire to implement programs that would require vast expenditures by the government. We, as readers of this book, realize that the government gets its money from taxes, which constitute a burden upon the productive forces in our capitalist economy. Increasing taxes saps more and more of the economy's potential to create wealth.

Government can also acquire funds by borrowing, otherwise known as deficit spending. This technique is good for politicians, because it moves the day of reckoning out to the distant future, when our ambitious politicians will have retired from office. So they get the advantages of profligate spending now without any responsibility to pay the bills later.

Another method government can use to raise funds is to simply print new money. But this causes inflation, which raises prices and thus increases the cost of goods to all consumers. Inflation becomes apparent to the public fairly soon after the new money is pumped into the economy. By raising prices, inflation effectively steals money from consumers, especially those widows and orphans who are living on fixed incomes. Inflation is unpopular with voters who understand it.

Our candidate, A. Hack, speaks in generalities about his goals and ambitions, but gives no details as to how he plans to accomplish them. If he were to explain his methods, logic would force into view the contradictions between his goals and how he plans to achieve them. The details are thus best left until after the political campaign.

Our candidate concludes his notes for making speeches with an attempt to include all possible voters in his pitch to win the election. Finally, he wonders whether anyone will believe his promises. This statement will never see the light of day in any actual speeches, but gives a clue about how he really thinks.

Many voters realize that most of the things a candidate says during his campaign cannot be expected to last into his administration, if he is elected. Nobody who speaks the whole truth about his ideas during the campaign could ever actually be elected, or so is the belief among political campaign organizers. Note that this belief implies that any candidate is expected to lie, or at least to practice deception when speaking to his constituency. Practical voters understand that so much of a candidate's political speech is posturing and puffery, so they base their decisions on whom to vote for on other cues about his record, personality, good looks, charisma, reputation, or party affiliation. Some of these criteria may not be valid indicators of a candidate's fitness for office, but every voter is entitled to make his own decision. Each voter decides based on his own thoughts and feelings, and marks his ballot in the privacy of the voting booth.

Thus, political campaigns are about manipulating the psychology of as many voters as possible. The concepts of truth, honesty, justice, and the way a country ought to be run, are not the primary drivers during a campaign, although no candidate would ever publicly admit to such a thing. So politics is actually a game, like football or Monopoly or poker. Especially like poker, with its bluffing and psychology of deception.

Now that we have seen some of the things that A. Hack might like to say during his speeches, let us look into the private thoughts of our hypothetical candidate to see what he considers while planning his political maneuvers.

People have been telling me what to do all my life, and I am sick and tired of it. I must grab the opportunity to turn the tables, and politics will be my ticket to prestige and respect. I must claw my way out from the bottom of the heap, from the depths of oppression, towards the pinnacles of political power. It will be my turn to tell others what they must do.

I wish to become a big shot and get to hobnob with the wealthy and famous celebrities of the nation and the world. I will feel important for a change. Famous and powerful people will listen to what I have to say, or at least they will pretend to be interested in what I say. In like manner, I will pretend to be interested in what they say, because we all are playing the same game, and engage in artificially stroking each other's egos. Have you ever actually listened to the politicians in the halls of power addressing each other?

"The chair recognizes the Honorable Senator from the Great State of Pennsyltucky." Wouldn't it be more efficient to simply say, "Go ahead Mr. Washington?" No, we must overuse words and become sickly sweet to our opponents (whom we cannot stand) because we might need to ally with them on some future legislation.

"I beg to respectfully take exception to the remarks regarding our esteemed colleague from Montorado."

Ha! I can easily learn to talk this way, because I want to rub elbows with kings and princes, have dinner with leaders of the world, move among the international jet set, all at the expense of taxpayers.

When I become mayor, I will have the city police commissioner working for me. I will subtly manipulate his ability to harass my political enemies. The power of the police department can influence the behavior of many people in public service, business and industry.

When I am governor I will have an attorney general to decide which laws will be enforced on a statewide basis. My ability to destroy opposition will be enhanced a hundredfold. But subtly, of course, with very small steps at any one time. With the aid of the legislature, we will write new laws, always with the goal of increasing the power of the political class. We will gradually raise taxes over the years and slowly move the power of money away from those who earn it to those of us who can take it away from them, and expend it on our politically expedient goals.

When I am president, the whole world will be my oyster. Think of the power and prestige vested in that oval office. The opportunities are limitless. I will be commander in chief of the greatest military power in the history of the world, with nuclear weapons at my disposal. Why should I be satisfied with running the country when the entire globe is still available? Today the presidency, tomorrow the world! King Hack, Absolute Monarch of Planet Earth. Doesn't that have a fine ring to it? The King is A. Hack. Long live the King.

But wait. I must not get too far ahead of myself. I must take small steps toward my goals, so that the voters will not see their freedoms slipping away. I must consider the limitations on political power in our society today. What is the line I cannot cross before the citizens will demand impeachment? What egregious corruption committed by a politician in office would result in his removal?

Murder. Yes, a politician must not blatantly kill anyone in the furtherance of his career. It is OK for a president to order the military to kill enemy soldiers in the hostilities of war, because that is his prerogative in defense of his country. But if a senator became excessively irritating in his opposition to my political ambitions, I would not be justified in taking him out in a mafia-style hit. Too bad, because this technique used to be acceptable behavior in the politics of ancient Rome. Julius Cesar was assassinated at the forum on the ides of March in 44BC, and the politicians involved in the plot continued with their careers. Alas, times change.

Burglary is probably out as an option as well. President Nixon was eventually removed from office after the press pinned on him the botched burglary at the Watergate complex. I must take that lesson to heart and avoid any actions that would place me in the direct path of responsibility for any burglary.

Bribery is also a category to be shunned. In 1973, Vice President Agnew got nailed for accepting a bribe while in office. Actually, he pleaded no contest to not paying income tax on money received while governor of Maryland, but the charges were related to an alleged history of taking bribes. More recently, the governor of Illinois was removed from his position for trying to sell a vacated senate seat, when he might have stayed in the clear by merely appointing a close political ally who could be counted on to support his interests. At any rate, bribery is frowned upon by the typical voter.

Cover-ups are another very ambiguous activity that must be avoided. The news can be so easily manipulated, a politician needs the acquiescence of the news media to get away with cover-ups in his bag of tricks. A politician should therefore associate himself with the political party that has the news media in its pocket.

Lying is certainly acceptable behavior. I must practice the art of deceiving people. I must be able to look them in the eye and make false statements without the slightest hesitation. Tell people the things I know they want to hear. Promise them benefits from their government, when I have no intention of actually delivering. I will say anything I need to please the audience that confronts me. Besides, everyone expects politicians to lie through their teeth during political campaigns, and transferring this practice to one's administration is a simple tautology. Words are so flexible in meaning, any statement may be twisted to mean something else, and be explained away at a later date. Remember the famous presidential prevarication: "It depends upon what the meaning of the word "is" is."[1]

Stealing, although related to burglary, can be made acceptable via the proper obfuscating manipulations of facts. Raising taxes for some pet project, in collaboration with the legislature, is actually stealing from the taxpayers, although it is wrapped in legal legitimacy. By the wave of a pen, a percentage of the hard-earned funds of citizens may be taken for any purpose the legislators may decide upon. Bit by bit we will take more. It is convenient for us that the national economy is so large that no one ever notices how we are slowly killing this golden goose. No, that cannot be the case. We are merely making it mildly ill, with perhaps a little flu during the winter season. Yes, our vast economy will undoubtedly survive these minor stresses. At any rate, the health of greedy businessmen is of no concern of to those of us in power. The larger is government, the larger is my power to maintain my position at the head of it. The more people employed by the bureaucracy the harder it is to remove them and shrink the influence and power of us, the entrenched manipulators, the political class.

Cheating is simply a way of life for the successful politician. Deception must always be practiced in order to beat the opposition. A long established aphorism tells us that all is fair in love and war.[2] I say all is fair in politics, and the ends justify the means.

In kindergarten we teach children to never lie, cheat or steal. But when we graduate to the lofty status of politician, the tables are turned and we revert to the opposite extreme. Politics is a form of anarchy, the anarchy of words. In politics words are our weapons. Lying, cheating and stealing with our words are the ways of life and survival. Any resulting actions are acceptable, such as the ruination of an opponent's career, with the only provisos being to avoid outright murder, blatant burglary, unadulterated bribery, and obvious cover-ups. I think I am capable of remaining within these boundaries as I seek advancement in the high-powered realms of government.

Power and control are the favorite foods for any politician, so I must plan to gain power in every possible way. Control over voters is an important consideration, because voters must be used to get me into office. It is a good thing that many voters are so gullible. I might even say they are stupid, but I must be careful not to think like that, since I don't want this attitude to become apparent for anyone to see. But many voters are easy to lead around by the nose. All you need to do is promise them freebies, make it easier for them to get stuff from the government than it would be for them to earn it for themselves. So, in my speeches and appearances I must appear to sincerely desire to help the plight of the voter.

How will I know what they want? I will look at the polls to see what is the opinion of the most folks at the moment, and adjust my point of view to conform with that. I need not bother to appear consistent over a period of time because voters have no memory. They are only interested in what they hear today, and they must like what they hear from me today. Some news people like to point out inconsistencies and flip-flops from politicians, but voters do not pay much attention to muckraking reporters. Yes, I will stick my finger in the air of the political winds to see which way the electorate is blowing today. That will determine my current stand on any issue.

I must look presidential at all times, calm, collected, in charge. I must have a clever remark for all occasions. I must learn to deflect any question by stating a fact on some subject of concern to voters. I must be able to dominate a conversation by taking the offensive in every situation. Never answer a question from a reporter when you can make a statement about the concerns of the day. Emphasize the plight of the poor, the energy situation, high prices, injustice for this group or for that minority.

In my public appearances I must always stress that everything I do is for the good of the people. However, I must never let on that I, in my lofty position of authority, am the one who gets to decide what is good for the people. All my decisions will be ultimately for the acquisition of personal power, or when that is not feasible, to enhance the power of the political class, which will eventually result in my own benefit. Of course, I must occasionally provide some crumbs for the voters, like some minimal tax cut, which will be greatly overemphasized by the propaganda machine of the popular press. Isn't politics grand? Power to the people, as long as I am in charge.

Everything I do must be carefully planned to advance my career. Each step along the way must look good on my resume. I must take any job that will widen my experience in the bureaucracy. Sometimes in the early years the pay is not all that good, but I am not seeking monetary wealth, I am ultimately seeking power. Besides, politics may be the only career field where the workers get to vote themselves a raise every year. The money will certainly follow once the power is achieved.

I am beautiful people and you can trust me to watch out for your interests in Washington. See how I have a pretty smile and I am such a charismatic speaker. Vote for me, vote for me, vote for me.

Notes:

[1] President Clinton in testimony before the Starr hearings, regarding his relationship with Ms. Lewinski, 17 Aug 1998.
[2] Attributed to John Lyly, in *Euphues,* 1578.

CHAPTER TWENTY-THREE

GOVERNMENT

Ethics in Government

THE previous chapter about A. Hack demonstrates that it is possible for some people to seek success in political office, not because they are concerned about changing the world for the better, but merely because they seek power, fame and fortune. Anyone who has read this far should recognize in this behavior-pattern the time-tested methods of anarchy from the animal world.

This is not to say that all politicians are in the arena strictly for personal aggrandizement at the expense of taxpayers. We realize there are many thousands of dedicated public servants who do perform their jobs with integrity and honesty, and who seek to give their full day's effort in return for their salaries. These men and women should be complimented for their hard work. Their daily labor provides them the rewards of a job well done, and gives satisfaction while they work to advance their careers, since they are (or should be) motivated by their own rational self-interest.

Many people begin their political careers with a sincere desire to improve the lot of mankind, and wish to fight corruption in the halls of government. But once they have tasted the "honey of power," they are constantly tempted towards the dark side. People who resist the siren calls of corruption, and maintain ethical behavior, uphold the human ideals of virtue. They resist a natural tendency to descend towards the animal behaviors of instant gratification and vice.

Ethical behavior, the decision to promote goodness and avoid evil, may be measured by the degree of wisdom exercised in the use of power. However, there are no units established for a measurement of virtue. What would be the miles, dollars, gallons, or hours to rate the quantity of good-ness? What symbol would we use to represent the amount of virtue? Perhaps a "virt" or a "holy" could be proposed as a candidate for this job.

Since there are no virts in common usage, we must evaluate each ethical decision on its own merits. Remember that evil is enabled or empowered whenever one person or group uses his power to deny a right to another person or group. Good from evil is easy to distinguish in some simple cases, like when you instruct your child not to hit his sister. Also, it is moral to slap your child's hand away when he is about to stick his fingers in the lamp socket. Other ethical situations are more complex, as when two opposing armies are facing each other across a neutral zone. Armed conflicts are the result of many preceding decisions having been made where virtue and ethics have been largely ignored.

In deciding an ethical question, when many variables are involved, the best option would be to compare two situations, differing in some small detail, and choose the more virtuous one. To decide any particular question, we might look at how an individual's power is used to uphold the rights of his fellow citizens, and see if his choice provides for the most beneficial outcome for the greatest number of people. On the other hand, we might ask if an action denies the rights of a citizen or a particular group. A balance of power between competitors is to be desired, where one party does not feel he has a significant advantage over the other.

Analyzing particular cases to score on the basis of virtue is beyond the scope of this book, so we won't launch a discussion about it. However, the reader may find it instructive to consider various ethical dilemmas he has encountered in his own life, and judge the outcome based on his understanding of the principles. Extremely complex scenarios might be constructed in pursuit of this method, but remember that nearly any situation may be broken down into simpler cases. We trust that our readers have the ability to make the distinctions necessary to judge the results.

Corruption

Returning to the question of corruption in politics, one might ask whether it is even possible for anyone to behave in an ethical manner while holding elected office. For the sake of argument, let us postulate that it is possible for a politician in elected office to conduct his official business in an ethical manner. After all, we can look around the world and identify many governments that are clearly dictatorial and consistently violate the human rights of their citizens. When we look at our own government we see a much more benign situation where citizens are permitted to earn their livings in relative freedom. Our government must therefore be more ethical in nature than the more authoritarian regimes. Ethicalness, like any virtue, must lie along a line of degree, somewhere between criminality and justice.

Only one individual at any one time is allowed to exercise the office of mayor, or senator, or president. Therefore, competition between qualified contenders for a particular office will be intense. An individual must play the game of politics to get elected, and the successful candidate must persuade the voters to select him instead of the others. Can this competition be conducted in an ethical manner?

What better way to answer this question than to ask the successful candidates themselves? Perhaps we could ask our politician to tell the story of his own rise to power, and describe how he followed ethical principles to attain his current leadership position in government. Here are some suggested queries to challenge the politician you wish to interview.

Do you consistently violate the rights of your constituents?
Did you conduct your political campaign in an ethical manner?
Do you conduct your political office in an ethical manner?
Do you consider the ethical dimensions of your actions in government before you make a decision?
Have you ever made a political decision where you felt you were getting close to the margin of ethical behavior? On which side of the margin?
Can you give an example where you have upheld the interests of the common citizen over the wealthy special interests that fund your campaign?
Can you give an example where you made a politically expedient choice, but show how it was actually the ethically correct decision?

The politician will, of course, try to defend his integrity. Most people consider themselves honest and upright, even if they do end up in the political arena. But the politician is likely to perceive these questions as hostile, and may have a tendency to retaliate against the questioner. Especially if the politician becomes tangled in contradictions of his own making. So be aware of the hazards if you choose this technique.

Certainly, the voters place some degree of trust in their political candidates, and this implies the voters believe the politicians are not complete crooks; otherwise they would not bother voting. Most people believe that government does perform valid functions in society and deserves some degree of support from the citizenry.

You, as a voter, are the final decider when you exercise your wisdom in the election of contenders for public office. You get to make your own judgment on whether to believe them, and which candidate to support.

Problems with Government

Now let us consider a few items that we, as typical citizens, find objectionable about dealing with a government agency. Also, we should see if we could propose a way to make its service more satisfactory while still accomplishing the intended function.

One function of government that most people are familiar with is the Department of Motor Vehicles or DMV. This where you go to get a driver's license, obtain license plates for your car, or record the title for your new vehicle. We have all waited in line at one of these government bureaus to transact our business with the state. Each DMV is set up by a state or county government, has its own rules and regulations, and it is the only location where the particular service is offered.

Perhaps you have gone to one of these agencies to get your license plates. You wait in a long line before you get to talk to the person behind the counter, only to learn you have been waiting in the wrong line.

"Oh, you want a license plate? This is the driver's license line; the license plate line is over there. Yes, you need to go to the end of the line and start over. Can't you read the signs we have clearly posted where you entered the room?"

After waiting in the license plate line, you finally reach the clerk, only to be informed that you have filled out the wrong form.

"Oh, you need plates for a *new* car? This form you filled out is only to renew plates for a car where you already have the plates from last year. Go back over to that counter by the wall and get the proper form, and fill it out completely before you get back to me. Yes, you will have to go to the end of the line again. It would be unfair to the others waiting to butt in front."

When you finally return to the clerk with the correct form, filled out properly, he puts his rubber stamp on it and directs you to the cashier's line where you may pay the fee with a check or money order. Cash is not accepted, because of the security problems associated with handling large quantities of real money. Of course, the cashier's line is the longest one in the room, because the people from all the other lines end up there eventually.

Once you have paid the fee, you get to stand in the line for picking up your license plates. Notice that a police officer is always present on the premises to maintain order among the frustrated citizens.

Could you design a more efficient operation for this DMV office that still meets the legal requirements for issuing license plates to citizens? Of course you could, and so could anyone with a high school diploma. So why does the government maintain such an inefficient operation? Because it has a monopoly with the sole power to issue license plates. It does not have to compete with any other agencies in the business of the DMV. Once it is set up, and staffed with a particular number of government employees, it can continue to operate as long as it is funded by the state legislature. It doesn't need to earn a profit, it doesn't need to be efficient, it doesn't need to be convenient for the citizens it was established to serve.

If we were to turn over this DMV function to the private sector, a businessman would probably set it up more like a bank, where any clerk could handle any function required by the customer, be it license plates, titles, or driver's licenses. The clerk would also be able to perform the cashier's function, and accept cash, too. The businessman running this operation would need to compete with other businessmen in the same market, and thus he would strive to make the experience pleasing to his customers, so that they would return to his place of business the next time, rather than go to his competitors. On busy days he would have more clerks on duty, or he could extend his hours of operation. He would be competing with others for your business. The one who provided the most satisfactory shopping experience would earn the most business and thus earn the most profits. The most efficient businessman would earn the contract for the next year, thus reducing cost to the taxpayers.

If it is so obvious that the private sector could provide the same functions as government agencies, but with more efficiency and at lower cost, why doesn't the government adopt the better practice? Power. The government bureaucracy is a lifelike creature that strives to survive in its environment. It grows and extends its tentacles into more and more areas of influence, unless it meets competition from a larger special interest. Unless it is challenged by a large enough number of disaffected citizens, the legislature will continue to fund its inefficient operation. Most people have enough to worry about in their own lives without trying to challenge the wasteful practices of government, and the common belief is that you can't fight city hall. So government grows bigger and bigger, sapping ever more and more of the productive forces of a free economy. The burdensome interference of power-hungry legislators grows with the increase in government control over the liberty of citizens. Remember that profit is the food of business. A business will die if it cannot earn a profit in its market. Government agencies have the unfair advantage in that they do not need to worry about profits. Power is the favorite food of politics, and government is a political creature.

Misdirection

Were you ever misdirected by a government employee? Did you get faulty information that caused you to spend time solving some problem that later turned out to be unnecessary, so you had to start over? This practice has become known as the bureaucratic runaround, which is a fine art practiced by too many government employees.

A particularly stark example is provided by a retired county worker who liked to tell a story about the stupid citizens who would come into his office seeking copies of documents his agency was in charge of maintaining. He would carefully explain, using the bureaucratic language of his department, how that document was actually maintained by the office in the basement of city hall, three buildings down the street. When the customer left, our bureaucrat would make a bet with his colleague at the next desk as to how long it would take before the citizen came back to their office, still looking for the same document. When the citizen returned, our bureaucrat would apologize profusely about misunderstanding the nature of the document the citizen was seeking, using obtuse terminology to obfuscate his deception.

While this game can be very amusing for the government employees, it is actually a minor crime (intentional deception, lying) perpetrated against the unsuspecting citizen, and illustrates just another type of government waste.

How does this government employee get away with this type of behavior? He knows his job is secure as long as he does not cause embarrassment to his boss. He has no incentive to serve his customers efficiently. He is on a specified salary that will increase only with his seniority in the bureaucracy. It makes no difference to him career-wise if he is helpful and pleasant to his customers or if he is obstructive and gruff. His customers are stuck dealing with him, because his government agency has the monopoly on providing the service. The brief power wielded by his position of authority in a government agency is easy to abuse if he allows his ethical integrity to slip.

For this reason alone, a single-payer medical insurance system is a frightful concept. Granting a monopoly to the government, on paying for medical care, or any other business that is the real job of professionals in the private sector, guarantees fraud, abuse and inefficiency. It invites political, bureaucratic decision-making and incompetent control over a business that should be the province of doctors and other medical professionals. Competition between businesses in a free market is the most efficient method to provide any product or service to mankind.

IRS

The Internal Revenue Service (IRS) has a toll-free number you may call for help with interpreting the complex tax laws. Let us say you rely on the advice you get from one of these consultants, and fill out your tax forms accordingly. When it later turns out that the consultant gave you faulty advice, you are still the one responsible for the error, along with the resulting taxes, penalties and interest. But, hey, the advice was free. Well, it wasn't really free, it was provided by the taxpayers who funded the government agency. Is this not also waste, this service of advice without accountability? In our view this is a form of government malpractice with no accountability.

Water board

In June of the year 2010 the city of Charlotte, North Carolina, raised its water rates by 15 percent. This increase seems a little excessive to those of us who run businesses and wish to be fair to our customers. But the city was beset by a national recession, and Mother Nature refused to be so generous with her usual provision of rains, so the rivers and aquifers were running low. The city had already proclaimed watering restrictions, and limited lawn and garden watering to certain days of the week. The patriotic citizens responded with conservation efforts and cut back their water use to an impressive degree. The water department discovered that this reduced flow of water also reduced the flow of dollars to the city in payment of water bills. Thus the necessity for a healthy increase in water rates.

In later months, nature inevitably reverts to her average rainfall, and restores the flow of river and the level of aquifer. Do the city fathers also respond with a decrease in water rates? The reader is encouraged to investigate this question to satisfy his or her own curiosity.

Similar scenarios are repeated by government agencies across the country as standard operating procedure. In many cases the citizens, who have important matters requiring attention in their personal lives, simply don't notice. So the government gets away with another free ride on the backs of an inattentive electorate.

Gas Shortage

Here is a little story about how the government contributes to the suffering of its citizens by the unintended consequences of ill-considered legislation.

The people of Asheville, North Carolina, and surrounding areas, suffered a gasoline shortage in September of 2008, which lasted for about a month. Nearly everybody in the region was inconvenienced by this economic disruption to his or her normally carefree existence.

The underlying cause was the double-whammy of hurricanes Gustav and Ike. Hurricane Gustav struck Louisiana on September first. The storm was promptly followed by Ike, twelve days later, that hit Texas on Saturday, September 13. The storms disrupted the refinery industry and shutdown gasoline production for a time. The pipeline that carries gasoline from

Texas to the distribution center in Atlanta was affected by the interruption. Gasoline tanker trucks, which deliver the product from the distribution center to the neighborhood gas stations, were idled for a few days.

First news of the impending shortage in Asheville was announced Monday on one of the local radio stations. The reporter said that some of the gas station operators in town had been informed by their suppliers to expect disruptions in gasoline delivery. The announcer cautioned his listeners not to panic, and advised them to "not" go out and top-off their tanks, so that other citizens would have the opportunity to buy gas when they really needed it (wink, wink).

So what happened? Naturally, everybody who heard the report jumped in his car and rushed down to the local gas station to fill up before everyone else heard about it. The next day, an article in the newspaper described the developing shortage, with more cautions for people to avoid dashing-out to top-off their tanks. Of course, it was too late, because the gas stations were already sold out, and closed for the business of selling gasoline.

Since this is America, many people were confident the economy would rapidly respond to the emergency and soon replenish gas supplies, restoring their customary domestic tranquility. They were partially correct. After a month or so, gas stations were back to serving their customers in the usual fashion, without long lines, but the availability of all three grades of gas took a while longer to return to normal.

During the crisis, news reports were full of stories about people in gas lines waiting for two hours or more before reaching the pump. Some folks actually ran out of gas while waiting in line. Many were turned away when the gas station sold out. An occasional fracas broke out between frustrated citizens competing for their turn at the pump. Gas stations were limiting the dollar amount or number of gallons a particular individual was permitted to purchase during his session. Police responded to several fights, and their presence helped to maintain order.

Some charitable folks, or shall we call them enterprising business persons, delivered free pizza to the drivers waiting in line. Angels at other locations handed out complimentary donuts and coffee. Such behavior speaks well of the Americans who went out of their way to assist their fellow man in a bad situation, but the near riot conditions at some gas stations also demonstrated the dark side of people caught in a trying situation.

By October 16, about 34 days after the crisis began, a major grocery store chain in Asheville that also sells gasoline reported their stations were effectively back to normal. One might reasonably ask why it took a month for a gas shortage to be resolved when the people living in New York, Chicago, Los Angeles, and Denver weren't even aware of any gas shortage. Certainly, a fleet of tanker trucks from the Chicago area, where there was plenty of gas, could have delivered gas to Asheville in three days or so, if they had the incentive.

The culprit is the government of North Carolina, by having passed anti-price-gouging legislation, and these enlightened leaders have also guaranteed a similar crisis the next time any commodity becomes temporarily unavailable. In 2003, the North Carolina legislators noticed that some merchants had raised their prices in response to the difficulty of obtaining things to sell during natural disasters. Now anyone who actually attended his college classes in Economics 101 might recognize this universal principle as the law of supply and demand. However, the legislators observed that some merchants were trying to sell such things as gasoline, generators, batteries, drinking water and ice for exorbitant prices. This was simply not nice, and it was so very not nice, that the legislators decided to make it a crime. These representatives of the people therefore drafted legislation that seeks to "prevent merchants and others from preying on the public at a time of disaster by selling goods or services at unreasonably excessive prices."

North Carolina defines price gouging as "intentionally charging an unreasonably excessive price under the circumstances for goods or services that are used by North Carolinians during an emergency." This prohibition applies to all parties in the distribution chain, including the manufacturer, supplier, wholesaler, distributor and merchant.

Who, we might ask, determines when a price is "unreasonably excessive?" The Attorney General of North Carolina will look at the vendor's price before the disaster and compare it with the vendor's price after the disaster. This one man, or his deputies, will tell you, Mr. GasStationOwner, after the fact, that your price was too high under the circumstances. There is a civil penalty of $5000 per violation. A person who is the victim of price gouging can bring a civil action for damages (which may be tripled), attorney's fees and court costs. So, if you are a GasStationOwner, or other business operator, you should be aware of this anti-price-gouging law.

What happens when our GasStationOwner knows about this law? Say he has been selling his gasoline for $3.60 gallon (the typical price in Asheville before the shortage), and he learns that his supplier will not be able to make any more deliveries until several days after the usual schedule. He now knows that the gasoline in his underground tanks is worth more to him than it was yesterday. What he now wants to do is raise his price to the point where he will slow his sales so that he will not sell out until just before his tanker truck arrives to refill his storage tanks. That way he will be able to stay open for business continuously. Can he raise his price to $3.70 per gallon, a silly little dime? Maybe $3.75 would be fair for his customers. How about $3.96, which would be a ten-percent increase? Why not a 25% increase to $4.50?

Mr. GasStationOwner has no way to tell, until he actually raises his price to X, sells it for that, waits a few weeks for the Attorney General of North Carolina to review his higher price and decide that, yes indeed, his price increase was "unreasonably excessive." Perhaps our businessman could call the Attorney General's office to ask how much he is allowed to increase his price today, along with every other merchant in Western North Carolina. Certainly the North Carolina Attorney General's office has the telephone lines and personnel to efficiently handle this volume of calls.

So our GasStationOwner fears the government's power to penalize him for raising his price, realizing that he cannot afford a $5000 fine, if he is later found in violation. So he leaves his price the same at $3.60 per gallon. When the hoards of customers arrive to clean him out at the now artificially low price, his tanks are soon empty, and he must shut down his business for a few days, and lay off all his employees, until the next tanker arrives to refill his storage tanks.

Does this not cause our business owner to be worse off than he would be if he were allowed to raise his price and stay open for business? Does this not cause his employees to be worse off because they become unemployed for a few days and do not earn their hourly wage while waiting for the next tanker truck to arrive?

How does our gasoline consumer behave in this situation? He hears on the radio that a shortage of gas is likely to develop, so he runs over to his local gas station and fills up. Then he goes home and promptly takes his other car to fill it up too, even though he doesn't really need the gas right now. The result is that the gas station quickly runs dry. A typical station, under normal conditions, will get gas deliveries about every two days. During panics, customers can drain the tanks dry in six to eight hours.

But let us say, just for the sake of argument, that there are no government price controls, and the free market determines the price of gas. In this case, when our gasoline consumer hears on the radio that a shortage of gas is likely to develop, he runs over to his local gas station to fill up. But our clever GasStationOwner is ahead of the game and has already raised his price in order to slow his sales. The customer must now decide if he truly needs to fill his tank today at the higher price, or if he should buy some smaller number of gallons that he actually needs. Also the consumer will be less likely to top off his other two vehicles at the higher price. If his business requires him to drive many miles every day he will think it worth the price to pay more for gas in order for him to continue operating his business. Other people, who do not need to drive very far every day, will stay home until the strong American economy quickly restores supplies to the gas stations and prices revert to their formerly reasonable levels.

How do the business operators in the supply chain respond when free market rules apply? They see that a certain region is running low on gasoline so the price there will be rising. They prefer to sell their product for a higher price, so they divert their tanker trucks to make deliveries in the higher price region, rather than sticking to their usual routes where prices are lower. If the price justifies it, a tanker trucker from Chicago would rather drive his load to North Carolina than sell it in Illinois where he could only get the cheaper price. This automatic response of free market capitalism ensures that gas is delivered to the areas where it is needed with the least delay.

What do business operators in the supply chain do when government price controls are in force? Since they don't wish to be harassed later by the Attorney General, they stick with their established price and make no effort to better serve their customers in the zone affected by the disaster. Why stick your neck out when you know there is no profit to be earned?

So now we see why government price controls guarantee shortages and extend the time that citizens must suffer economic disruption. Nevertheless, our citizens must be much happier because they have a visceral hatred of anyone who would take advantage of them by price gouging. We all would much prefer to see the same old price on our gas station sign, even if the sold-out sign is up as well.

Yeah, OK, but what about our government punishing the greedy bastards who engage in "real" price gouging? Capitalism has an automatic solution for that problem as well. When a customer feels that he has been taken advantage of by some vendor, he will simply not buy any more stuff from that vendor. He will instead go down the street and patronize the guy's competition. The greedy gouger will see his sales fall off after the emergency is over, and if enough of his customers are dissatisfied with his prices, his product, his service or his attitude, they all will go to some other vendor. The gouger's business will go down the tubes. Capitalism automatically resolves the problem, without any interference from the government. When the government regulates prices, it causes people to act in ways that are not beneficial to the economy as a whole.

America was founded on the concepts of individual freedom. Should not the owner of any property be free to determine at what price to sell it? Gasoline in the storage tanks of a gas station certainly qualifies as the property of the gas station owner.

Should one man in high government office have the power to decide, after the fact, that some merchant in Western North Carolina, trying to earn an honest living, sold his own property at too high a price? In some countries a man with this kind of power is called a dictator.

So how does a government bureaucrat in America obtain the power to decide how much some owner was entitled to sell his property for? Anti-price-gouging legislation. Some of us might argue that this law is unconstitutional, and no doubt several judges would agree with us. But anti-price-gouging laws exist in several states.

Constitutionality

Speaking of government forays into unconstitutional behavior, several books have been written about this particular subject. One we can heartily recommend is *Constitutional Chaos,* by Andrew P. Napolitano, a judge of the Superior Court in New Jersey. Subtitled *What happens when the government breaks its own laws,* this book points out that government makes laws so that citizens may be punished for lying, cheating and stealing. Such laws are enforced vigorously, yet the government frequently lies to, cheats and steals from citizens without being held accountable. Judge Napolitano fearlessly reports the corruption he observed from his unique perspective, while on the inside of the U.S. court system. He provides many more examples of how our leaders in government misuse their power to the detriment of freedom and liberty of ordinary citizens.[1]

His chilling insights should be more widely perceived among the voting public in America, so that more citizens will demand greater ethical standards from their political leaders. Allow us to once more point out that the purpose of the Constitution is to protect the citizens of our country from the power of the government. Many of your leaders in government appear to be hostile to this concept.

In this chapter we have looked at a few examples of government insufficiencies. These are but a tiny fraction of the thousands of ways our governments waste resources and manpower, and interfere with the creation of wealth by citizens attempting to engage in legitimate commerce.

Notes:

[1] See Napolitano.

CHAPTER TWENTY-FOUR

BETTER GOVERNMENT

NOW that we have observed that governments seem to engage in practices that are inimical to the welfare of citizens, we should consider the
actual purposes of government, and define the valid functions that an ideal
government should provide. Note that we are operating under the assumption that a valid government should be established to serve its citizens, and
enable them to safely engage in those acts of commerce that are beneficial to
them. An ideal government should encourage its people to interact for their
mutual benefit, to stimulate the creation of wealth, and enhance domestic
tranquility. It should permit the people to engage in their own rational
self-interest.

Contrariwise, if the primary purpose of a government is to enslave its
people merely to serve the interests of the governing class, we can also find
such models of oppression in the world of today. A current example of this
type may be found in the North Korea of Kim Jong Il. Basically, this society
is a prison on the scale of a nation. The government takes authoritarian
control over every facet of a citizen's life, and exercises its power backed by
the threat of violence in a military regime. Any wealth created by the citizens through their labor is appropriated by the government. In our view this
is no different than theft on a national scale, which allows the powerful to
live extravagantly on the wealth produced by the common people, who are
forced to live in poverty.[1]

However, the purpose of this chapter is to investigate better forms of
government, so let us review the forces that lead to the establishment of any
government in the first place.

When people get together to form a group or a tribe, the pecking order
principle goes into effect, and the members of the group are sorted into

a hierarchy. In a primitive society, one of the individuals becomes chief, usually because he is the biggest or meanest. In more advanced societies, sometimes the chief is automatically determined, because he is the one who called the meeting. If you have ever been a member of a new group at your workplace, you have seen this group dynamic play out. In 1965, Bruce Tuckman wrote an article about the stages of social interaction in group dynamics, and labeled them forming, storming, norming, and performing[2] Most people gain an intuitive appreciation of this concept when they first hear of it. The next time you are involved in a new group situation, watch for these stages as they develop.

Once a new tribe has become established as a lifelike creature, it will need to compete with other tribes in its vicinity, and another pecking order dynamic will develop among the tribes. The interactions between the individuals and groups of the various tribes, the life forms and lifelike forms, become extremely complex, but a hierarchy of behaviors soon develops. As the population grows and tribes form into city-states, kingdoms, nations and empires, the pecking order principle still applies, and every lifelike creature competes against the others for domination, territory, influence and power. The history of peoples on our planet has been one of continuous intertribal warfare, with brief interludes of peace, growth and prosperity. After a benign period of relative abundance, the barbarians would rise up again, and society would devolve back into anarchy, continuing the cycle.

Despite numerous setbacks, civilization advanced and the standard model of government became the kingdom, where power was concentrated in one individual who controlled nobles, who controlled the peasants. The king claimed ownership of all land and property, and was free to use it or distribute it as he saw fit. As civilization advanced under this model, the nobles began to demand access to more of the power the king had customarily reserved to himself. In 1215, the Magna Carta marked a major turning point in history, where King John of England agreed to allow his nobles certain rights to conduct their lives with more freedom, and to recognize that a king may be bound by the law.[3] King John did not offer these rights out of the goodness in his heart; they were extracted from him under the threat of civil war by his barons. Some of the rights thus granted seem intuitively obvious to us as modern day citizens, but the written Magna Carta was the origin of them in law. The most notable concept that has survived from Magna Carta into the law of today is habeas corpus, or the protection against illegal imprisonment.

In following ages, the nobles succeeded in extracting more and more power from the various kings, as parliaments and legislatures took over decision-making and the establishment of laws. The death of King Henry VIII in 1547 marked another turning point in history where the absolute power of the king, the divine right, began fading to a significant degree.

When the thirteen colonies formed in the New World, the colonists discovered the advantages of freedom, and learned they could govern themselves more satisfactorily than being tied to the policies of a distant king. The founders of the United States wrote a constitution defining the limited powers of a federal government, separated into three branches of executive, legislative and judicial. The three branches were designed with checks and balances to prevent any one from becoming too powerful. The guiding principle was that the new government should derive its just powers from the consent of the governed. Under this concept, individual freedom and liberty were released among the citizens, creating the most successful nation the world has ever seen.

Note that the purpose of the Constitution, and of Magna Carta before it, was to protect the citizens from the power of government. More basically, the idea is for the rules in the foundation document to protect the individual from the power of the group. This principle is still true today, and is even more important as government grows and tries increasingly to invade the rights and liberties of its citizens.

Since we, as modern people, have a vast historical database of the successes and failures in the many types of governments, we should be able to select a style of government that would be most advantageous to a civilization. We have previously discovered that virtue is best served, and evil is significantly discouraged, when a balance of power exists between competing human life forms and lifelike forms. The government selected should thus be a republic or a democracy to spread power most widely, and to allow the largest number of citizens to influence the leaders they select to govern them. The government should base its laws on the primary imperatives of civilization, which are to deter killing and stealing. Our ideal government will also strive to facilitate trade in free markets that permit people to engage in practices that enhance their own rational self-interest. The invisible hand of commerce, operating under the forces of capitalism, will then produce a vibrant and successful economy, and a strong, fair and free society.

A government is also a lifelike form that must compete against other governments for survival. It thus has the imperative to protect itself from the competing governments (nations) that wish to kill it or steal its stuff (property). A government lifelike form will have cell analogs to the biological life form, and these cell analogs are, of course, its citizens. A government will therefore need to field an army. Recent experience has shown that a volunteer military force best fits this requirement, in order to preserve the freedom and liberty of its citizens.

When a government makes a law it presumes it has the power to enforce that law. To enforce a law it must have coercive power over the individuals in the group, its citizens. In action, this is the power of the group over the individual. The government will thus create a police force and system of courts to enforce the laws and decide questions of dispute between citizens.

When an individual desires to join a group, he must agree to abide by the rules of the group. So to become a citizen, the man gives up his option to take the law into his own hands. He gives up his option to exercise force, violence or coercion against any other individual in his society. He agrees to respect the rights of the others, as defined by the government. When he has a grievance against another man and cannot settle his complaint with peaceful negotiation, he must go to the group for resolution, and accept the group's judgment. When he does this he will either win or lose, but he is bound to be satisfied with the outcome by going through the lawful process. He does this by taking his grievance to his police department or to his lawyer and the justice system of the courts.

The police departments, and the law and court system, are staffed by professional people whose duty it is to investigate crimes, and to determine the guilty party in each case. The individual victim of a crime is not allowed to perform this function for himself, because he does not have the training and independent judgment to arrive at unbiased decisions. He would likely come to a hasty conclusion blaming an innocent party, and thus compound the injustice. The power of the group is better able to achieve justice for both the victim and the perpetrator.

Every citizen must follow this same process, regardless of his profession. The butcher, baker or candlestick maker, the chief of police, the mayor, the governor of the state, or the president of the country must all embrace independent investigation of disagreement, misdemeanor or felony, whether he is victim or suspect. He must never allow his personal interest to interfere with the fairness and balance of the law applying evenly to all citizens. In any investigation, an unbiased third party, familiar with the appropriate law, should be employed to decide. A properly functioning law and court system provides this service to society. Thus a major purpose of government is to guarantee the rule of law over the rule of men. This is another example of a balance of power enhancing virtue.

Note how everyone understands this concept of fairness, but every individual also harbors the animal instinct to watch out for himself, so the integrity of enforcing the law without bias is frequently compromised.

When a government makes a law to forbid stealing or theft among its citizens, this concept implies an underlying right for an individual to own property. Carried further, this principle requires our ideal government to make laws to enforce contracts. Contracts are agreements between citizens to define the privileges and obligations of the parties over some form of property.

Note that in a socialist government, where the state or the group retains ownership of all property, or even a particular item of property, agreements or contracts between individuals regarding that property have no validity. The socialist concept destroys any motivation of the individual to respect property, since he feels he owns it as much as does anyone else, and he wishes to maximize his own benefit from it. Thus his behavior towards that property reverts to anarchy. He cannot respect another man's rights to an item of property when the other man has no unique claim to that public property. Therefore, contracts under socialism become impossible to enforce.

Returning to consideration of our ideal government, let us summarize the ideas we have presented in this chapter. The ideal government should:

1) Maximize virtue and minimize evil.
2) Be organized as a constitutional republic in which the just powers of the state are derived from the consent of the governed.
3) Operate under the rule of law.
4) Establish an army to defend its citizens from foreign power.
5) Reserve the exercise of force, violence and coercion to the state, under carefully defined restrictions.
6) Establish a fair and equitable legal system to enforce the rights of all citizens.
7) Enforce contracts.

In order to meet these goals, it is essential for the people who operate a government organization to exercise their virtues of honesty and integrity.

Rights

These defined functions of government lead us to consider the rights that a government should guarantee to its citizens. We will start with the rights extended to citizens of the United States, which are found in the Declaration of Independence and the Constitution.

People are entitled to life, liberty and the pursuit of happiness. They retain the right to self-defense, which is grounded in the imperative of life, which is survival. The right to self-defense leads to the right to bear arms.

We have the right to express our opinion on any subject, which leads to free speech, and freedom of the press. We are granted the right to form groups with likeminded people, which results in freedom of religion, freedom to peaceably assemble, and to petition the government for redress of grievances.

We retain the right to be secure against unreasonable searches and seizures in one's person, houses, papers and effects. This rule derives from the basic prohibition against theft by individuals, which carries over to protect people from the power of the group, or the government.

If accused of a crime, the citizen has the right to trial by jury, is protected against double jeopardy, cannot be compelled to testify against himself, nor be deprived of life, liberty or property without due process of law. The accused is entitled to a speedy and public trial, and the assistance of council for his defense. This is the habeas corpus principle that flowed from Magna

Carta. An accused may not be held for excessive bail, have excessive fines imposed, nor be subjected to cruel and unusual punishments.

Slavery is proscribed in our society, as an extension of liberty and citizenship to ethnic groups, the members of which were previously classified as property rather than persons.

The right to vote is extended to all citizens regardless of race, color, creed, place of national origin or sex, but limited to those over a certain age of majority.

The preceding list covers most of the rights granted to the people of the U.S., but many more human rights have been proposed by various well-meaning groups.

One well-known version of this type of document is the *Universal Declaration of Human Rights*, which was adopted by the Untied Nations General Assembly in 1948, with the goal of eradicating the atrocities observed during the two world wars. The UDHR consists of thirty articles, which generally cover the rights mentioned above, with such additional rights as:

Social security, a right to work under favorable remuneration, equal pay for equal work, limitation of working hours and grants of periodic holidays with pay, an adequate standard of living, food, clothing, housing, medical care, unemployment and disaster compensation, and a right to education.

By now the reader should be able to recognize such additional rights as socialist concepts where grants of free property are awarded to people who have not earned them. Since Chapter 18 in this book we have been emphasizing the primacy of the individual and his own responsibility to care for himself and his own interests.

People must be permitted to suffer from their own mistakes; otherwise they will not learn their lessons on how to take care of themselves. An individual who depends on others to get him out of jams will thus become a burden on the rest of society. He will not be a producer but only a consumer. He will be like the young adult who refuses to leave home and go out into the world by himself to earn his own living. After he has 20 years of education he still finds it easier to continue sponging off the old man who cannot bear to release the child to the realities of the world. When we move from the family model of father and son, to the larger model of government and citizen, we can see the similarities.

A human child is like any other animal that must learn from his mother how to survive in the big bad world. If he fails to learn the lessons on how to flee when the predator appears, he will not be around tomorrow to contribute to the welfare of the herd. A poorly trained or over protected citizen likewise will become a drag on his society rather than a contributor to its success. Problems of the human condition may best be resolved by people working in an environment of freedom for their own rational self-interest. The people demanding additional rights, such as the ones proposed by the UDHR, are merely feeding at the public trough without an obligation to provide for their own welfare. When a government provides these additional rights, they must be first financed by taxpayers who are productive, who do the work that generate the assets, which are then taxed.

Charity

How then do we as a community care for those individuals who are less able to care for themselves? Are we not obligated as virtuous members of humanity to provide for those among us who are less fortunate? We can see by looking around us that many human beings are inherently compassionate for their fellow man. Why? Because most of us grow up in a loving family environment where we eventually realize that we can accomplish more when we cooperate with others, rather than when we only fight for narrow personal selfishness. We discover that when we get along with our fellows it also serves our rational self-interest.

Look in your local telephone directory, the yellow pages, and count the number of churches, synagogues, and mosques that are to be found in your own community. Most of these religious organizations will be supporting charities. Membership in these groups is voluntary, because the government is prohibited (in the U.S.) from establishing a mandatory state religion. The charitable functions of these groups arise from the teachings of their founders, and must strike a sympathetic note in the hearts of the members because so many of these groups exist, and membership is voluntary.

Now turn to the "charities" section of the phone book and count the number of secular organizations, which are not sponsored by religious groups. All of these charitable organizations are funded by voluntary donations from people who might instead spend those same dollars on more self-serving pursuits. Ergo, humans have heartfelt compassion for those less fortunate than themselves.

Note that all of these charities exist on top of, or in addition to, or despite, the government-mandated charities that are financed with your tax dollars. We are obligated to pay our taxes, whether we want to or not, because the government has the power of the group to put us in jail or otherwise restrict our freedom if we do not comply with the tax laws. Nevertheless, all of those voluntary secular and religious charities also exist in our society, because we, in our modern civilization, are so generous. It is in our rational self-interest to support our less fortunate brothers, because we would expect our community to give us a hand if we found ourselves on the wanting side of the ledger. The famous Golden Rule becomes operative: Do unto others, as you would have them do unto you. The concept of rational self-interest is a corollary of the golden rule.

Is there a limit to our capacity for charity? When we observe that a receiver of our largess seems to have a limitless capacity to accept more help without any attempt to try to make it on his own, perhaps we would become less inclined to continue our generosity. Does a government program that offers free assistance have a similar feedback loop? What about the honest employee who is laid off from his job and goes on welfare or on government provided unemployment insurance? When he goes seeking a new job, is he "really" looking for a job, if the pay scale is only a little greater than his welfare payment? Perhaps he might find it easier to game the system and remain on welfare for the maximum time, than to seriously seek employment.

What about the able bodied worker who cannot bear to get out of bed in the morning to go to his job? When he is late for work too many times he gets fired. Does he deserve assistance from a government program? How many government workers must be employed at taxpayer expense to keep track of all these details?

Let us speculate, just for the sake of argument, that the government gradually eased away from supporting so many of its "charitable" giveaways. Would not the victim of some employment misfortune be more motivated to fend for himself if he knew the government would not automatically bail him out? Would not the natural charitable instincts of our civilization fill the void? No doubt a more efficient distribution mechanism would arise due to "market" forces in the charitable "industry." Governments need not force charity out of the pockets of the citizens. The voluntary goodness in everyday people can handle the necessity. Furthermore, what do wealthy industrialists do with their obscene hoards of riches? After they have provided thousands of jobs to facilitate the livelihoods of their employees and suppliers, they choose to give much of it away to worthy causes. Andrew Carnegie is a famous example from a century ago. Bill Gates is a famous example from our contemporary society.

The wealthier a society becomes, the greater is its capacity to share its wealth with those less fortunate. In Chapter 7 we defined wealth as goods made by man, and discussed how wealth is created by the labor of man. Note that government does not create wealth; it can merely appropriate wealth by its power over the individual, its power to tax. A government may redistribute wealth, but it must obtain wealth by taking it from the individuals who produce it. Any government should thus establish an environment that encourages its citizens to create wealth. To this end, we would suggest free trade in a capitalist system to motivate people to act in their own rational self-interest, with as little government interference as possible. We have seen that laissez-faire capitalism best fits the bill.[4]

Notes:

[1] For an interesting account of one person's "vacation" to partake of the thrills offered by the Democratic People's Republic of Korea(sic), read the 2008 article by SungHa Park in The Wall Street Journal, *Road Trip in a Strange Land; Tourists Now Can Drive to a North Korean Resort.* See Park.

[2] See Tuckman.

[3] See Magna Carta.

[4] Laissez-faire: from the French for "allow to act."

CHAPTER TWENTY-FIVE

OTHER FUNCTIONS OF GOVERNMENT

PERHAPS the reader has noticed a developing theme of this book, that government control should be reduced to achieve a more advantageous balance of power in civilization. The government should allow individual liberty, freedom, and opportunity to flourish among its citizens, so they might act in their own best interest, and thus create the greatest wealth and prosperity the people's ingenuity can accomplish. The rising tide will lift all boats, says the popular metaphor, and all sectors of society will benefit from the prosperity generated by ambitious people. The productive citizens who earn the profits and who are allowed to retain their earnings will do the best, while the less productive will also benefit from the inevitable gains in societal infrastructure and the increased charitable assets that prosperity pumps into private and public organizations.

In keeping with another theme of this book, competition is the basic conflict between any two lifelike forms. In this case we are considering the government vs. the populace or the electorate, which is similar to a king vs. his subjects, or more generally as the rulers vs. the ruled. The government has power over the people, yet the people are the source of wealth that the government needs to survive. The people need the government to provide them with a secure environment in which to pursue their commerce, so they put up with the government's control over their lives, yet they resent the government's intrusions into their freedoms. Over time, an equilibrium develops between the opposing forces, and life goes on under a balance of power that is constantly shifting to a small degree. The government, as a lifelike form, a bureaucracy, wants to grow and increase its influence. The electorate sometimes notices the government's attempts at power grabs, and resists the passage of new laws by writing letters to the editor and to their congressional representatives. When the government goes too far, the voters do not reelect the incumbent legislators, and replace them with new representatives.

We wish to emphasize that individual freedom and the liberty of good people to choose their own way is the source of progress in any society. Governments, by over-exercise of their powers, limit the people's ability to achieve their potential. Although we might apply this idea to any country in the world, we need look no further than the United Sates to see that government has grown too powerful for the good of modern civilization.

In the previous chapter we discussed a few of the valid tasks of government, which have been called the protective function, wherein the government creates rules for order and security in its society. Government should provide the people with protection for their lives, properties and liberties, to insure that their possessions are not taken from them by force, violence, fraud or theft. The government should prevent people from harming one another, encourage harmonious interaction, and enforce contracts. When people are confident they will not be cheated, they will have the incentive to work and create prosperity for themselves and for society.[1]

If the wealth people earn is taken by intruders, or by the government in the form of taxes, onerous regulations, or inflation, they will have little incentive to work hard and take necessary risks. If the government handles its protective function poorly, private ownership rights will suffer. Bad people will take property that does not belong to them, or use it without paying. Markets will not reflect the true cost of doing business, and the economy will stagnate. When freedom and individual initiative are allowed to flourish, people will instinctively generate abundance.

Governments have another valid function, which is to provide those things that are known as public goods. This is also called the productive function, where government takes over activities that are not handled well by private businesses. When no direct connection exists between the producer of a good and the customer who uses it, a free market fails to develop. Examples of the productive function of government are national defense, roads and bridges, flood control dams, and the local fire department. How would a conventional business charge its customers for the benefits of a flood control dam? If a certain customer refused to pay his monthly bill, how would the company withhold its flood control from his property? By the government creating a taxing district to distribute the costs among the people living downstream from the dam, the people who benefit pay a proportional amount. On the other hand, the government would have no business running a manufacturer of light bulbs or of automobiles, because these are private goods. If a customer refused to pay for his light bulbs he could not take them home from the store. Neither could he use his neighbors' light bulbs for free.

Air and water pollution result because of the difficulty in tying the use of these resources to paying customers. All people get their air for free so they are not careful to treat it with respect and not damage it for use by the next guy. As a result, most metropolitan area governments have an ordinance against burning trash outdoors or in fireplaces. Smoke dirties the air and makes it unhealthy for the neighbors to breathe.

Lakes, streams and rivers are likewise difficult to restrict to people who will pay for their use of the water. A plot of land, on the other hand, can be titled to an individual or corporation with clear property rights. When an owner is done with his land he will want to sell it for the best price, so he will maintain it in good order during his ownership. When the government leases national forest land to a lumber company for harvesting the mature timber, it should require as part of the deal replanting of new trees to restore the resource for the next generation, and a future harvest. If the lumber company owned the land itself, we can be sure it would carefully prepare for the next crop, as would a farmer who owned his cornfield.

So now we have a complete picture of the valid functions of government.

Protective functions:
Provide for the national defense.
Protect citizens from criminal behavior.
Enforce contracts.

Productive functions:
Provide for public goods.

All other needs of society should grow out of the natural spirit of the people, working in their own rational self-interest, through free trade under free competition in a capitalist environment. It is human nature for people to sew and reap. If the government does not interfere with the harvest by imposing taxes or limiting prices, people will have the incentive to sew and reap with exuberance.

What are some of the specific things governments do today that are counterproductive and should be avoided or discontinued? In the book *Common Sense Economics* (see Notes, below) a list of seven items may be found in Part III, Section 10, under "A Positive Program for Prosperity," which includes a paragraph expanding upon each item. The following list includes several of their ideas.

A. Allowing able-bodied citizens to feed at the public trough without reasonable limits or without an obligation to regain their own ability to fend for themselves.
B. Providing subsidies to special interest groups.
C. Failing to require a balanced budget, except perhaps in time of war.
D. Taking of private property for public use without paying the owner full market value.
E. Interfering with free competition in trade.
F. Imposing taxes, tariffs or quotas on either imports or exports.
G. Attempting to regulate prices, either as a maximum or minimum.
H. Regulating wages or compensation, either as a minimum wage or as a maximum remuneration for highly paid executives. Free market forces will reliably and automatically find the best prices for products, commodities and services when unhindered by government interference.
I. Spending money it does not have.

Bills authorizing government expenditures are currently approved by a majority vote in the legislature. Many of the abuses in government would be eliminated if expenditures were subject to a two-thirds or three-quarters supermajority vote. Special interests would thus find it more difficult to impose their self-serving and unnecessary costs upon the rest of society.

Before concluding this chapter, we would like to expand upon two subjects that are not widely understood among many of our citizens today, credit and minimum wages.

Credit

What is the one subject that causes the most difficulty in any economy? Credit, or when viewed from the other side, debt. Credit allows people to have things now, yet pay for them later.

When credit is granted wisely it has the potential to multiply economic strength and permit people to achieve greater benefits than they could if they were only allowed to invest the wealth they had already earned.

Many people see the advantages in being able to borrow enough money to buy a house to live in while taking on the obligation to pay it back over thirty years. We can understand how a corporation might take out a loan to purchase the equipment to outfit a factory with the goal of manufacturing trucks, and also provide employment for hundreds of workers. These projects can be successful and pay back their loans over the life of the projects, but interest rates for such loans must be high enough collectively to cover the loans that do default.

When a debtor falls hopelessly behind on his payments and his creditors hound him unmercifully, he will declare bankruptcy, and basically seek to start his financial life over from zero, rather than keep trying to dig himself out from his substantially negative position. In this case his creditors take the hit, which spreads his losses over a larger number of people. Presumably, the creditors each hold a smaller portion of the debtor's losses, and have the capacity to absorb the pain, yet continue in business. We could also view this situation as the larger economy contracting to cover the losses.

When credit is granted to people who have no chance of ever paying back the loan, much less of paying both the principal and interest, a built in default is inevitable. When credit is extended to people who may not have the capability to eventually pay it back, the interest rate needs to be high enough to cover the creditor's risk that the debtor will default. When too many debtors are granted credit that overwhelms their ability to repay, a recession results, which was the case leading to the recession of 2008 and 2009. The entire economy must bear the burden of the defaulted loans, so everyone must pull back on their expenditures, which requires less and less output from the economy, which further reduces demand and employment, thus deepening the recession. This vicious cycle has been described as a self-eating watermelon.

Governments are particularly fond of spending money they don't have. It allows the politicians to give away free goodies to their constituents, which is viewed by many voters as party time. Government calls this technique "borrowing" when it recognizes that it has an obligation to pay the money back later, or merely "deficit spending" when it does not. The federal government also has the option of printing new money, which causes inflation. The end result of these three techniques is the same, in that the economy has less of the capital it needs to function smoothly.

Unwise credit expansion is the cause of the boom-and-bust cycles we see consistently in the history of civilization. Many economists actually understand these phenomena and know how to smooth out the cycles to avoid recessions and depressions. However the vast majority of politicians, who are responsible for making the laws that the rest of us must abide, either do not understand economics, or do not want to. We suspect that many politicians find the wielding of power, regardless of the consequences, to be much more fun than would be responsibly managing the interests of a prosperous civilization.[2]

Minimum wage

What is a reasonable minimum wage? One dollar an hour? Ten? $100? Every increase in the legally required minimum wage merely eliminates more entry-level jobs from the economy. If a job's costs exceed the job's benefits to the employer, the job will be eliminated. Any wage or salary is an expense to a business. If the expense exceeds its usefulness to the business it will be dropped. If a ten dollar minimum wage is good for a worker, then a $400 minimum wage should be even better. Most workers would jump at the chance to earn $400 per hour, wouldn't you? But most people can see the job-destroying nature of a $400 minimum wage, or at least spot its inflationary potential. Should not any worker be entitled to a living wage so he can survive on his job? How many hours a week should he be required to work before he is allowed to rest? Who gets to decide these questions? Free markets under free competition automatically find the fairest price and wage for everybody, worker and employer alike.

Can you hire a young person to babysit at your house for a few hours for reasonable wage? How can you determine what that wage should be? Ask the babysitter how much she will charge for her services, or offer her some hourly rate that the two of you can agree on? That seems like a reasonable, arms-length negotiation without any threat of violence or coercion on the part of either party to the agreement. But wait. The government has a minimum wage law. Does it apply to this simple arrangement? The government has child labor laws that protect innocent youth from exploitation by greedy industrialists. Do these laws apply to your employment of this young person? How about Social Security withholding from the funds you pay the child? Is she your employee or an independent contractor? Certainly she qualifies as a domestic servant under the nanny law. What happens if the baby falls out of the crib while the babysitter is watching TV in the next room? Does the babysitter have insurance for such an occurrence? Who is able to sue whom, and should they try? Do you sue the child or her parents? Can the babysitter sue the homeowner for misrepresenting the safety of their house? Can you sue the manufacturer of the crib?

Your government has an employee on the payroll who can answer all of these questions, if you want to spend hours on the phone trying to locate the proper department where you might pose your concerns. Most parents anticipating a night out will merely ignore all of these legal complications and hire the neighborhood kid to babysit for them, regardless. Have our babysitter employers thus committed a crime? Want to turn them in for a reward? Should any of this be the government's business?

Many a politician has gained notoriety by being snagged in the trap of the nanny tax. They hired someone to care for their child and paid them under the table, without accounting for Social Security tax. Their political opponents love to expose such transgressions, but you, as a private citizen, are less likely to get caught. If the government did not impose a minimum wage, or try to tax every conceivable monetary transaction, many of these questions would never arise.

Now that we have discussed the valid functions of government and a few of the many pitfalls of government excess, we know the guidelines to establish a prosperous civilization. Perhaps, if mankind ever gets the opportunity to set up an independent colony on a new planet, the lessons of freedom and capitalism will be allowed take root. These guidelines may also be used to reform the destructive policies of existing government.

Note how this opportunity to create an ideal government also occurred just before the founding of the United States. Unhappy peoples had fled oppressive regimes looking for the freedom offered by a new, primitive, empty continent, where they might have only nature to contend with. The imperious kings, who formerly claimed to own and control everything, were left far across the sea. The brilliant and inspired leaders who founded the United State of America in the late 1700's, created a society based upon the precepts of liberty and freedom, operating under free trade in a largely capitalist economic system, resulting in the most prosperous and uplifting civilization the world had ever known. The successes achieved by the United States of America during her first 150 years provide a shining example for the rest of humanity to observe and emulate.

Notes:

[1] *Commonsense Economics,* by Gwartney et al., is a brief and enjoyable introduction to the principles of economics that anyone should be able to read in a few days. We recommend it for all readers. Much of the material in this chapter is derived therefrom.

[2] We can heartily recommend four more books that expand upon the economic concepts we have mentioned in this chapter, and elsewhere throughout the book:
Economics in One Lesson, by Hazlitt, is a classic introductory economics book that has been used by educators for several decades. It should be required reading for anyone entering politics.
The Way the World Works, by Wanniski, is a clear account of supply side economics that includes numerous insights on a complicated subject.
How Capitalism Will Save Us, by Forbes et al., is an excellent account of economic principles written for the general reader.
Capitalism, by Reisman, is the magnum opus on economics that deals with every conceivable topic in the field. Be prepared to spend many days working your way through this thousand-plus page wonder.
See the bibliography for reference information.

CHAPTER TWENTY-SIX

COUNTY GOVERNMENT

LET us open this chapter with a brief discussion of how health, wealth, productivity and profit fit in with life, business and government.

It is necessary for your good health to divide your time between physical activity and sleep. Many people follow the custom of splitting their daily time into thirds; eight hours for work, eight hours for sleep, and eight hours for playing and tending to personal needs like eating. Sleeping and eating may be considered administrative functions of your life. While the administrative hours are important to your survival, the productive working hours are the ones that create wealth and pay the bills.

In the business environment, your employer wants to pay you only for your work hours. When your boss walks by, he wants to see you busy working at your job, not playing solitaire on the computer. He wants you to be productive while on company time. He is running a business that needs to make a profit by efficiently producing its products and services.

The customer of your business wants to pay only for the product or service you offer, not for extra fancy packaging or unnecessary administrative expenses. Your competitors strive to minimize their administrative costs, and so do you. Increasing productivity is important so that your business will earn more profits.

For any enterprise to be productive in the economic sense, it must be organized to earn a profit, otherwise it will be only a consumer of resources and not a contributor to productivity in the economy. Productivity implies that something new is left over, something of value that another person wishes to buy, after the effort and materials have been expended in the creation of the product. The success of productivity in the economy is measured by profit. A business that succeeds is one that earns a profit. A business that fails is one that cannot manage to earn a profit. Just like in natural selection, the life form that grows and prospers in its environment succeeds and propagates into the future. The life form that fails to grow withers and dies, and is eliminated from the ecology. A business is a lifelike form that must follow similar rules. Note that a government cannot be a profit making enterprise. Government is a parasite upon the productive members of society. Government gets its nourishment from taxes, which it takes from its citizens giving them no choice. The citizens do not choose to pay taxes because they want to, they are forced to pay or they will be punished. Although a government does provide services necessary to enable commerce, it is always an expense upon its citizens, it is an administrative function. Governments are also lifelike forms, which strive to grow and expand their influence and power, so they always reach beyond their valid functions and invade the territory that should remain in the free market economy. Therefore government is inevitably a burden on society, always a consumer, never a producer.

In the previous chapter we discussed the functions that an ideal government should concern itself with, and we looked at a number of ways that governments waste time, money and resources. Citizens are unavoidably beset with several layers of government. In the U.S., these governments include the federal level, the state, county, and finally the city or municipal governments. We have one federal government, 50 at the state level, some 3140 county (or county-equivalent) governments, while city governments are the most numerous at approximately 20,000. These numbers should give you an idea about the potential for mischief that your political leaders can get into. Every one of these government units has the power to tax (which is also the power to destroy),[1] and therefore they all have a responsibility to prudently exercise their powers for the benefit of the citizens. Or contrariwise, they have the power to oppress citizens to the benefit of the political class.

Let us now choose an actual example of a county government and analyze it in light of these ideas. We will look in Western North Carolina at Buncombe County,[2] because that is where the author lives, and he will find it convenient to access information about his local vicinity. Buncombe

County is one of 100 counties in North Carolina, and we will declare it to be of a "typical" size, since it is neither a major population center, nor a particularly rural area.

Buncombe County has a population of 206,330 (2000 census) spread over an area of 656 square miles. The major city and county seat is Asheville with population 68,889, and the other incorporated communities are Biltmore Forest (1440), Black Mountain (7511), Montreat (630), Weaverville (2416), and Woodfin (3162), containing a combined city population of 84,048, which leaves 122,282 people living in unincorporated regions of the county. This represents 41 percent urban population and 59 percent rural, if we may define these terms loosely.[3]

If we wish to estimate how many of these folks could have jobs and thus be contributing to the economy, we should subtract the people younger than 18, and also the seniors older than 65. The county records that split out these data tell us that 45,129 (22 percent) are younger than 18 while 31,776 (15 percent) are 65 and older. This leaves 129,425 possible workers.

Employment statistics for the county show a labor force of 106,066, with 100,924 actually employed. The employed people represent 49 percent of the overall population, or 78 percent of our estimated possible workers.

How many of these workers actually contribute to economic production? We concluded earlier that government activities are always administrative in nature and are thus burdens upon the productive forces in the economy. Since government workers are paid from tax receipts, we must subtract them from the list of economically productive laborers.

The county statistics split out worker categories as:

Private wage and salary	78979
Self employed	8118
Unpaid family workers	237
Government workers	13590
Total	100924

Presumably, private wage and salary workers, and self-employed people are working for profit making enterprises, and may thus be considered productive in the economic sense. We therefore subtract the government workers and unpaid family workers to arrive at our estimate of 87097 economically productive workers in the county. These are 42 percent of the total population and 82 percent of the labor force.

We can easily understand how less than half the workers are supporting the entire economy, because many people have spouses, children and aging parents to support. However, a generous portion of government employees (overall 13 percent of the employed) would certainly be more productively utilized by the private sector in profit earning endeavors.

Let us look at the voter registration records to determine how many people are actually interested enough in politics to want to influence the direction of their government. Of the total county population, 161,201 are over the age of 18, so most of these folks should be registered to vote. Voter registration in 2000 was 138,608, which represents 86 percent of the voting age population.

How do these county numbers compare with the statistics of the entire U.S.? The voting age population was 205,815,000 in 2000. 156,421,311 were registered and 105,586,274 actually turned out to vote. This is 76 percent registration and a 68 percent turnout of registered voters for the election. So Buncombe County voters are ahead of the nation is this respect. Voter turnout is usually in the 50 to 60 percent range for voting age citizens, or about 70 percent of registered voters in presidential election years, and down around 30 percent of voting age people in off-year elections.

Note that, as a reader of this book, you may compliment yourself on being an interested citizen. If you have not yet registered to vote, go out today and take care of this important privilege of your free society.

Large numbers

Before we discuss the county budget, we should note that not many people have an appreciation for the meaning of large numbers. We find it difficult to get our minds around the actual size of a billion dollars, because we have no reference for how much stuff that amount of money would buy. A million is 1000 thousands. A billion is 1000 millions, and a trillion is 1000 billions.

Most of us can internalize the amount of money we typically spend for groceries, or would have to pay to buy a car, or the amount we earn in a year. The average annual salary of a worker in the U.S. is $34,718. We can appreciate the price for a typical house, which is about $200,000. But when we hear about billions of dollars in the budgets of states or countries we really have no idea what that means.

To put it all in perspective, let us say that you wanted to buy up all the property in Buncombe County so you could build a fence around it and kick out all the people you don't like. How many dollars would this project cost to purchase the property?[4]

First, we need to count the number of houses, business locations, and empty lots in the county, and figure out how much each one would cost to buy. The county assessor is charged with the responsibility to determine the value of each parcel of real property in the county, for purposes of computing property tax bills. His estimates are based upon market value, but typically lag actual value by a few years because the numbers are updated on a four-year basis. Also, a farm property might be assessed at $25,000 for tax purposes, but when the owner decides to sell it for a housing development, he would be asking millions.

Of course, many properties are exempt from tax, because they belong to religious organizations, national forest, state or local park districts, government installations, etc. These exempt properties account for 43 percent of the county area, where 18 percent is totally exempt and the other 25 percent is partially exempt for land use purposes or discounted for elderly owners.

Nevertheless, if we add up all the assessed valuations, we will have an estimate of the amount we need to spend in buying as much of the county as possible.

Buncombe County has approximately 120,000 real estate parcels ranging from the largest, the Biltmore Estate at 8000 acres, down to the smallest condominium at maybe 500 square feet. The county provided the following estimates of total assessed valuation in July of 2009.

Residential properties	$18,864 million
Commercial properties	4,995 million
Industrial properties	324 million
Total	$24,183 million

So this rough estimate tells us it would cost us about 24 billion dollars to "buy" all the saleable real property in Buncombe County.

Expanding on this idea, we could estimate the value of the real estate in the U.S. If we make the wild assumption that Buncombe County is typical of all counties in the U.S., we could multiply our value of $24 billion by the 3140 counties and arrive at a price of roughly $75,360 billion to buy all the real estate in the country.

To check if this is a reasonable result, we could multiply the total population of Buncombe County by 3140 to yield 648 million, which is higher than the U.S. population of 282 million, by 2.3 times. This shows that Buncombe County has a larger population than the average county in the U.S. So we apply this 2.3 as a correction factor to reduce the value for the U.S. property to 32.7 trillion dollars. This exercise in fantasy yields a set of ballpark figures to help us understand the meaning of large numbers.

Cost for a week's groceries	$200
Average new car price	$20,000
Per capita personal income	$29,847
Average annual wage per job	$34,718
Average price of a house	$200,000
County population	206,000
Country population	282,000,000
Value of county property	$24,000,000,000
Per capita income x population	$8,400,000,000,000
U.S. Gross Domestic Product	$10,000,000,000,000
Value of country property	$33,000,000,000,000[5]

County budget

Returning to the statistics for Buncombe County, the annual budget for FY2009 was $316,801,139. County revenues, or sources of funds, break out as follows:[6]

Property tax	49.8 percent
Intergovernment	14.7
Sales and services	13.2
Sales tax	12.9
Other taxes and licenses	3.7
Appropriated fund balance	3.6
Other/transfers	1.6
Permits and fees[7]	0.6

The four largest categories account for 90.6 percent of revenues. Property tax is the largest source of county funds. This is the annual ad valorem tax applied mostly to real property owned by county residents and businesses. Intergovernmental revenues are received from federal agencies, state agencies, municipalities, and other counties. These funds are simply tax dollars transferred from other taxing districts to the county. Sales and services are dollars obtained by charging county customers for property and services provided by the various county agencies. Sales tax revenues come from the 2 percent tax on retail sales in the county (this on top of the 5.75 percent state sales tax, for a total of 7.75 percent).

County expenditures, on the other hand, break out as follows:

Human services	29.8 percent
Public safety	24.2
Education	21.3
General government	7.6
Insurance	5.2
Economic and physical development	3.3
Solid waste	2.6
Culture and recreation	2.5
Occupancy tax[7]	1.7

Human services, the largest portion of county expenditures, is actually government-supplied charity. It includes such things as social services, health center, Medicaid, animal shelter, child-care services and aging services, among others. Earlier chapters in this book have shown how government welfare is destructive of the need for people to care for themselves and pull their own weight. Public welfare is not included in the valid functions of an ideal government, as discussed previously.

Public safety, on the other hand, is a valid function of government. This category includes such services as the sheriff's department, emergency medical services, and court support.

Education, another biggie, covers expenditures for public schools in the county, Asheville city schools, and the Asheville-Buncombe Technical Community College. Public education has a long history in the United States, and every citizen who has grown up in the system has an opinion about it. Much ink has been spilled over its successes and shortcomings, but the administration of public schools has become a massive bureaucracy, and largely a government monopoly. Charter schools have become a competitive threat to the entrenched public schools' regime, and teachers unions resist all attempts to invade their established territory. Although charter schools demonstrate the superiority of competitive merit, they will continue to face an uphill battle for survival. Parents who are seeking better schools for their children represent a powerful force for change to a more efficient, competitive system.

A convincing argument to convert the public schools into a privately run system may be found in the book *The Machinery of Freedom* by David Friedman. Refer to his Chapter 10, "Sell the Schools."[8] In a competitive system, merit would determine the survival of the best, and eliminate the inadequate. The current system promotes too many ill-educated students, and allows failing schools to continue in operation.

If the economic drag of taxes for human services and education could be eliminated, this county government budget would be cut in half, releasing those funds to work in the economy providing those services in a much more efficient manner and expanding the economy in the process.

In this chapter we have taken a brief look at one government entity, one county government out of more than three thousand. There are more tens of thousands of municipal governments soaking up tax dollars and sapping economic strength from you and your fellow citizens.

Remember that government subsidy means economic waste. People working for their own rational self-interest in a free capitalist system create the highest degree of wealth obtainable, which benefits all members of society, both rich and poor.

Notes:

[1] The quotation, "The power to tax is the power to destroy," is attributed to Chief Justice John Marshall, whose dates are 1755 to 1835, in his opinion of 1819 on McCulloch vs. Maryland.

[2] Buncombe is pronounced "BUNK-um."

[3] The numbers used in this chapter are taken from various sources that are believed to be reliable, but our goal here is to make estimates with no particular necessity for precision. This should put us in the ballpark, so to speak, for purposes of this discussion.

[4] To buy an entire county would not actually be a practical thing to do, because somebody would eventually figure out what you were trying to get away with. Owners would refuse to sell you their property for anything near its assessed valuation, and others would refuse to sell at any price. To corner the market on all saleable property in a county would take careful planning and numerous front companies to disguise your ultimate plan.

[5] Numbers in this table are for U.S. baseline year 2000.

[6] These data are from the Buncombe County Annual Budget Report of 2008–2009 (FY 2009).

[7] The columns in these two charts do not total 100% due to rounding errors.

[8] See Friedman.

CHAPTER TWENTY-SEVEN

RECYCLE CITY

ALAS, now is the time to slaughter some sacred cows.[1] Actual sacred cows are a feature of Hindu culture, where cattle are revered for their gentle nature and for their many generous benefits freely offered to mankind. Milk, cream, butter, cheese, and manure are a few of the useful products attributed to cows. Also, some people believe that cows house the resurrected souls of human ancestors. For whatever reasons, cows are protected by law from molestation or maltreatment by people. They are free to roam the streets, trample your garden and eat the flowers from your window boxes. We might consider this practice as animal rights taken to a ridiculous extreme, but from a believer's perspective, it is eminently logical.

What sacred cows do we have in our own culture? How about recycling? Do you recycle a considerable portion of your trash? Of course you do, it is an ingrained part of our culture. You, like your humble author, have been recycling newspapers since you were a child, with the willing approval and guidance of your mother. After all, we must certainly reduce waste, conserve our valuable resources, and save trees from unnecessary destruction. Back in the olden days, let us say the 1950's, before the government mandated curb-side recycling in every city in America, the schools had newspaper recycling day. We would neatly tie up our old newspapers in a bundle with string. On a special day each month, we carted them over to the school parking lot and stacked them in neat piles. The class that recycled the most newspapers won a reward, and was honored by a plaque in the school trophy case.

Nowadays our city or county governments mandate that we dutifully sort our trash into bins of cans, glass, plastic, newspaper, cardboard, mixed papers, etc., and place them out at the curb for collection on the appointed day. And we also pay an extra fee on our trash bills for this privilege.

Is all of this extra labor and effort upon our trash actually worthwhile from an economic standpoint? Let us analyze recycling from a slightly different perspective.

Take the common practice of owning a set of china dinnerware. We may consider the re-use of these plates as a form of recycling, because we do not throw them away in the trash after each use. We need to wash the china we use every day, but we consider this more worthwhile than buying new plates all the time. On the other hand, we might just as well buy paper plates at the grocery store and throw them in the trash after each meal. This would avoid the hassle of washing dishes. Which of these options is more economic?

At the grocery store we have the choice of many types of picnic supplies and items for more formal dining. We find single-use paper plates, thin plastic dishes we could re-use a couple times, plastic dishes as a substitute for china, and house-brand china. If we go to a fancy department store we could spend all our money on fine china, but a reasonable everyday set in a quality brand would cost about $120 for a 16 piece, 4 place setting.

Here is a price summary from our local merchants:

Style of dishes	cost per qty	per plate
House brand, foam	$1.98 for 50	$0.0396
House brand, paper	$4.98 for 115	$0.0433
Heavier duty, foam	$2.78 for 50	$0.0556
National brand, paper	$2.78 for 20	$0.139
Heavier duty, paper	$2.45 for 16	$0.153
House brand, red plastic	$2.78 for 15	$0.185
National brand, clear plastic	$2.77 for 8	$0.346
Inexpensive china	$1.00 for 1	$1.00
Budget china set	$20 for 16	$1.25
National brand, heavy duty plastic	$2.40 for 1	$2.40
Everyday china	$20 for 4	$5.00
Quality national brand china	$120 for 16	$7.50
Fancy department store china	$25 for 1	$25.00
Famous European brand china	$140 for 5	$28.00

As far as acquisition cost, this summary implies that a quality national brand china dish at $7.50 would need to last for 173 uses (about 6 months) before it economically surpasses the cheapest paper plate. But, alas, we need also to account for the maintenance expenses of our china, in washing the dirty dishes. Someone might suggest that we include our cost for trash collection as an additional expense for throwing away the soiled paper plates. But we need not consider this expense, because we must pay for trash removal anyway on a flat rate every month, whether or not we throw away paper plates.

What expenses of dish maintenance should we consider? There is the labor of rinsing dishes and loading the dishwasher, but we will ignore labor cost because nobody will pay you to do your own dishes. Besides, you could spend the same amount of time preparing the meal and cleaning up afterwards, whether you use paper plates or fine china.

We need to pay for the water used by the dishwasher, for heating the water to washing temperature, for dish soap, and the electricity to run the dishwasher. Let us assume a two-person household that eats three meals a day using six dishes plus two for a snack in the afternoon, for a total of eight china dishes per day that need to go through the dishwasher after dinner.

Our dishwasher runs for 90 minutes and uses a total of 13.2 gallons of water, in six fill-and-drain cycles.

A residential water bill in Asheville has recently charged $59.50 for 5 ccf, which is 500 cubic feet.[2] At 748 gallons per ccf, this works out to 3740 gallons for $59.50, or $0.0159 per gallon. The cost for the 13.2 gallons consumed by the dishwasher is therefore $0.21.

We need to pay for heating the water to 140 degrees Fahrenheit from the 58 degree underground supply, for a temperature rise of 82 degrees. If we use our electric water heater, we need to compute the energy consumed in kilowatt-hours. It takes one British Thermal Unit to raise one pound of water by one degree F, and a gallon of water weighs 8.33 pounds, so it takes 8.33 Btu to heat a gallon of water by one degree F, or 683 Btu for 82 degrees. A kilowatt-hour is equivalent to 3412 Btu, so it takes 0.2 kwh to heat each gallon of water. At $0.12 per kwh, we have a cost of $0.024 to heat each gallon, or $0.317 for the 13.2 gallons.

At our local grocery store, a 75 ounce bottle of automatic dishwasher liquid soap costs $6.86. We use maybe two ounces per wash, which works out to $0.183 for soap.

The dishwasher will run for 90 minutes to complete the washing cycle, and we guesstimate a continuous power consumption of 200 watts for its motor, which yields 300 watt-hours, or $0.036 at $0.12 per kwh. We will not use the drying feature of the dishwasher because that uses a power-hungry, 800 watt heating element. Just let the dishes air-dry over night.

Summarizing these costs we have:

13.2 gallons of water at	$0.21
Heat the water for	.317
Soap consumption	.183
Electricity to run the dishwasher	.036
Total to wash a load of dishes	$0.75

We need to divide this number by two, because the dishwasher has a top rack for glasses and other small items, as well as a bottom rack where the dishes go. The bottom rack has room for 24 dishes, so we need to divide the result by 24 to come up with the expense-to-wash per dish of $0.016. Since it costs less to wash our china dish than to buy a new paper plate at $0.043, we can conclude that recycling the china for everyday use is economically worthwhile.

If we were to stick with the cheapest paper plates ($0.0433), at eight dishes per day, times thirty days per month, this yields $10.39 per month for paper plates that simply go into the trash. Dishwashing expense for the same number of china dishes ($0.016) is $3.84. By using china we save $7.05 per month. This is nearly enough to purchase one china dish of the quality national brand at $7.50, which implies that purchasing a set of sixteen china dishes is economically justified if they will last for more than 17 months, which is a reasonable expectation.

Note that we get to decide whether to use paper plates or china plates, and how fancy we want to go with the expense of our fine china. The government does not direct us to a particular brand or style. We get to make the choice in a free market without government interference in this decision.

This is an example of recycling that makes economic sense and fits in with our desire to own fancy stuff. We are still free to buy paper plates if they fit our needs for a picnic or other occasion where china would be cumbersome.

Compare the recycling of china to recycling of newspapers. Do you recycle newspapers because it is of economic benefit to yourself, or because you grew up with your mother telling you to do it? Perhaps you believe that recycling newspapers is good for the environment, good from the standpoint of saving trees or keeping excess waste out of the county landfill. But if it were economically worthwhile, wouldn't someone offer to buy your old newspapers from you at a price that would motivate you to go to the effort of saving them for him?

Your government tells you to recycle your newspapers. They provide you with special bins for this service, and add a fee to your trash bill to pay for it. You do not recycle because it is of economic benefit to yourself. If it made economic sense, the trash collection company would hire workers to separate newspapers from the trash stream so they could sell it to the company that makes recycled paper. But this effort is not economically feasible, so your government requires you to do the labor for free, before the newspapers go into the trash stream. Note again that the government charges you extra on your trash bill for you to do the labor that is not economic for any businessman to bother with.

When your author was a young man going to college he drank a considerable amount of soda-pop and thought it would be a good idea to recycle his soda-pop cans. At the time such cans were made from steel, the same material that manufacturers use to make automobiles. Everybody is familiar with the auto junk yards that dot the landscape, and such businesses resell used fenders, doors and other parts to repair cars that have suffered accidents. The residual scrap metal is sold to steel mills to use as a resource of ingredients for making new steel. This is recycled metal, which makes economic sense because it supports the business of all those junkyards.

Certainly, fifty pounds of empty steel soda-pop cans would be equivalent to fifty pounds of automotive scrap metal, so our environmentally aware college student called every junk yard and metal recycler in the vicinity of his university town. Sorry, nobody wanted them. Why? Because it was not economical for them to bother with the hassle of dealing with old soda-pop cans. His yearlong collection of perfectly good recyclable metal thus ended up in the trash stream.

To further belabor the point, how can we tell if some activity, such as recycling, is actually worthwhile from an economic standpoint? If you own some kind of resource that has economic value, somebody will want to buy it from you. If two or more people want to buy your stuff, you may hold an auction and sell it to the highest bidder.

Let us say your land is situated over a deposit of crude oil. An oil company will come by and ask if they can drill a well on your property. If they offer to pay you for the privilege and give you a cut of the oil they extract, you might go for the deal. If you have a large mound of empty aluminum beer cans, perhaps an aluminum recycler will pay you 40 cents per pound and offer to cart them away for free. If, on the other hand, you have a dumpster full of soiled baby diapers, you will probably need to pay someone to haul them off to the dump, because this particular "resource" has no value to anybody else. If some activity is economic, someone will voluntarily go into the business and try to earn a profit from it. If some activity is not economic, but a majority of the legislators deem it desirable from a political standpoint, they will pass a law to make it mandatory upon the citizens. If a government must subsidize an activity, it has no economic merit. A common example, aside from the recycling mandate, is a city bus service. The Asheville Transit System operates a citywide bus service that earns only 16 percent of its revenues from fares, or put another way, from the customers who actually use the service. The remaining 84 percent is subsidized by the government via taxes, from federal and state grants, the city's general fund and fees derived from such things as parking meters.

To demonstrate how far politicians will go to distort market forces, we need only to look at the city ordinances. Asheville, like many cities, has an ordinance that makes it illegal to "steal" "trash" from bins set out at the curb for collection on recycle day.[3] Does this law not stretch logic to a ridiculous degree? How could somebody possibly steal something that someone else has thrown away as utterly useless? Perhaps one man's trash becomes another man's treasure.

One morning we heard the radio news report that certain human scavengers had been observed sneaking aluminum cans from neighborhood curbside recycling bins before the city truck could collect them. Market forces in the economy had raised scrap aluminum prices to the point where empty beer cans became more valuable. Some poor people were trying to earn a few bucks by being industrious in attempting to recycle aluminum. But the city does not allow this practice, in favor of keeping that revenue stream to itself. Poor people are not allowed to try to fend for themselves; they must instead accept government handouts that politicians determine are appropriate for them. This is one more example of government interfering with the natural, free-market instincts of human beings.

The rule to remember is: If government has to subsidize an activity, it is an economic waste. A free market would better utilize the resources, personnel and capital diverted by government mandates, thus generating true wealth by profit-earning industries that compete to produce products and services that people actually want to pay for.

Are we saying in this chapter that you should not recycle your newspapers? No, of course not, but we are in favor of freedom. As a citizen of the United States, you should be free to choose your own life style and incorporate recycling if you prefer. Nothing is wrong with being frugal, if it your own decision. If your government instructs you to be frugal, it is rationing.

We noted in Chapter 14 that economic or money expense is not the only thing we take into account when deciding what to do. We value things based on our sentiments and judgment about what is right. We like to own fine china because we inherited it from our grandmother, or because we worked for twenty years to be able to afford it. Some folks don't like to eat off paper plates because they get soggy half way through the meal. In many cases a paper plate is not adequate for the task, where a china dish fits the bill.

We elect our representatives to champion our desires in the legislature, and if they are doing their job correctly, we wanted them to establish a city bus service so people without cars can get around. And if we trust in the democratic process, we must have wanted the politicians to deny us our freedom of choice in whether or not to recycle newspapers.

Now that you know the economics behind recycling, you may make an educated choice on the subject, rather than just blindly following your government's instructions.

Notes:

[1] We realize that the term "sacred" has previously been rejected from use in this book as a word that is too closely associated with religious doctrine. However, we may be permitted to use it in this chapter in its idiomatic sense.

[2] This water bill includes fees for city sewer facilities as well, but it seems reasonable to include these charges as part of the water cost.

[3] City of Asheville Code of Ordinances; Chapter 15, Solid Waste Management; Article III, Recycling; Section 15-51, Regulations; Paragraph (c), Scavenging and Unauthorized Collection of Recyclable Materials.

CHAPTER TWENTY-EIGHT

POPULATION

ANOTHER widespread myth in our society concerns the subject of a population explosion among the human inhabitants of our planet. This concept first gained popularity back in 1798 when Thomas Malthus, whose dates are 1766 to 1834, published his work in *An Essay on the Principle of Population*.[1]

Malthus' logical reasoning proposed the concept that the fertility of the population would inevitably produce larger numbers of people faster than the ability of those people to produce enough food to feed everyone. The natural result of this situation would be widespread starvation and death for vast swaths of humanity. Although he made no prediction as to the dates when this tragedy would visit the population, his ideas led to a considerable debate among his contemporaries, and influenced the writings of many other scientists and philosophers. After publication of his first book, Malthus continued his career and revised his book five times from 1803 to 1826, to answer challenges from his contemporaries and to continue promulgating his ideas.

We, as modern people, are able to look back in history for the intervening 200 years to see whether Malthus' dire predictions were ever realized. We see that no great dying off of humans, due to lack of food, ever occurred. The population of the world in 1800 was about 900 million. The population of the world today is 6.8 billion, an increase of 655 percent. Between then and now the industrial revolution intervened and created enough wealth and increase in productivity per worker to feed the many new, hungry mouths. The worst declines of population in Europe occurred between 1347 and 1351 due to the bubonic plague or Black Death, which eliminated up to 50% of the population.[2] Major recurrences of the disease continued to plague Europe up until 1530, but these periodic disasters occurred long before Malthus appeared on the scene. Since then, the major destroyers of populations were probably World Wars I and II, which accounted for an estimated 20 million and 55 million deaths, respectively.

Despite the continuing prosperity among ever greater numbers of human beings populating our planet, the discredited concept of a population explosion keeps working its way into the public psyche.

The Malthusian ideas regained traction in popular culture during the 1960's and 70's with the publication in 1968 of *The Population Bomb* by Paul Ehrlich.[3] He predicted the same type of societal collapse for the same reasons. He claimed that a lack of food to feed the burgeoning population would surely result in famine and suffering for hundreds of millions of people within the next 15 years. He claimed that time had already run out for humanity to do anything about the coming disaster.

Again, we can look back at the history of the past 40 years and see no great famine. The population of the world in 1970 was 3.7 billion, in 2010 6.8 billion, an increase of 84 percent. The population of the U.S. in 1970 was 203 million, and became 313 million by 2010, an increase of 54 percent. We still have plenty to eat and the growing variety of restaurants provides an ever-expanding set of dining experiences.

The definitive debunking of the population doomsayers was published in 1981 by Dr. Julian L. Simon in *The Ultimate Resource.* Fifteen years later, in 1996, the author published an expanded edition, *The Ultimate Resource 2.* The later book allowed the author to confirm his earlier findings and present further scientific evidence to support his thesis that population growth contributes to prosperity and an increased standard of living, not decline and starvation.[4]

Dr. Simon's major idea is that over the history of civilization, and particularly over the history of the United States, commodities become cheaper rather than more expensive. This applies to such items as metals (copper, steel, aluminum), energy supplies (oil, electricity), and agricultural products (corn, wheat, potatoes), which is to say, food. If a runaway population increase were actually starving out masses of people, the law of supply and demand would force the prices of foodstuffs higher, because food availability per capita would decrease.

Graphs and plots of the data for each of the commodities show a declining cost over time, both when compared to the consumer price index, and again when compared to average wages.

These results are anti-intuitive and just seem to be wrong. In fact, Dr. Simon began his investigations of the population problem under the opinion that population was indeed about to overrun the ability of humanity to feed itself. He wanted to discover just how much time we had left to change our ways so that we might avoid disaster. However, the more research he performed the more he learned that the population inherently contains the self-correcting mechanisms that raise production and increase productivity per worker. He discovered that population is not only a growing consumer of limited resources, but is itself the ultimate resource that creates wealth and prosperity to a greater degree than it uses up existing supplies. Note that this conclusion aligns nicely with a major theme of this book.

Of course, this regenerating phenomenon is enhanced when people have the political and economic freedom to watch out for their own affairs. The country where this ability is held by the people to the greatest degree is the United States of America. Government power always threatens the freedom of the people to prosper by taxing ever-greater portions of their output, eventually reaching the point where people begin to lose the resolve to continue their efforts.

Self-regulation

What is it that holds a check on the growth of population in human society? Experiments in biology seem to imply an inevitable exponential growth when nutrients are available and there is still room to expand.

When times are bad and infant mortality is high, families have more children so that there will be enough workers to help support the parents in the coming years. This is the family or tribal model where the sons and daughters are loyal to their family, and work for the betterment of their small group. This model predominates in less developed countries where more people are poor and live closer to subsistence levels. They thus have greater motivation to work hard for their very survival. This more stressful life style leads to longer workdays and shorter life spans.

However, when we look at more developed countries we see a greater wealth per capita, and many more opportunities for varied career fields.

Close family ties become less important for survival, and the sons and daughters find opportunities for advancement in other parts of the country, far from their biological families. When times are good and prosperity reigns, parents make the conscious decision to limit their offspring to replacement levels. This phenomenon has been observed in societies everywhere around the world. A plot of birth rate versus per capita wealth across many nations shows a decline in birth rate as wealth increases.[5] It is a built-in feedback, self-regulation feature of life that derives from the blind forces of evolution, tempered by the intelligence of the human mind.

Fertility in more developed countries thus declines to replacement levels, so that any population gains must be made up of immigrants. Fertility in poor countries is always much larger as struggling people realize they need to grow their families to fend off poverty. Such larger numbers of sons and daughters who survive observe the expanded opportunities available in the more developed countries, so they become willing immigrants, and sometimes, illegal aliens.

A child is an investment in the future. An addition of a child to a family is at first a burden on the fixed budget, which allows less for other members of the family. But over the long term, the dependent baby becomes a productive worker and contributes more to the productivity of the community than he consumes.

In Chapter 13 we saw how life for the animals, the lions of the Okavango Delta, is limited by the resources provided by nature. Conversely, we saw how the humans may use their intelligence to grow resources and provide themselves with greater amounts of food than they could if they merely emulated the animals. Humans are indeed the ultimate resource. The population bomb is a myth. Increased human populations breed prosperity.

Notes:

[1] See Malthus.
[2] See Gottfried.
[3] See Ehrlich.
[4] See Simon.
[5] Ibid. *The Ultimate Resource 2,* Figure 24-3.

CHAPTER TWENTY-NINE

STORIES

AT this point in the book we have covered all the concepts that our wise engineer uses to analyze the behavior of animals and humans he observes in the world. In this chapter, let us indulge in a little creative nonfiction and look at a few undocumented stories illustrating the problems that we creatures experience, and analyze them in light of the principles we have described. The purpose here is to stimulate your thinking about various situations, to see if you may apply the tools we have tried to impart through these pages.

Bugs and Birds

A hiker we know likes to tell stories about his encounters with wildlife. One time, on a hike through the piney woods, he noticed a dark spot on the trail ahead. Walking closer, he saw it was a beetle of some sort, maybe an inch long and a quarter inch wide, crawling slowly across the trail. He leaned over to take a closer look, feeling mildly repelled by this yucky bug, and resisted an urge to step on it. After a brief inspection, he decided to leave it alone, not wanting to interfere with the ecology of the woods. Just as he started off he heard a fluttering of wings behind him. He turned around in time to see a big black bird swoop down from a nearby tree and gobble up the beetle. Before flying away the bird looked at him momentarily, not to say thank you, but as if to remark, "Bud, if you're too damned stupid to pick up an easy snack when it's in front of your face, you deserve to starve to death."

Moral: Animals live in the anarchy of nature and must take advantage of every opportunity to feed.

261

This same hiker observed, while quietly sitting on the front porch of his cabin in the woods, that the songbirds fluttering past would often snag moths out of the air. He could hear the bugs snap as the bird's little beak closed upon them.

Perhaps you have observed a flock of birds in the early evening darting back and forth at treetop level, flying erratically in all directions, but not really going anywhere. They are actually catching dinner on the fly.[1] Ornithologists will tell you that one insectivorous bird will eat more than 100 bugs in a day.[2]

In Denver, Colorado, at many intersections, birds may be found building their nests on top of stoplight poles. Their little birdbrains harbor the faulty belief system that the cars waiting at the stoplights are actually predators in the neighborhood that want to harm to their babies. Thus these birds spend a lot of time whooshing past the windshields of the cars, trying to drive them away from their precious nests. This activity seems to us to be a waste of time and effort, but then we humans also undertake a lot of worthless pursuits.

Moral: When you understand the big picture, you can avoid a lot of unnecessary effort.

Bees

One fine day in North Carolina a homeowner went out in his backyard to cut the grass with his power lawnmower. Halfway through this task he felt a sharp pain on his left hand. Looking down he saw he was in the midst of an angry swarm of wasps. He had innocently pushed his mower over the insects' hideyhole in the dirt.

An observer watching from a safe distance would have seen a comedy routine of a frantic gardener waving his arms, running away from his lawnmower across the yard, yelling, cursing, and slapping at the numerous bees flying around his head and crawling all over his jeans and t-shirt. The victim's wife, who had been tending some flowers in a garden across the yard, got into the act, too, with a hastily retrieved can of bug spray from the garage. Once the attacking swarm had been dispersed from his personal space, the homeowner looked across the yard to see his lawnmower sitting where he left it, roaring at full throttle over the hornets' nest. Some three dozen, highly irritated yellow jackets were buzzing around the machine, having no success in driving it away. Rather than just letting it run out of gas, he picked up a broom handle, trotted past the machine and swatted the throttle lever, shutting it down.[3]

This episode discouraged our homeowner from any further gardening activity that afternoon. Besides, he needed to treat his stings, and later visit the hardware store to buy a can of wasp poison.

That evening he pushed the silent lawnmower away from the hole in the dirt where the bees made their home, and expended the entire canister of poison into the nest, thus putting an end to the problem.[4]

But is that really the end of the story? Is there an ethical dimension to this event that needs to be considered? Did the human need to destroy the whole colony, or was there an alternative to allow this small batch of creatures to continue existing in nature's harmony?

If we look at the situation from a dispassionate perspective, perhaps the whole episode was unnecessary. The bugs did not need to attack the human. They could have allowed him to cut the grass unmolested. Their hive might have suffered the loss of a few individuals to the blades of the lawnmower, but if they had left the human alone, he would have finished cutting the grass, and not even have known they were there. If they had not attacked, their community would still exist in peace.

But neither the individual bees nor the hive community possesses the intelligence to understand this bigger picture. So the insects attacked the human invader in self-defense, which is the natural right of any self-respecting creature. The human, being attacked in his own home territory, responded to the threat, also in self-defense, eliminating the whole hive, feeling there was no reasonable alternative.

One would like to think that mankind can get along in his complex world environment, respecting the diversity of his fellow creatures who also strive to exist in whatever niche they can carve out of the ecology. But life is an unending competition for resources and territory, so the struggle continues.

Moral: When different species contend, killing results.

A reviewer of this chapter has expressed the opinion that it's a good thing the bees don't have the intelligence to appreciate the big picture. Since they live in the anarchy of the natural world, they would not use the intelligence to become a peaceful, live-and-let-live community, but rather a more formidable force in competition with the rest of us.

Robins

One lovely spring morning a man and his wife were looking out their front window when they noticed a pair of robins building a nest in the tall bushes next to their front porch. The humans were thrilled to have a front-row seat on this display of budding life in nature. Imagine their pleasure to discover, after a few days, a pretty blue robin's egg in the nest. They would get to witness first-hand a hatching baby chick and be able to observe the adult birds raising their offspring. Imagine their despair to learn upon returning home the next evening that the neighbor's cat had destroyed the nest and its contents.

Did the cat have to do that? After all she was well fed by her owner and was provided with the benefits of human civilization. The cat had no valid reason to be hunting in the neighborhood. But alas, a cat is a cat is a cat. And also a robin is a robin. The unfortunate birds had no recourse. They could not sing to the police and have the cat arrested. They carried no insurance on their home. They would just have to start over and build a new nest elsewhere.

> Moral: Anarchy rules in the natural world, even just beyond the human's windows.

It does no good to cry over the tribulations of animals, because this sort of thing happens everyday, everywhere throughout the world. However, the cat's owner did suffer misery when she learned, a year later, that her pet had been killed in the street. The cat, in pursuit of some mission known only to herself, darted under a passing car at an inopportune moment.

As sensitive humans, who feel that justice should be available to all creatures, we must continually remind ourselves that no good nor evil may be ascribed to the actions of animals.

Territory

An elderly lady owned a small dog, a fluffy blonde Pomeranian, that was always happy, friendly and vigorously wagging his tail. He got along well with people, liked both children and adults, and wanted to be part of whatever activities the humans enjoyed. He would bark (yip) with enthusiasm whenever anyone surprised him, and would run from one person to the next in any group to have his ears scratched and keep track of whatever was going on. He was sociable and wanted to be everybody's friend. He would play with anyone who paid attention to him, and enjoyed the company of strangers when they came to visit. When nothing exciting was going on, the dog would sit calmly with his human guests. When his mistress sat on the sofa to read a book, he would be there on her lap or resting quietly beside her on the cushions.

Nevertheless, when he was in his own private territory, this gentle, friendly pup had a mean streak. An old-fashioned wicker chair in the living room had a basket-like base under the seat that provided a cozy cave where the dog liked to rest. If anyone, including his mistress, put their fingers or toes under the chair, the dog would vigorously defend this territory with growls and snaps of his sharp little teeth. But once he came out of this personal cage he would suddenly transform back into his adorable, charming, friendly self again. He wouldn't hold a grudge against anyone for having disturbed him in his house. It was as though he could turn off his aggression like a light switch.

Moral: Animals have an intense territorial instinct that civilization cannot erase.

Otters

Animal rescuers certainly have strong feelings about their duty to help disadvantaged creatures survive in competition with uncaring humans. Sometimes the animals suffer destruction of their habitat by accidents caused by human inattentiveness. A good example is the 1989 Exxon Valdez oil spill on Prince William Sound in Alaska. When the oil tanker went off course and ran aground, millions of gallons of crude oil spilled into the sea and washed ashore. As a result, vast swaths of wildlife were wiped out. Birds, sea otters, salmon, killer whales, and many other creatures were coated with oil, or had their food chains despoiled.

Several human organizations leaped to the rescue and expended great efforts to save the animals lucky enough to fall under their care.

Sea otters in particular benefited from the attention lavished upon the innocent animal victims of the disaster.

Sea otters in particular are much more deserving of human attention than might be other creatures. Sea otters are so adorable! They have such sweet little faces. We love to watch them play and zip about in the water having fun. We can identify with them, and know that they deserve our respect and regard. However, certain other animals of a similar size and fuzziness definitely give us feelings of revulsion. Rats might be an example. We are so much less likely to want to help out rats in their hour of need, even though in the scheme of nature they are no different from any other creature trying to carve out a niche to survive in the ecology. Note that our language does include a term for such out-of-favor creatures; vermin.

But returning to our friends the sea otters, some 357 were rescued from the contaminated waters of Prince William Sound and cleaned of the crude oil in their fur.[5] Of the ones that could be nursed back to health, 197 were released again into the wild where they belong. More than one of these restored otters were promptly gobbled up by killer whales in the vicinity. While feeding Orcas was certainly not their original intent, the animal rescuers undoubtedly spent more time, money and effort in their endeavors than was really justified for the overall welfare of life in the biosphere. Since Exxon paid $18 million towards the otter rescue effort, we have no doubt the Orcas could have been fed with much cheaper fare. Also, we wonder if the portion of otters eaten by Orcas, at a per otter rate around $90,000, qualifies as the most expensive business lunch on record.

Moral: There is more than one way to skin a cat.

Camping

Responsible campers know the mantra, "Take only pictures, leave only footprints." The park rangers will gladly instruct you in your responsibilities to preserve the natural heritage of the park system. They will tell you to stay on the trail, don't cut through the woods. Never pick wildflowers or take away pretty rocks or interestingly shaped sticks. Leave the forest as undisturbed as you found it. Camp only in established campgrounds. Build fires only in provided firepits. Do not harvest dead or down firewood. If you are hiking through the back country and need to make a pitstop, leave the trail and bury your waste six inches deep, 100 feet from any trail, campground or water source. Don't clean your dishes or bathe with soap in a stream. Pack out all your trash. If you carried it in, you can carry it out.

Note that the animals who live in the wild are never subject to these same regulations. A bear is allowed to defecate in the woods whenever and wherever he happens to get the urge. He may strip the bark off trees if he so desires. A moose is permitted to urinate in the creek if he should happen to be standing there when the time comes. He is free to eat whatever vegetation suits his fancy. Birds are noted for decorating freshly washed automobiles, to the point where some people believe they do it on purpose. When the bear population increases to a certain density, the park will be closed to human visitors.

Moral: Government regulations blatantly discriminate against people in favor of dumb animals. When in the national parks, wild animals enjoy rights denied to humans. The people are required to observe their civilized manners while the animals may continue in their gross and uncouth habits.

Armored Cars

If we, as everyday humans, lived like the animals in a true anarchy, what would a visit to the grocery store be like? First of all, would the concept of a grocery store actually be possible in a true anarchy? If everyone merely grabbed what they wanted when they saw it, could a vast array of products exist on rows of shelving in a large building where citizens may wander freely down the aisles? Would the customers bother to stop at the cash registers in the front of the store to pay for their selections? Maybe, if the grocery store kept a large crew of soldiers to maintain order among the customers. Visualize the chaos that would occur daily in such a grocery store, if the common people had no respect for the property rights of others, and had no compunctions against theft. It would probably more resemble the proverbial bull in a china shop, except with a whole herd of bulls.

If some unfortunate individual had an auto accident in a true anarchy, how would passers-by act towards the victim? Would they show compassion towards their fellow man and call the police and rescue squad to assist the victims? Or would they merely take advantage of the disabled victim by stealing his wallet, cell phone, tires and battery, and depart leaving him to worry about his own welfare? Does this kind of behavior actually exist in our enlightened civilization? Unfortunately, yes.

On 8 January 1997, in Miami, Florida, a Brinks armored car on I-95 was involved in an accident on a bridge at Northwest 17th Street in the Overtown neighborhood. The wreck spilled $3.7 million in cash, coin, and food stamps on the roadway, tumbling down the bridge embankment and blowing around in the wind. While the driver and his fellow Brinks officer lay bleeding in the wreckage, the residents of the neighborhood and passers-by on the highway descended on the scene and helped themselves to whatever they could pick up and carry off. The police arrived on the scene and tried to chase away the scavengers and recover coins and bills from more than 100 people harvesting the scene. Despite their best efforts, $500,000 of the cash disappeared into the communities of South Florida.[6]

The accident occurred in a poor neighborhood, so some newspaper commentaries about the incident were sympathetic of the human vultures who benefited from the misfortune of the persons and corporations who actually owned the property stolen from the scene of the accident.

Contrast this scenario to a similar accident involving a Loomis Fargo truck that crashed on I-25 south of Denver on the icy morning of 3 December 1997. The truck swerved to avoid another vehicle that made a rapid lane change, tipped over on its side and burst open, spilling coins and cash all over the highway. Many passers-by stopped to aid the injured driver and call emergency responders. These citizens helped collect the spilled cash and return it to the armored vehicle. The driver of a snowplow volunteered to help scrape the slippery coins off the highway onto the shoulder.[7] These everyday citizens did the right thing morally, came to the aid of the accident victims, and returned the spilled cash to its rightful owners.

This second incident was not reported by the news media, other than a brief mention of the accident in a Denver newspaper.[8] Presumably, people acting in a civilized manner are not considered newsworthy (which may be a good thing).

In the first incident, the people responded in an animalistic, anarchistic fashion, grabbing whatever they could get away with. In the second case people acted as only humans can, with respect for the rights and property of others.

> Moral: We live in a world where the forces of animalism live along-side, and compete with, the civilizing forces of virtue and humanism.

Unplugged

When Jake was in college it was his habit to use an electric shaver every day as part of his morning routine. He lived in a dormitory where he had to go down the hallway to the central bathroom to shave, shower, and brush his teeth.[9]

One morning when he awoke before sunrise, he discovered that the electric power to his dormitory was off. As a former Cub Scout, he was prepared for such an emergency. He lit his flashlight, gathered up his towel and other gear, and headed down the hall to the bathroom. He set his items on the sink and placed the flashlight on the little shelf in front of the mirror so he could see to shave. He plugged in his shaver and turned on the switch. The shaver did not make its usual buzz, because the power was still off. In the dim light, as he looked at the shaver in his hand, it dawned upon him that he was operating on habit, rather than thinking through his actions before he tried them. Embarrassed, he looked around to see if any of the other students in the bathroom had noticed his gaffe. Luckily, nobody was paying any attention, so he pulled the plug on the shaver and wrapped it in his towel. That day he went to class unshaven.

Ken is another character who noticed he made silly little mistakes in his daily activities. One day his wife told him she wanted a bookshelf for a particular corner of the bedroom, so he decided to build it himself in the garage. He set up a workbench along with a table-saw he borrowed from a neighbor, and a few power tools including a drill and a belt sander.

The garage had only one electrical outlet, so Ken ran a heavy-duty extension cord across the floor to the table saw. The cord had but a single socket on the end, which required changing the plug when he needed to use a different tool.

Visualize the busy woodworker in the midst of his project. He takes a freshly sawn shelf from the table-saw over to the workbench, measures to the spot where he wants to drill a hole, marks it with a pencil, clamps the work piece to the bench, picks up the electric drill, aligns it in the proper orientation and squeezes the trigger. The drill fails to turn, because it is not plugged in. So Ken growls in frustration at being stupid, returns to the saw to unplug it, plugs in the drill, re-lines up the drill on the work piece, squeezes the trigger and drills the hole.

Concentrating on doing a good job, Ken spends a few minutes measuring the correct place to draw a cut line on the next board. He takes the work piece to the saw, adjusts the rip fence just so, grasps the board so as to keep fingers away from the blade, slides the board back and forth a few inches to make sure everything is clear, reaches down to turn on the power switch, and the saw fails to start. The drill is the tool currently connected to the power cord. Ken rolls his eyes, takes a deep breath, counts to ten, and changes the power cord. After repeating this mistake a third time, Ken finally goes down to the basement and finds a power strip with multiple outlets for the end of the extension cord. With all his tools powered up he can concentrate on his project without worrying about swapping cords every time.

Several times a year, small planes do not arrive at their intended destinations because they run out of fuel during the flight. Proper preflight planning requires the pilot to ensure he has enough fuel to reach his primary destination, plus more than enough to reach an alternate airport. Running out of gas while airborne is considered pilot error, as are the previous examples of being unplugged.

Moral: Pilot error can cause minor irritations, or major disasters including death for hundreds of people.

Have you ever run out of gas while driving your vehicle down the highway? Most inconvenient, usually not disastrous, but also avoidable with proper planning. Larger systems have many more opportunities for errors to creep in because many more people are involved who are subject to making mistakes. Many employees do not even care if they make mistakes as long as they can continue to receive their paychecks. Individuals form habits and stick with them, even when such behaviors make no sense toward the goals of the organization.

Governments, being among the largest of organizations, are fraught with opportunities for error. Many of the leaders in government harbor faulty belief systems, or are merely in the game for power and personal aggrandizement. Either way they make errors in the proper conduct of their responsibilities. People who have faulty belief systems are in a situation similar to the man who tried to use the unplugged tools. The consequences of their actions do not result in the ends they desire. Some people realize their mistakes shortly after they make them. Others, especially the ones with faulty belief systems, never realize they are being counter-productive, and keep on doing the same ultimately destructive activities. Thus it is that socialism silently works its destruction throughout the economy, unnoticed by the unsuspecting victims. While those of us who do understand the big picture try to educate the misinformed, we are opposed by the political class, with its vested interests in the status quo, striving to expand its power and control.

Moral: Competition for power and control often blinds people to the unintended consequences of their actions.

Production versus Q.A.

What conflicts arise inside a company in the normal conduct of its business? How do the employees view their responsibilities?

Take the common example of a business organization that manufactures widgets. This company is large enough to be divided into departments to keep the management focused on efficient operation. Let us say this company is organized into departments for Accounting, Engineering, Production, and Quality Assurance. The accounting department handles the company's money and makes sure its suppliers are paid in a timely manner, and that the employees receive their paychecks based on the hours they have worked. Engineering designs the widgets and makes sure they can be manufactured from materials that are readily available from the company's suppliers. Production builds the widgets and ships them to customers. Quality assurance monitors production to make sure the widgets meet or exceed the requirements specified on the engineering drawings.

The production department measures its success by the number of widgets it can ship every month, which determines how much money the company can earn from its customers. Quality assurance, on the other hand, slows down production by insisting that the widgets meet strict requirements for wonderfulness. Q.A. knows that low quality widgets provided to customers will lead to fewer repeat orders. The highest quality widgets will encourage customers to demand more widgets from our company, which helps our company grow and beat the competition in the marketplace. Note how Q.A. regulates the flow of widgets through production by providing a feedback loop. Q.A. may also decide that some requirement on an engineering drawing, a blueprint, or some other specification, is too restrictive and does not address any need the customer actually desires. Q.A. can ask that the drawing be revised to eliminate this feature and thus improve flow through production. All of the numerous feedback loops among the various departments in the company eventually create a balance or equilibrium of forces that produce a flow of quality widgets to satisfied customers.

Where does conflict arise among people who work for this company? The manager of production is an ambitious man who wants to advance his career and have an ever-increasing salary. He knows his production department is scored or measured by the number of widgets he can build in a month, so he strives for increasing productivity from his workers. He can achieve this goal by instructing his assemblers to eliminate unnecessary motion in their work by keeping their widget parts close at hand. An assembler shouldn't have to walk across the factory to get a new box of tips when her current supply runs out. The manager should hire a lower paid worker to deliver these new parts to the assembler in time and carry away the empty box. By paying attention to these details the production manager keeps his operation running smoothly.

But the production manager resents the manager of quality assurance, because he feels the Q.A. manager just slows down production. Q.A. insists that the new tips, which have been received from an outside supplier, be inspected before release to the production floor. Each tip must be measured with a micrometer for dimensional conformance to its specifications. Also, Q.A. inspects the finished widgets before shipment to be sure they meet requirements. Any defective widgets are sent back to production for rework, if they can be fixed. Such rework makes the widgets more expensive to produce, so Q.A. wants to make sure quality is built-in to the product during the manufacturing steps, where it belongs.

By being resentful of the Q.A. manager, the production manager is missing the big picture of his company. He should appreciate that excellent widgets for their customers is the ultimate purpose of the company, and even though he is measured by the number of widgets shipped each month, it is also in his interest that the widgets be of the highest quality. Good widgets are better than many widgets. Quality trumps quantity.

Shipping boxes of gravel at the end of the month is a technique that more than one company has tried. They want to appear to have met their quota for output of widgets when they have actually fallen short. So shipping out a few boxes of gravel along with the boxes of widgets gives them a temporary reprieve. When such accounting irregularities are revealed to the public, the company's share price declines suddenly, the responsible personnel are fired, and the CEO must resign. Fraud is no substitute for truth. Stockholders deserve to know the actual condition of the company.

Empire building is a common problem among management organizations in large companies. A Q.A. manager may wish to grow the size of his department so that he may wield power over a larger number of employees and gain influence and importance in the company. It becomes a case of putting his departmental interests above the overall company interests. It is a narrow view. He is more interested in advancing his career than in providing quality products from the company. He is thinking from A to B when he should be considering A to B to C.

Labor unions try to protect the union's workers regardless of the success of the company. They promote work rules that narrowly define the kinds of jobs each employee may perform, make it difficult for the company to layoff a non-productive worker or surplus labor, and regulate wages at higher levels than may be found in the larger economy. These practices interfere with the feedback loops that would regulate the needs and functions of the company, making its processes less efficient, more costly, and thus less competitive in the larger economy. This is the reason that management so vigorously opposes unionization.

It is so easy to lose sight of the overall mission of your company. Managers engage in empire building to enhance their own importance. Employees game the system to squeeze out benefits for themselves at the expense of company efficiency. Inappropriate metrics for employee evaluations distort the goals the workers should strive towards.

Moral: A man will often look no farther than his own nose.

Dreams from My Father

Did you ever have a dream in which you solved some mystery and became convinced you had discovered the secret of the universe? Then, after you awoke, you could not quite remember the details so the secret became lost to the world? Such a tragedy!

This same experience has happened to so many people that a common response has been to keep a pen and note pad at the bedside to record such revelations before the memory fades.

Your author has also tried this technique with fascinating results. One morning he sat bolt upright in bed knowing he had found the answer to all the problems of humanity. The one word he wrote on his notepad: "Cebibels."[10]

On another occasion he wrote several words, certain he had discovered a secret that would change the course of human history: "A monkey rice of waiting."

A third revelation delivered: "Make the meet mix the match." Perhaps the third word might be spelled "meat."

If you have concluded from these true events that dreams are utter nonsense, you are correct.

Certainly, dreams have occasionally provided the inspiration for significant advances in art and science. But dreams themselves are meaningless random wanderings of the sleeping mind that serve to sort through the waste memories of the previous day and to prepare the brain cells for a fresh workout the next day. Random juxtaposition of seemingly unrelated topics has been known to provide sudden insights to problems that are stewing in the subconscious mind, and dreaming, as well as day dreaming, can enhance this effect. Although assigning "meaning" to dreams can be a fun stimulant for conversation, claiming such meaning as truth is clearly fraudulent.

That said, here is our own interpretation on the meaning of dreams. Just before you wake, you may notice that your dreams become more and more ridiculous. This is a clue to your subconscious mind that it is time to wake up. When you do awake, you are pleased to realize all that tempestuous activity was just a dream. We call this phenomenon S.W.U.D. (read: S, triple-U, D) for "Stupid Wake Up Dreams."

A popular fallacy is that a particular dream represents a prediction of the future, or an example of guidance for conducting one's life. Where do people get these ideas? Is it all just wishful thinking? Is there some historical precedent? We don't need to search the literature any further than Genesis 41 to find an early example of dream interpretation. It seems that Pharaoh dreamed of seven fat cows and seven skinny cows, then seven ripe ears of corn followed by seven withered ones. Pharaoh asked his own viziers to tell him what it all meant, but they demurred. However, Joseph, a Hebrew in his prison, told him God was trying to inform him that he would experience seven years of plenty followed by seven years of famine, so Pharaoh had better prepare his countrymen to make hay while the sun shines. Joseph was placed in charge of the project and made a great success of his predictions.

Henceforth, people have been proclaiming the true meaning of dreams. Today you may even look online to find current practitioners of this art. We would advise against purchasing any of these services. Spend your money on ice cream, instead.

Moral: Place little credence in the predictions of soothsayers.

Astrology

Astrology is a lifelike form that competes for survival in the marketplace of ideas. It has a long history, starting in antiquity, and has developed a large and complex structure. We might say astrology is closely related to dreaming, except that it is a conscious attempt to derive guidance in human affairs from movements of stars and planets. Such interpretations are supposed to predict future events or give clues on how to handle current situations, based on the zodiacal sign you were born under.

An astrologer may make whatever statements and predictions he likes that suit his fancy at the time, but that does not make them true. The next astrologer will give you a different set of predictions, and you may check with several others until you find the one you like. How all this may be considered as truth is a mystery to those of us who have a more scientific outlook.

Where does an astrologer get his inspiration? Perhaps he may believe he receives visions from the gods, or maybe he is just practicing fraud against gullible marks.

In ancient times, shepherds, watching over their flocks by night, became bored enough to gaze into the heavens and observe the wonders of the astronomical display above their heads. Certainly, they thought, all this must mean something. Let's see if we can make an interpretation.

Do you see that pattern in the stars? There, that one above Orion? Does it not look sort of like a bull if you connect the dots? The bright star, Aldebaran, could be the eye and those stars to the right look like the horns. Let us name it Taurus, because that is the Latin for bull, and is also close to the Greek word, tauros. Now everyone knows that a bull is plodding and deliberate, so if the Sun was near the constellation Taurus when you were born, you must also share these characteristics. If we can persuade the king to agree with us on this interpretation, he will make it the law, and everyone will be forced to believe it unto eternity, because our king is the greatest. If you choose not to agree with the king on this matter, he will send some soldiers to your house to change your mind.

Moving closer to our own times, one may find astrological advice on the Internet. We would like to quote here a paragraph or two of text from a particular astrological website, but we can't get permission. This book takes a scientific view of astrology, which declares it to be nonsense, so the website owner will feel we are denigrating his profession. He will be highly insulted, and will withhold permission to reproduce his work. This attitude on the part of our astrologer implies that he actually believes in what he is doing. He has invested a considerable amount of time and effort learning his trade, and would be devastated to actually realize he has based his career on a faulty belief system.

Since we can't include a direct quote, you may view a surfeit of astrological predictions and commentary by doing your own Internet search. We might suggest entering "astrology" and "Chiron" in your search engine, which should result in more than a million hits.

One example might be that during 2009 the planets Jupiter and Neptune, and the asteroid Chiron[11] reached alignment in the slow march of their orbits around the sun. Several astrologers assigned "energy" to this triple conjunction and concluded that it could influence the direction of the stock market, among other claims.

Are we deeply inspired by this pseudo-scientific symbolism, or are we astute enough to recognize it as fraudulent drivel? Or perhaps we should be more diplomatic and classify it along with amusing parlor games like Trivial Pursuit.

In 2009 there was indeed a conjunction of Neptune, Chiron and Jupiter, which will happen periodically as the planets and moons revolve in their orbits. These occasional alignments do not have meaning for how we should conduct our lives any more than the periodic alignments of the gears in your grandfather clock. However, note that the periodic alignments of the hour and minute hands on the face of the clock (which are proportional to the positions of the gears) do seem to regulate our lives. We use these clock alignments to determine our daily feeding schedules and decide when to get out of bed and go to work. We are also careful to align our clock hands with the position of the sun in the sky, and bump them ahead or back by an hour when daylight savings time goes into effect, or standard time returns. These events are defined by acts of the legislature. Alignments of the planets are not subject to such practical considerations.

However, since the planetary alignments may not be reset according to standards determined by the legislature, perhaps we must adjust our life activities in accordance with the meanings of their positions. But then we need to determine what are their proper meanings. Each astrologer gets to decide for himself what meanings to ascribe to such positions. You may ask your favorite astrologer to cast your horoscope, but when you are not pleased by his answer, you may pay the next astrologer for a different opinion, and repeat the process until you find the answer you want. This is not science.

Some folks will actually spend good money for an astrologer to cast them a personal horoscope. Although we are in favor of individual freedom, where people may spend their money in whatever way they please, we would advise against spending money on astrological advice.

Moral: Place little credence in the predictions of soothsayers.

Streetlights

Do you know anyone who has the uncanny ability to cause streetlights to go out when traveling along the avenues of her city at night? Perhaps you have noticed this phenomenon happening to you as well. Certain individuals think they have an aura that causes them to affect the streetlights when they are in the vicinity. What is really going on here?

A common failure mode of streetlamp units is for them to become intermittent before they actually fail permanently. Heating and cooling cycles caused by the weather and by the on-off, night-day use cycles of the units stresses the copper wires in their electrical ballast transformers. When one of these wires finally breaks, it causes an open circuit, which turns off the lamp. When the unit cools down, the wires touch again, turning the lamp back on. These intermittent on-off cycles can continue for several days before the unit finally dies.

The folks who think their magical powers cause the lights to go out as they approach, and come back on as they depart, are actually fooling you, or themselves.

Moral: The first explanation that comes to mind is not necessarily correct.

Checkout

A clerk in our local grocery store likes to tell the story about how she was personally responsible for shutting down all the checkout stands in the store at once. While she was busy scanning a customer's purchases, she noticed a box of mushrooms in the basket she had never seen before. She didn't know the store stocked this particular item, so she stopped to look at it for a moment. Then she scanned it and her cash register immediately shut off. So did all the other checkout stands along the front of the store. She was sure that one strange item she scanned had caused the outage.

Of course, the system shutdown was not caused by the barcode on her box of mushrooms. The actual cause was a circuit breaker supplying the row of cash registers. When it tripped, the clerk had just scanned the mushrooms, a mere coincidence.

But it made a good story to relate to her customers while they were waiting for their groceries to be toted up.

Moral: The first explanation that comes to mind is not necessarily correct.

Stock

Can you beat the stock market? This is a question that has been considered by millions of people. We can use the principles discussed in this book to provide some illumination on this subject.

Beating the stock market means being able to predict the future. This is a hazardous undertaking because you have less than a fifty-fifty chance of being correct. Your goal is to buy a stock for a low price and then sell it later for a higher price. Once you buy the stock you want it to go up, but the possibility exists for it to go down. Since it can go either up or down, you might think you have a fifty-fifty chance to make money. But you must also pay transaction costs and taxes, so there is a built in bias to lose money. This fact is related to the second law of thermodynamics, which tells us that there is no free lunch.

However when we look at the long-term history of stock market averages we see an inexorable rise. This bias for an increase is still apparent when the data is corrected for inflation. Is there some underlying cause of this happy condition?

Yes, because the stock market is a living thing, or in our terminology, a lifelike creature. As a lifelike analog it has an inherent tendency to survive, grow and compete in its environment. Thousands of people (the cell analogs) are attracted to join in the endeavor. The successful investors grow their money and expand their participation, while the unsuccessful investors eventually give up on stocks and seek out other activities in the economy. The underlying principle for this industry is that of a free market, laissez faire capitalism. Transactions are entered into by willing buyers and willing sellers, with no threats nor coercion on either side.

The companies and businesses that survive and thus remain in the stock market must earn a profit, and will also be staying ahead of inflation. As long as the stock market exists it will be made up of successful companies.

The unsuccessful ones die off and drop out of the market. These features help to explain the long-term upward bias of the stock market.

Does any of this apply to you as an individual investor seeking to earn a few bucks on your portfolio? You may take advantage of the long-term upward bias of the stock market by buying into an index mutual fund, but then the question becomes which of many to choose from. You must also consider your time horizon, as to how long you have available to stay in the market to ride through the inevitable declines. As in any other endeavor in life, you need to consider the big picture and avoid the narrow view, you must think from A to B to C.

Many people choose to play individual stocks, thinking that they have as much ability as the next guy to choose promising candidates. What a lot of beginning investors do not realize is that they are competing against a vast number of competent, experienced players in the market. Thousands of people are employed by the investment industry. Many of these people spend full time analyzing and sorting through stocks and other investments, and a lot of them have sophisticated computer programs to crunch the numbers for them. Do you, as an individual investor with limited experience and little spare time to devote to the enterprise, have any chance at all competing against these professionals? Yes, because the market is so big and so diversified you can carve a niche to survive in its ecology. Since you also have the opportunity to fail miserably, you must be continually observing and changing as the market evolves. Just as in the real world, life in the markets is not easy.

The stock market is continually changing and evolving as new players join and others drop out. New "systems" may be developed that work amazingly well for a time, but soon fall out of favor when they stop working so reliably. This happens because the stock market is a true marketplace, a free market where everybody has access to the same information. When too many players are using the same system or technique, others find out about it and act to counter it. A free market is the place where pure competition reaches its peak in striving for success.

Note that many politicians will have an inherent hatred for free markets. When politics is viewed as the lusting after power and control, politicians will try to limit and regulate free markets to direct benefits to the political class and their own favored interests. Free markets defy politicians because commerce seeks the freedom and liberty of individual investors to pursue their own interests.

Moral: A stock market may be used as a simplified example of a living organism, a lifelike creature, embodying the ecological rules of any living system.

Incompetent and Oblivious

Another feature of the faulty belief system is that people like to try things for which they are woefully unqualified. Would you try a do-it-yourself brake job on your car if you had never done one before? You might be successful at it if you are mechanically inclined, are handy with tools, and get some instruction beforehand from your friendly local auto parts store.

How about trying to fly an airplane? Most folks know how to ride a bicycle and drive a car, so they figure that flying a light plane should be a natural extension of those skills, especially if they think they understand the physics involved.

If you wish to learn how clueless you really are, take a few flying lessons. When the flight instructor gives you control of the stick and rudder, you are guaranteed to feel like a complete klutz, an accident waiting to happen. (If you are already a pilot, merely think back to how you performed during your early lessons.)

Anybody should be able to walk onstage and do a standup comedy routine, right? You already know what's funny and what's not, so you just need to memorize a few jokes and practice your delivery.

This idea was tested by two professors at Cornell University who wrote a paper on the subject: *Unskilled and Unaware of It: How Difficulties in Recognizing One's Own Incompetence Lead to Inflated Self-Assessments.*[12] The authors, Justin Kruger and David Dunning, set up experiments to evaluate subjects' competence and self-assessment in three topics; humor, grammar and logical reasoning. In all cases, the more unqualified were the subjects, the more over-confidence they held in their own abilities. Each of us has probably recognized this phenomenon while observing others trying to do something new, and even in looking at our own performance, if we can set aside our ego and be completely honest with ourselves. Incompetence coupled with over-confidence is daily demonstrated by politicians who are affiliated with the party in opposition to your own, and frequently by those of your political persuasion.

Moral: Be skeptical of self-proclaimed experts.

Qualifications

If a student wishes to become an engineer, he or she must go to college for four years, study subjects such as chemistry, physics, calculus, psychology, economics, history, English (yes, science students must also pass a few humanities, too), and take a significant list of electives in their particular engineering specialty. Once the graduate has his degree, he must go to work for a corporation in the industry to get a few years experience in the discipline. After a considerable time of working in the field, the engineer-in-training may actually become competent to practice engineering as a profession. In many branches of engineering, the aspirant must also pass a professional engineering exam under the auspices of state board of examiners, much like passing the bar exam to become a lawyer, or doing a residency to become a doctor.

On the other hand, what are the qualifications to become a politician? Let's start at the top: To become president of the United States, a candidate must be at least 35 years of age and be a natural born citizen of the United States. That's it! Of course the aspirant must persuade a large number of the electorate to vote for him, which is no mean feat. So the politician must have a thick skin and enjoy the rough and tumble of the political arena. He might start his career on a city council, go the mayor route, or work his way up through the state legislature before hitting the national scene. In Chapter 22 we have already considered a hypothetical politician's outlook, but in politics there is no requirement for the candidate to have passed a test on economics, spent time running a business, needed to worry about making a payroll, have any experience in foreign affairs, or obtained any other life experience that might qualify him for the position of power he wishes to attain.

The constitution imposes no test for education level nor competence upon our leaders. The voters get to decide who their leaders will be based on what each individual voter knows about the candidates. Political parties thus go out and pitch their candidate based on his or her image, which they have largely created themselves through advertising.

Many voters are gullible and misinformed. They think only from A to B and miss out on C, D, E and F entirely. They are easily led around by the nose, with no concept of the kind of lessons presented in this book. Politics is the anarchy of words. Politicians' favorite foods are power and control. Remember this when you hear any politician speak, and be skeptical about everything he says.

Moral: Let the buyer beware.

Notes:

[1] Pun intended.

[2] Chester Reed, *Bird Guide* (New York: Doubleday, 1951)

[3] The power lawnmower in question was of an earlier model, before the government mandated safety feature that shuts off the engine when the handle is released.

[4] Note we have used several terms here to identify the stinging insects, including bees, wasps, hornets, and yellow jackets. The homeowner did not bother to positively identify the actual species, either.

[5] See Wohlforth, *Otter Rescue,* Anchorage Daily News.

[6] See New York Times, *Rain of Cash.*

[7] From a private conversation with Leo LeBoeuf, who was at the time a firefighter in the Volunteer Fire Department of Larkspur, Colorado.

[8] See Miniclier in The Denver Post.

[9] Jake and Ken are fictional characters used here to illustrate features of human behavior.

[10] Pronounced: sebby bells.

[11] Chiron is an unusual object orbiting the sun between Saturn and Uranus. It was discovered in 1977 and has been classified (by astronomers) as both an asteroid and a comet.

[12] See Kruger and Dunning.

CHAPTER THIRTY

RECIPE FOR DISASTER

A college chemistry professor asked his students to consider a philosophical question. What if all the things we think we know and believe are wrong? What if we are really just part of an experiment in the corner of some grad student's laboratory? Perhaps the whole world, our great civilization, and our supposed accomplishments are merely reactions in a puddle of chemicals sloshing around in a big terrarium. Perhaps we are not even the main point of the experiment, but just an artifact on the periphery. Furthermore, what happens to us when the PhD candidate finishes his thesis, closes the valves and shuts off the electricity? When he graduates, he may decide to toss the whole works in the dumpster, including us. After all, under his microscope we look just like so many microbes squirming around on the agar gel.

Not too likely, you might object, but let's consider this scenario as the plot for a science fiction story. Go back to when our grad student, let's call him Prometheus (just to be obscure), was deciding on the subject for his thesis. After he determined he needed a terrarium to house his project, he wanted to populate it with creatures of some sort. Perhaps Prometheus had some new ideas on how to manipulate DNA and to engineer biological molecules to perform particular functions.

Prometheus designs his creatures to have two legs, that way they will have to walk around upright. Give them two arms with hands and opposable thumbs, so they can learn to handle tools. Give them a big brain so they can think about the consequences of their actions. Make them mostly hairless so they will be forced to invent clothing. Assign them a lifetime of about 70 orbits, and give them the ability to pass along only their physical characteristics to their offspring, but none of the things they learn during their lifetimes. That way, if they really want to advance, they will have to learn how to cooperate and work together, and if they are very clever, perhaps they will invent writing.

Prometheus sets up the initial conditions in the terrarium, and lets the experiment run until most of the reactants are consumed. As time goes by, he will take a few measurements every week in the hope that some significant results appear in his data. Prometheus will not be allowed to interfere with the actions of the creatures in his terrarium. His professor has warned him that if he should alter the conditions of an experiment while it is in progress, the scientific community will look upon his results with skepticism.

After a few semesters, Prometheus has collected enough data to satisfy his professors and complete his thesis, so he moves on to the next phase of his career. He no longer has any motivation to maintain his experiment, so he abandons the creatures in the terrarium. Does this not sound like a recipe for disaster, at least for the experimental subjects?

But let us say the professor in charge of the chemistry department sees some potential for another PhD candidate to continue the experiment and investigate what is happening in a different part of the terrarium. In fact, the professor observes that the experiment seems to be developing unexpected features. These may keep many advanced students busy for an extended period of time. So Prometheus' experiment survives its initial designer. At least until the grant funding the professor's project is not renewed. Regardless, does this not sound like a disaster in the making?

Of course, we are using our story about Prometheus' experiment as a metaphor for the human condition. What happens to the individual human over his lifetime in the terrarium? He is born helpless, and must be cared for by his mother and family. He needs to be educated in the ways of his tribe, because he starts out with only his animal instincts and no knowledge about how to survive in his society. As he grows up, he needs to gain in knowledge and strength to become a functioning member of his community. If his mother or family fails him in his upbringing he may turn into a destroyer rather than a producer. Once he gains the ability to provide for his own needs, he can support himself and contribute to the needs of his tribe, or he can become a burden on others, and drag down the accomplishments of his society. Let us say our individual turns out well and contributes to the advancement of his civilization. Soon he will reach middle age where his physical strength starts to wane and he can no longer work so hard or so long during his time on the job. As he advances into old age he will also lose his mental sharpness and will eventually need to have assistance with his daily care. Then he will die, whereupon his accumulated store of lifetime knowledge and wisdom will be lost to his immediate community and the world. His slot in society will be filled by a new baby, who starts out knowing essentially nothing, and must be trained from zero. The experienced citizens must have some way to pass along their knowledge and wisdom to the new generation. Writing, books and continuing education provide a large part of this necessary service to humanity.

But note that every opportunity for success also offers one for failure. How many possibilities for disaster are included in the previous paragraph? Perhaps the stupid people will outbreed the smart ones. Maybe the ones who resort to violence for mediation of every dispute will overwhelm the people who want to cooperate and get along with their neighbors. We have seen how this anarchic scenario has predominated in the realm of animals. Although this tradition caused the early Earth to become a balanced ecology with an amazing diversity of living things, humanity grew out of this phase, discovering that cooperation was more advantageous to the general welfare than constant intertribal warfare. Today we still see that less developed countries have a higher fertility rate than more developed countries. Increasing wealth and opportunities discourage large-size families, because the additional children are no longer required to insure survival for the family group.

Perhaps feuding families or tribes would predominate over more cooperative groups. The Montague and Capulet families had been feuding for generations, and the original disagreement that set them off had long been forgotten. Nevertheless, their hatred was stoked by each new occurrence of theft or murder between the families. But a pair of youngsters from opposite sides met, unknown to their parents, and discovered mutual attraction. Romeo and Juliet managed to make a tragedy out of their treasonous liaison, but other affairs have led to eventual reconciliation between families. Love knows no boundaries. Over the generations, conflict can be translated into cooperation.

Although Shakespeare successfully embellished an old tale in writing

Romeo and Juliet, the same kind of situation arises time and again as history unfolds. The feud between the Hatfield and McCoy families is a more recent example from U.S history of the 1880's.

People are always failing to learn the proper lessons from their experiences, and go on to repeat the mistakes of their predecessors. As George Santayana wrote: "Those who cannot remember the past are condemned to repeat it."[1] The animal passions of hatred and revenge arise in the hearts of men, whereas the virtues of tolerance and cooperation are more difficult to instill. A faulty belief system can become so firmly established in a community that it is nearly impossible to remove. An examination of history may easily lead us to conclude that the customs of mankind are a recipe for disaster.

Are we Smarter Now?

Two of the themes of this book are to demonstrate that civilizations have improved over the ages, and to encourage people to strive for further advancement.

We have certainly come a long way since ancient times, but are we any smarter than the sages of antiquity? Aristotle, Cicero, and Machiavelli are but three examples out of thousands of great thinkers who long ago figured out how the world really works. Few writers were lucky enough for their works to survive the fires, floods, eruptions and wars during the years separating their times from ours, but these men thoroughly understood the concepts of science, philosophy, mathematics, literature, poetry and music, from their own times. If we could somehow bring Aristotle back to life and let him debate modern Nobel Prize winners, would he be able to hold his own? Certainly, a sage from antiquity would need some time to become educated about the advances of modern man, but the evidence of his writings indicates he would have the intellectual capacity to understand all the concepts we have today.

So maybe we, or at least the most intelligent among us, are no smarter than the old-time giants of literature. But we, as average citizens of the world, are better educated than the average citizen of antiquity, or even of a few hundred years ago. Before the invention of movable type printing, notably by Johannes Gutenberg around 1439, literacy would have been restricted to elites and the clergy. Since then, mankind has prospered under increasing levels of education for the masses. Today, literacy has increased to 99 percent of the population in the United Sates, and 82 percent world-wide.[2] Some countries suffer literacy rates as low as 30 percent, but these countries also suffer under atrocious governments, dictatorships, lack of human rights, and widespread poverty. Probably two-thirds of illiterates in the world are women, indicating the outdated cultural practices of many societies.

Our civilization clearly has plenty of room for improvement in providing human rights and better education for people around the world, but we should feel proud of ourselves for having advanced this far.

Since individual humans today have probably not gained much inherent intelligence over the sages of olden times, is there anybody among us who has reached his ultimate potential? What are humans capable of? Do we still have untapped depths of resources? Certainly, we have capabilities we do not understand, or have not yet investigated to any significant degree.

Memory

Let us look at human memory for example. Everybody wishes for a better memory. If we could remember things we heard the first time, we could spend a lot less time in school, and could avoid making the same mistakes over and over. Actors would have an easier time memorizing their lines. We could remember the names of people we met last week, and not have to be embarrassed asking them for their names again. Wouldn't it be nice if we could store new memories in our brains with the same facility as a computer? The computer memory needs to be told a fact only once, and it can go back to access the information again and again whenever it is needed. It does this by setting individual memory cells, called bits (implemented by individual transistors), to a particular state, a 1 or a 0. Information such as "George Washington was the first president of the United States," would be stored as several bytes (8 bit words) of information.

The human memory, however, is more difficult to program, because memories are stored in biological neurons that take more time to grow new connections than the time needed for merely switching a transistor. Neurons must be stimulated the same way many times in order to form a memory that will still be accessible after a few days. So we make up for the deficit by writing ourselves little notes on scraps of paper.

Nevertheless, we can do fairly well with short-term memories, and we do have a kind of access to memories where we don't think we can remember.

We might ask a young student to tell us about things he should have learned in history class.

"Who was the first president of the United States?"
"Uh, I used to know that, but I can't remember."
"Was it James Madison?"
"No."
"Are you sure it wasn't Madison?"
"Yes, I'm sure."
"Was it Ben Franklin?"
"No."
"Are you sure?"
"Yes, I know that."
"Was it George Washington?"
"Yes, now I remember."
"Are you sure?"
"I'm positive."

We might call this a partial memory, or one that has not yet completely formed but can be triggered by someone else providing the proper clues. A lawyer might say, "Let me refresh your memory," when interviewing a witness. Most people have experienced the phenomenon called déjà vu, where the individual feels certain he has been here before, but has no reliable memory of when or how. Also, when you go somewhere new, you learn that you can find your way back to it the next time, even though you could not tell anyone how to get there. This is because you find clues you recognize along the way.

Find the restaurant

An instance of hearing something once can be enough to implant a memory of the event, although it might not be accessible as a memory that can be recalled at will. Here is a little story to illustrate the technique.

When your author was on a business trip to Boston many years ago, he and a group of colleagues had promised to meet a client for dinner at a particular restaurant the client had recommended. Boston is one of those cities where it is easy to get lost, if you are not familiar with the territory. We had the name and address of the restaurant, but as strangers to Boston, we didn't have a clear idea about how to get there. One of our party thought she knew the way, so we jumped in our rent-a-car and headed out, but we soon became lost in the maze of Boston's streets. We stopped at a convenience store to ask directions, but the clerk behind the counter had never heard of the restaurant. A customer in the store overheard me asking and came to the rescue.

"I know how to get there from here, but it's rather complicated," he said.

"Well go ahead and tell me," I replied, "and we'll see."

"OK," he said, "the first thing is to go down this street to the right until you cross the railroad tracks. Then look for a car dealership on the right that has a long building with really big windows. When you get to the next stoplight, turn left, but I can't remember the name of the street. Follow that street for about half mile till you see a whole bunch of electrical wires crossing above the road. Turn right at the next stoplight. After a while you'll go under a rusty old railroad bridge that has ivy hanging all over it. Then you'll come to a fork in the road where there is a big old white house with columns. Bear to the left and go for another half mile or so when you'll start to see a neat row of manicured bushes. Turn left at the light, and your restaurant is on the left after a few blocks."

I didn't think I could remember all that, but didn't want to ask the helpful stranger to go through it again, so I thanked him and went back out to the rent-a-car. My colleagues wanted to know what I found out, but I couldn't remember the instructions well enough to repeat them.

"Go that way," I said to the driver, pointing to the right. Sure enough, we soon crossed the railroad tracks and I spotted the car dealership.

"Left at the light," I remembered. When I saw the power wires above the road I visualized turning right. I couldn't remember what was next, but when I saw the ivy covered bridge, I knew we were on the right track.

"Bear left," I said when the white house came into view, right on schedule. When the row of neatly trimmed bushes turned up I knew to take the next left and look for the restaurant.

I was astounded at our good luck as we arrived at our intended destination. I could never have recited the directions back from memory, but the friendly stranger had provided my unconscious mind with enough clues and mental pictures to follow the trail he had described.[3]

Of course, some memories we don't need to keep forever, and we wouldn't want them cluttering up our storage capacity. So we need to delete unimportant information. Who would want to maintain the memory of a grocery list from three months ago? Do you really need to keep all your checkbook transactions from last year in your brain? No, your written checkbook register is a more appropriate memory device for this kind of information. So fading short-term-memory is a blessing. But if you could recall all this trivial information, you might be considered a genius, and could have your own TV show.

Savant

Certain people have an uncanny ability to memorize enormous quantities of information. These folks were previously referred to as idiot savants, but that terminology now has negative connotations, so the condition is referred to as savant syndrome. These people are often afflicted with autism or other severe disabilities, but retain an ability to perform amazing mental feats that are beyond the capabilities of a genius level of intelligence. An individual with savant syndrome may be able to instantly tell you in which years your birthday falls on a Monday. Another will be able to add long columns of numbers faster than an accountant with a calculator. Ones with the musical talent can playback an entire piano concerto perfectly after hearing it once, or a sculptor can carve a perfect three-dimensional reproduction of an animal after glancing once at a two-dimensional photograph[4] A further mysterious feature of the syndrome is that its practitioners cannot explain how they do it. The ability seems obvious to them, so why should you ask? You might as well try to explain how you keep your heart beating all night when you are asleep.

How would you like to have the ability to memorize the phonebook in one reading? Or learn all the information in the periodic table of elements at one sitting? A doctor might find it convenient to have an entire pharmacology available for instant recall without reference to his printed library. The savants show us that this ability exists in the human mind, but is not accessible to normal people.

Surgery

In 1940s and 50s the neurosurgeon Wilder Penfield (1891-1976) discovered he could elicit old memories in epilepsy patients by electrically stimulating certain areas on the surface of the brain. Doctor Penfield developed a technique where he could perform brain surgery on awake patients (under local anesthesia), and ask them which muscle twitched or what sensory experience occurred when he probed a specific point. He wished to excise only the brain tissue that caused the epileptic seizures, and the patient could report when he elicited the aura that always preceded a seizure. When the doctor stimulated a certain part of the temporal lobe, a patient reported a sudden, vivid memory of a long-forgotten incident in her life. Another stimulation of the same spot would again elicit the same memory. Penfield was thus able to map the brain to show which regions controlled which motor, sensory, or memory functions.[5] His research suggested that the human memory might "record" a running history of the person's life, although particular "memories" might not be available for conscious recall. Further research has not confirmed this hypothesis, but no one currently understands what information lurks in the unplumbed depths of the human brain. Perhaps some as yet undiscovered stimulation technique will reveal more details of this mystery.

Clinch

We would like to think that human life is not entirely a recipe for disaster. Rather, we would prefer to say the human condition is fraught with potential for improvement. If we consider all the evidence presented in this book, however biased it might seem, optimism should prevail. Although we may indeed spend much of our lives a mere eight feet from certain death, the life force inherent in every individual, the instinct for survival deeply embedded in all of our human organizations, will continue to fend off Chaos for more than the next 48 hours.

Notes:

[1] American philosopher George Santayana (1863-1952).

[2] Literacy data from *The World Factbook*, an online database of the Central Intelligence Agency of the United States.

[3] This tale has been reconstructed from an incomplete recollection of the event by the author. Thus the details are not accurate, and attempting to find the actual restaurant (if it still exits) in Boston from this description would be futile.

[4] See Treffert.

[5] See Penfield.

CHAPTER THIRTY-ONE

BALANCE OF POWER

LET us summarize the major points we have covered in this book. The most basic meaning of life is competition in the struggle for survival. We have seen what life is like for animals, mostly consisting of anarchy and violence. We have also noted that humans can and do act like animals to a large extent. However, humans have discovered that they can suppress their anarchistic reflexes, and embrace virtue and cooperation. They are the only creatures who can think from A to B to C, and act in their own rational self-interest. Unlike the animals, humans can distinguish between good and evil, if they choose to do so.

Rights

When people form into groups for their mutual benefit, they establish a set of rules for everyone to follow. Advanced tribes have determined that life, liberty and the pursuit of happiness are to be considered basic human rights. Since people are also living creatures, their imperative for survival grants them the basic human right to self-defense. When someone tries to deprive them of their rights by force or violence, they are entitled to respond in like manner. In civilized society, a person who initiates force, coercion or violence, anyone who tries to kill or steal is a criminal, subject to disciplinary action by the group.

Wealth

After a while the members of a successful tribe will discover that they have more wealth now than they did when they started out a few years ago. They may even come to understand that wealth is created by people making products and supplying services that other people want to buy. This universal feature of reality implies a profit motive, in that when you have customers, you must satisfy their needs, or the competing business down the street will lure them away. Contrariwise, when you have no customers, you have no market in which to sell your product, which in turn implies you go bankrupt and your business dies. This fact helps to explain why people strive for production and seek to avoid destruction.

Government does not create wealth, but rather consumes wealth. Government is always an administrative function that is a burden upon the wealth creating private sector, which is motivated and constrained by the profit motive. Government is funded through taxes, which are extracted from the citizens by the threat of force, not because the taxpayers want to pay taxes for the obvious benefits the government provides.

Freedom

When humans understand the true source of wealth, they realize they must have the political and economic freedom to work for their own benefit. They need property rights and protection from criminality. Government's true responsibilities are limited to protecting citizens from foreign invasion, providing a police force to discourage criminality, maintaining a court system to enforce contracts, and providing for public goods. Taxes should be adequate to support the valid functions of government, but must not extend to redistributing wealth from rich to poor, or from politically un-favored to favored groups. Free market capitalism is the most efficient method for generating wealth, both for the benefit of individuals and for society in general.

The terrible and glorious truth is that even though all men are created equal, and individuals have unalienable rights to life, liberty and the pursuit of happiness, people are not automatically entitled to equality of riches nor equality of outcome. The second law of thermodynamics may be said to apply as well to the activities of man (TANSTAAFL).[1]

Charity

Although the civilized human may be primarily concerned with his own personal well-being, he is also compassionate for his fellow man. He wants all his neighbors to be treated fairly and to have a chance to live up to their own potential. The human therefore has a tremendous capacity for charity, and will help his neighbor who has fallen on hard times. He will voluntarily donate to local religious organizations and secular charities without direction from any governmental body. However, when the government forces him to contribute through taxes to its selected beneficiaries, he will resent the imposition.

Trust

Mutual trust is needed for the maintenance of peace and successful commerce between individual humans and between tribes. Lack of trust reverts behavior toward animalism and anarchy, regardless of the group size.

We saw in Chapter 12 that love and trust arise naturally in the family, the traditional unit of man, wife and children. We also saw that this love does not extend very far beyond the family because the breadwinner must compete in the business world with the many other family-heads. Society therefore needs to establish a set of common rules that everyone agrees to obey, which allows all individuals to compete for their own rational self-interest, while observing the rights of their competitors. They do this by obeying the two fundamental rules against killing and stealing, thereby granting their neighbors the rights to life and property ownership, and by not initiating force or violence against the fellow citizen. Very large tribes of humans have successfully implemented this way of life and have formed into the lifelike units called cities, states and countries. Wisdom is required by the leaders of a tribe to maintain peaceful commerce among the citizens.

However, in the real world of hundreds of different countries, the various tribes come from different cultures, which have arisen from different ideas about how they should be organized. Thus, not every tribe operates from the same set of rules. As a result, intertribal conflicts arise. The history of mankind has been a continuous record of intertribal warfare, which we still observe today, and we expect to continue well into the future. Great wisdom is required by the leaders of tribes when they must deal with other tribes.

In the world of today we may observe many countries where the governments honor their citizens by granting them varying degrees of human rights. We also observe many countries where dictatorships deny the citizens most human rights. We may also observe many inter-country relationships where the two governments cooperate with their neighbors for mutually beneficial commerce. We can find many examples, on the other hand, where certain countries try to deny their neighbors even the right to exist. So anarchy may be said to reign in inter-country relations, with occasional instances of cooperation. Government leaders need great wisdom to distinguish their international friends from their enemies, and act appropriately with friendship or hostility. We must recognize that there will always be barbarians at the gate.

Love is All You Need

Love is the highest form of friendship. Love based on mutual respect and trust is the most powerful uniting force for cooperation between humans. It is unfortunate that the word "love" in our language is so interchangeable with the word "sex." Sex drive, or lust, is an instinct like hunger or thirst that all animals have. Lust powers the necessity to propagate the species, and is a result of evolutionary forces that require sex for the continuation of the line. Our definition of love, for purposes of this book, separates lust from the meaning of love. Love is the feeling of belonging with another person, or a commitment to a family member.

Love may well be all you need, but it need not extend to all your neighbors or citizens of your community. Friendship is the answer, love being reserved for family members or the dedication to religious beliefs. Friendship is required for a successful civilization, and is possible when citizens trust that the members of their social group will not initiate violence against them, and will respect the rights of their neighbors.

Wisdom

Can we count on friendship to the point where we can trust our competitors? An independent watchdog can help. In sports, we can trust the other players because we have umpires. In the business world we have laws that intend to enforce contracts. In our cities and states we have a police force and a system of courts to arbitrate disputes between citizens. But we must always be alert to watch out for our own interests, because corruption and deception have a nasty habit of arising in our dealings with fellow humans.

Can we trust our competitors from different countries or their governments? Only with the utmost vigilance. Corruption is a way of life in many of the world's societies, because they have not yet grown out of their fundamental, anarchistic origins. Perhaps many of their leaders have not yet read this book, or have chosen to ignore their responsibility to act in a virtuous manner. Some chiefs subscribe to the socialist teachings of Karl Marx, and do not believe in the benefits of free market capitalism.

How do we know whom to trust? Essentially, we are all animals, so we should obey our natural instincts to distrust everyone. We need to experience mutual respect, before we trust those we deal with. We observe the actions of people as compared to their words. Once we decide to engage with another human, constant vigilance is required because we have no guarantee that things will continue as they have in the past.

Wisdom and strength are necessary. Wisdom in the use of strength is required. A balance of power between contenders is needed to promote goodness and discourage evil. Alas, life is not easy, nor will it become so in the foreseeable future.

Chances

Do we have a chance? Does civilization have a rosy future, or are we doomed to ultimate destruction? Good question. If we look at the big picture, it could go either way. If Mother Nature continues to grant Earth freedom from collisions with large interplanetary objects, we definitely have the opportunity to survive. If mankind can prevent terrorists and international criminals access to nuclear weapons, we will be less likely to destroy our own civilization.

If we look at the overall sweep of history we can have an optimistic outlook. We started out as cavemen at the beginning of human evolution. Our ancestors learned how to speak and how to write. We moved beyond the animal world when we graduated from hunting-gathering, and learned to raise crops and domesticate animals. We formed into tribes and villages, we expanded the population enough to spread out and inhabit the entire globe.

All this progress was held back by recurrent warfare, which destroyed property and wealth and killed off thousands of our fellow creatures. As a species we seem to have a problem understanding the benefits of cooperating for the common good. Despite such mass stupidity, history was blessed with occasional periods of amazing advancement. The European Renaissance of the 14th to 16th centuries is one example.[2]

Civilization has grown and prospered over the centuries because of the mysterious life force, which can be understood when we consider civilization as a lifelike creature. As a result of this advance, people are in general better off now than we were in the last century, and this pattern has continued from earlier centuries. The last 300 years is particularly notable in this regard. With the advent of the industrial revolution, people realized that moving to the crowded cities would provide them with more benefits of civilization than staying in the countryside to live on farms like their grandfathers.

Over the last three centuries growth in civilization has exploded. By whatever measure you choose; population, wealth, standard of living, we are better off now than were our ancestors. Would you really want to go back and live in your grandfather's day? People say they yearn for a simpler time, a more natural way of life, something more in harmony with nature. But if you are honest with yourself you will conclude that you really do like indoor plumbing, your computer and cell phone, and would not wish to give them up. Look back in history a mere thirty years. Personal computers had maybe 640K of memory. Radio-telephones were the size of half-gallon milk cartons. Today you appreciate the emergency services that are available when you dial 911. When you get sick you can find a hospital nearby with plenty of competent doctors and skilled surgeons who have advanced techniques and a full supply of antibiotics and wonder drugs. Our life expectancies are longer than were our grandparents'.

Regardless of the advances our civilization has made to this point in history, we all know we could do better. Many of our fellow humans seem trapped in a life of poverty and suffering. How do we change from the course we are on now to one that would be more beneficial to more people? How do we adjust the balance of power so the individual is not so threatened by the power of the group, the greatest offender being, of course, government.

Change must always be implemented incrementally, slowly, in small steps. Sudden changes disturb the equilibrium that develops in any stable society. Sudden, vast changes always revert society to anarchy, because individuals discover they can no longer trust the traditional methods in their lives that have been working fine for such a long time. So people revert to their animal instincts to watch out for themselves in survival mode, as would any other self-respecting creature. In a word, they return to anarchy. Revolution breeds warfare. Look at the history of any country. What was life like for people during the French Revolution of the late 1700s, the U.S. Civil War in the 1860s, or after the Russian Revolutions of 1917? Not at all pleasant.

Effective government requires wisdom from our leaders to implement policies that grow production and avoid destruction. Politicians need to honor their commitments to the Constitution and the public trust, rather than concentrating solely on acquiring ever more power and control, merely for the enhancement of their personal resumes. Remember the purpose of the Constitution is to protect the individual from the power of government.

As an individual, you should not resent another man his wealth, nor should he resent yours, because this would be a form of envy, one of the seven deadly sins. When a man resents his neighbor's wealth or covets his neighbor's property, he harbors an attitude that encourages his desire to steal it, thus violating the second of the two fundamental rules for civilization: do not kill and do not steal. If you wish to have what another man owns, you must trade with him in an arms-length transaction, where neither party has power of coercion over the other. Work to develop your own strengths, in mind and body and character. Be a Lady or a Gentleman and respect the rights of your fellow citizen, while demanding respect for your own rights in return.

A balance of power between civilized human beings is the secret to fighting evil and promoting virtue. Capitalism is the force of nature that provides for the creation of wealth and economic strength for any society. Embrace these concepts to enhance the growth and prosperity of your civilization.

There you go

In this book we have discussed many of the ways one engineer looks at life. We have attempted to explain how the world really works. Whether you agree or not, you now have insight from the perspective of someone who has carefully researched the big picture.

As a citizen of an exceptional country, the one country that leads the world in the benefits it provides its citizens, you have the freedom to conduct your life in the manner you deem most appropriate. Try not to waste this gift, purchased for you by the toil of your hard-working ancestors.

In any case, we wish you the best of luck as you carve a niche to survive in your ecology. May you succeed in striving after your own rational self-interest.

Notes:

[1] TANSTAAFL -- There ain't no such thing as a free lunch.
[2] If you are not already a student of history, a good place to start would be *Civilization, a Personal View* by Kenneth Clark. This book and companion DVD television series of 13 episodes presents the sweep of Western Civilization from the fall of the Roman Empire into the modern day. See Clark.
Another excellent book we can recommend is *The Black Death*, by Robert Gottfried, which gives a clear account of what life was really like for people of the Middle Ages. See Gottfried.

AFTERWORD

IF you disagree with everything we have presented in this book, you should burn it in protest. That way the next reader will be forced to buy a new copy, which will be good for the publishing industry, although it may represent a negative for the overall economy.[1] However, the heat energy liberated by burning this book may provide a useful benefit in helping to heat your home or cook dinner.

A book of this size, mostly paper of about 12 ounces, when burned in atmosphere at standard temperature and pressure should liberate approximately 1,417,000 calories, which is 5625 Btu, or 1.65 kilowatt-hours of energy.

For easy reference, here is a short table of approximate values for Heat of Combustion for various fuels:

Dry firewood	7,000 Btu/pound
Paper (recycled)	7,500
Coal (Lignite)	8,000
Coal (Anthracite)	14,000
Diesel fuel	19,300
Gasoline	20,000 Btu/pound

Caution: Burning trash may be restricted by law in your political jurisdiction, so check with your local authorities before lighting any fires.

Warning: Fire is hot, and may cause serious burns or even death. Always observe proper safety precautions when exposure to fire is possible.

Notes:

[1] See Hazlitt, *Economics in One Lesson*, Chapter 2, "The Broken Window," for the economic consequences of destroying property.

EPILOG

BEFORE I started writing this book, I didn't know all this stuff. Researching and writing the chapters became an education, and more importantly, a revelation.

I mean, there I was, a successful adult with a good job who lived a fairly comfortable life in America, among my family and friends. I was an engineer who possessed the rational thought processes for solving problems and learning about new things that I could apply to new situations. But unknown to me during most of my life, I harbored a faulty belief system.

Although I was not terminally naive, I trusted that most other people thought similarly to the way I did. I believed that nearly everybody, other than outright criminals, conducted their lives honestly, and attempted to deal with their fellow citizens fairly. I believed that our political leaders were mostly honest men and women who attempted to run the country with compassion for the individual citizens, the people being the assets of civilization, and the ultimate resource.

But my research has led me to the inevitable conclusion that there is enough evil and anarchistic, narrow self-interest in the halls of power to seriously endanger the future success of our republic.

A major revelation occurred for me about half way through the writing process. I brought home a particular book from the library, *Common Sense Economics,* which explained to me how our government ignores well-established, scientific, economic principles. Legislatures establish policies that destroy, rather than enhance, prosperity.[1] It made me angry to finally realize, I mean to truly understand, that many politicians who run the country are actually there to exercise power for their own personal benefit, not because they wish to provide an efficient economy that serves the most people. This discovery should also make you angry, and motivate you to help remove such people from leadership positions in our fine country.

Many of the people in charge of pulling the levers of power simply do not understand what they are doing, other than to protect their own lofty positions in the vast bureaucratic machine. Meanwhile, they inhibit the private sector from creating the wealth that would benefit the entire population.

It is like giving the keys of your 500-horsepower Ferrari to a seven-year-old boy. He has no driving skills, yet thinks he is invincible. He has a faulty belief system. He is going to wreck the car and kill himself along with innocent victims who happen to be in the way. Similarly, incompetent politicians running the economy grind the gears and stomp on the accelerator when they actually need to apply the brakes. They turn left when it would be more advisable to turn right. The only thing that keeps them from having already destroyed the country is that the economy is a living being, a lifelike form, which has inherent, self-correcting mechanisms to adjust its responses for survival, despite the destructive forces of the people running it. An engineer knows that when you don't understand how something works, you cannot fix it when it breaks. Even worse, you cannot tell when it is not operating properly.

I do realize that many of our leaders in politics are indeed honest and upright citizens. They wish to honor and uphold the Constitution of the United States, just as every one of them has sworn to do. They may have truly tasted the Honey of Power, yet have continued to resist the attractions of corruption. As yet they may not have been turned towards the Dark Side, but every human harbors some degree of the faulty belief system, and will also make occasional errors in judgment, despite noble intentions.

I was recently asked whether I am glad to have learned these lessons, or was I happier before I discovered how the world really works. Most likely, any new education has more benefits than hazards. You should be interested in studying about a disease once you discover you have it. To be forewarned is to be forearmed. Of course, it is always fun to be fat, dumb and happy, to be like a child who trusts his parents to watch out for him and supply him with plenty of food, shelter and toys. But, alas, we must eventually grow up and take care of ourselves. We need to compete with our neighbors to earn a successful living. But we may also compete while respecting the human rights of our fellow citizens. When we cooperate with the forces of capitalism, we compete for production, rather than merely competing for consumption, which is the way of animals.

Now that *you* know how the world *really* works, please join me in spreading the word about how government already controls too much power. Become a force to return power to the people. Restore power to people who wish to be left alone to pursue their own rational self-interest. Help eliminate wasteful government programs, expunge regulations whose only reason for existence is to protect existing entities from honest competition in a free marketplace. Re-ignite political and economic freedom so that we may pursue our lives in a free market where we will create the most successful economy possible, and promote the ideals of freedom and liberty in America.

J.D.W.
Asheville, 2010

Notes:

[1] See Gwartney.

BIBLIOGRAPHY

Dante Alighieri, *The Divine Comedy*, translated by C.H. Sisson (New York: Oxford, 1993) ISBN: 0-19-283073-2. Also available on the Internet from Project Gutenberg at: www.gutenberg.org/etext/8800,

Aristotle, *Nicomachean Ethics,* is available from The Internet Classics Archive at: classics.mit.edu/aristotle/nicomachaen.mb.txt.

Arthur Bloch, *Murphy's Law* (Los Angeles: Price/Stern/Sloan, 1977) ISBN: 0-8431-0428-7.

Kenneth Clark, *Civilization: A Personal View* (New York: Harper and Row, 1969) ISBN: 0-06-090787-8.

The Constitution of the United States is available on the Internet from Project Gutenberg at: www.gutenberg.org/dirs/etext90/const11.txt.

Peter A. Corning, *The Re-Emergence of "Emergence"* (Palo Alto, CA: Complexity, 2002) from the Internet at: www.complexsystems.org.

Charles R. Darwin, *On the Origin of Species by Means of Natural Selection* (Baltimore: Penguin, 1968[1859]). Also available on the Internet from Project Gutenberg at: www.gutenberg.org/etext/1228.

The Declaration of Independence is available on the Internet from Project Gutenberg at: www.gutenberg.org/files/16780/16780-8.txt.

Daniel C. Dennett, *Consciousness Explained* (Boston: Little, Brown & Co., 1991) ISBN: 0-316-18065-3.

Daniel C. Dennett, *Darwin's Dangerous Idea* (New York: Touchstone, 1995) ISBN: 0-684-80290-2.

Jared Diamond, *Guns, Germs, and Steel* (New York: W. W. Norton & Co., 1999) ISBN: 0-393-31755-2.

Steve Forbes and Elizabeth Ames, *How Capitalism Will Save Us* (New York: Crown, 2009) ISBN: 978-0-307-46309-8.

David Friedman, *The Machinery of Freedom* (LaSalle, IL: Open Court, 1989) ISBN: 0-8126-9068-0.

Peter J. Gomes, *The Good Life* (New York: HarperCollins, 2002) ISBN: 0 06 000075 9.

Robert S. Gottfried, *The Black Death* (New York: Free Press, 1983) ISBN: 0-02-912370-4.

James Gwartney, Richard Stroup, Dwight Lee, *Commonsense Economics* (New York: St. Martin's Press, 2005) ISBN 0-312-33818-X.

Edith Hamilton, *Mythology* (Boston: Little, Brown & Co, 1942).

Thomas A. Harris, *I'm OK – You're OK* (New York: Avon Books, 1973) ISBN: 0-380-0072-X.

Henry Hazlitt, *Economics in One Lesson* (New York: Three Rivers Press, 1979[1962][1946]) ISBN: 0-517-54823-2.

Thomas Hobbes, *Leviathan* edited by Richard Tuck (Cambridge: University of Cambridge Press, 2001[1651]) ISBN: 0-521-56797-1. Also available on the Internet from Project Gutenberg at: www.gutenberg.org/etext/3207.

Edward Hull, *The Wall Chart of World History* (London: Dorset Press, 1988) ISBN: 0-88029-239-3.

King James Version, *The Holy Bible* (London: Oxford University Press, undated).

Dereck Joubert, *Killer Pride* (National Geographic: Vol. 210 #3, September 2006).

Justin Kruger and David Dunning, *Unskilled and Unaware of It* (Journal of Personality and Social Psychology, 1999, vol. 77, no. 6, p. 1121), or on the Internet at: www.apa.org/journals/features/psp7761121.pdf.

Nicolo Machiavelli, *The Prince* is available on the Internet from Project Gutenberg at: www.gutenberg.org/files/1232/1232.txt.

Dana MacKenzie, *The Big Splat* (Hoboken, NJ: John Wiley & Sons, 2003) ISBN: 0-471-15057-6.

Magna Carta is available on the Internet from Project Gutenberg at: www.gutenberg.org/etext/10000.

Thomas Malthus, *Essay on the Principle of Population* (London: St Paul's, 1798) is available on the Internet from Project Gutenberg at: www.gutenberg.org/files/4239/4239.txt.

Stephen Marshak, *Earth: Portrait of a Planet* (New York: W.W.Norton, 2001) ISBN: 0-939-97423-5.

Karl Marx, *Communist Manifesto* (1848). Also available on the Internet from Project Gutenberg at: www.gutenberg.org/etext/61.

Karl Marx, *Critique of the Gotha Program* (1875).

Kit Miniclier, *Wrecks Tie Up Icy Stretch of I-25* in The Denver Post, 3 December 1997.

Ludwig Von Mises, *Socialism*, translated by J. Kahane (New Haven: Yale University Press, 1962[1951]).

Andrew P. Napolitano, *Constitutional Chaos* (Nashville: Nelson Current, 2004) ISBN 0-7852-6083-8.

New York Times, *Rain of Cash in Car Crash Tempts Poor from Miami*, 12 January 1997.

SungHa Park, *Road Trip in a Strange Land; Tourists Now Can Drive to a North Korean Resort*, The Wall Street Journal, Weekend Journal, 17 May 2008.

Wilder Penfield and Herbert Jasper, *Epilepsy and the Functional Anatomy of the Human Brain* (Boston: Little, Brown & Co., 1954).

Paul Raffaele, *In John They Trust*, Smithsonian Magazine, February 2006.

Donald B. Redford, *Akhenaten: The Heretic King* (Princeton: Princeton University Press, 1984) ISBN: 0-691-03567-9.

George Reisman, *Capitalism* (Ottawa, IL: Jameson Books, 1998) ISBN: 0-915463-73-3. Also available on the Internet at www.capitalism.net.

Rocky Mountain National Park Fact Sheet, *Elk and Vegetation Management Plan*, available on the Internet at: www.nps.gov/romo/parkmgmt/elkveg_fact_sheet_03-2008.htm or www.nps.gov/romo/parkmgmt/upload/elk_veg_newsletter_march_2008.pdf.

Solomon Schimmel, *The Seven Deadly Sins* (New York: The Free Press, 1992) ISBN: 0-02-927901-2.

Ted R. Schultz, *In Search of Ant Ancestors* (Proceedings of the National Academy of Sciences, 19 December 2000, vol. 97, no. 26, p. 14028).

Joseph A. Schumpeter, *Capitalism, Socialism and Democracy* (New York: Harper, 1950[1942]).

Charles Seife, *Decoding the Universe* (London: Penguin Books, 2006) ISBN: 978-0-14-303839-9.

Michael Shermer, *The Science of Good and Evil* (New York: Henry Holt and Co.,2004) ISBN: 0-8050-7520-8.

Julian L. Simon, *Ultimate Resource 2* (Princeton: Princeton University Press, 1996) ISBN: 0-691-04269-1.

W. Cleon Skousen, *The 5000 Year Leap* (Malta, ID: National Center for Constitutional Studies, 2009[1981]) ISBN: 0-88080-148-4.

Adam Smith, *Wealth of Nations* is available on the Internet from Project Gutenberg at: www.gutenberg.org/etext/3300.

Smithsonian Institution, website entitled *The Human Origins Program, Resource Guide to Paleoanthropology* at anthropology.si.edu/humanorigins/faq/encarta/encarta.htm.

Alan Sokal and Jean Bricmont, *Fashionable Nonsense: Postmodern Intellectuals' Abuse of Science* (New York: Picador, 1998) ISBN: 0-312-19545-1.

Darold A. Treffert, *Extraordinary People* (New York: Harper and Row, 1989) ISBN 0-06-015945-6.

Bruce W. Tuckman, *Developmental Sequence in Small Groups* (*Psychological Bulletin*, 63, 384-399, 1965). The article has been reprinted, and is available on the Internet at: dennislearningcenter.osu.edu/references/GROUP%20DEV%20ARTICLE.doc.

James D. Watson, *DNA* (New York: Alfred A. Knoph, 2003) ISBN: 0-375-41546-7.

Jude Wanniski, *The Way the World Works* (Washington, DC: Regnery, 1998[1978]) ISBN: 0-89526-344-0.

Charles Wohlforth, *Otter Rescue Questioned*, Anchorage Daily News, 17 April 1990.

CPSIA information can be obtained at www.ICGtesting.com
Printed in the USA
LVOW070249271212

313357LV00004B/702/P